THE BERNARD H. BRESLAUER COLLECTION OF

Manuscript Illuminations

THE
BERNARD H. BRESLAUER
COLLECTION OF
Manuscript Illuminations

William M. Voelkle
and Roger S. Wieck

assisted by Maria Francesca P. Saffiotti

THE PIERPONT MORGAN LIBRARY
New York

Exhibition dates:
9 December 1992 — 4 April 1993

Cover: The Lamb Defeating the Ten Kings (cat. no. 29)
Back cover: Francesco Sforza (detail from cat. no. 78)
Frontispiece: Penitent David (cat. no. 89)

Photographs for the Breslauer Collection are by David A. Loggie
and his staff at The Pierpont Morgan Library.

Designed by Klaus Gemming, New Haven
Typeset in Poliphilus and Blado by The Sarabande Press, New York
Printed by Schneidereith & Sons, Baltimore
Bound by Mueller Trade Bindery, Middletown, Connecticut

Library of Congress Cataloging-in-Publication Data
Voelkle, William M.
    The Bernard H. Breslauer collection of manuscript illuminations /
by William M. Voelkle and Roger S. Wieck assisted by Maria Francesca
P. Saffiotti.
            p.   cm.
    Catalog of an exhibition held at the Pierpont Morgan Library. Dec.
9, 1992–Apr. 4, 1993.
    Includes bibliographical references and index.
    ISBN 0-87598-095-3
    1. Illumination of books and manuscripts. Medieval—Exhibitions.
2. Illuminations of books and manuscripts, Renaissance—Exhibitions.
3. Breslauer, B. H. (Bernard)—Art collections—Exhibitions.
4. Illumination of books and manuscripts—Private collections—New
York (State)—Exhibitions.   I. Wieck, Roger S.   II. Saffiotti,
Maria Francesca P.   III. Pierpont Morgan Library.   IV. Title.
ND2920.V64 1992
745.6'7'0940747471—dc20   92-50519
                                                               CIP

CONTENTS

PREFACE

BERNARD H. BRESLAUER is known to many as a dealer in rare books and a discerning collector of fine bindings and important books on bibliography, including early sale catalogues. Few people, however, may be aware that he is also a serious collector of illuminated manuscript leaves, to which he has applied the same knowledge, judgment, determination, and zeal as he has to his other and better known collections. Indeed, the nature and scope of this collection is known to only a handful of specialists and friends. Consequently, we are deeply grateful to Mr. Breslauer, a Fellow of the Morgan Library, for permitting us to share his collection, for the first time, with a wider audience. Even those few who already know of the Breslauer Collection will be surprised by the depth and range of his holdings. Little could Mr. Breslauer himself have realized in 1967, when he purchased his first leaf, that a quarter century later his collection would rank as one of the most important private collections of single leaves, certainly the most important in the United States. Even within the last year, Mr. Breslauer has made substantial and important additions to the collection.

As the Introduction to this catalogue makes clear, single leaves were frequently collected because they have the direct appeal of small paintings. Their original function as parts of larger totalities, relationship to the texts they originally accompanied, and connection to the Church's liturgy were rarely acknowledged by collectors in the past. In this catalogue, however, William M. Voelkle and Roger S. Wieck have not only given a descriptive account of each leaf but also have identified, where possible, the kind of book from which each came, its precise textual and liturgical context. We hope that their many new discoveries will aid the public and scholars alike in heightening the appreciation of illuminated manuscripts, which contain the largest and best preserved body of medieval paintings.

Given the Morgan Library's particular strength in medieval and Renaissance manuscripts, which owes much to the passion of its two founders, J. Pierpont Morgan and his son, J. P. Morgan, Jr., and first director, Belle da Costa Greene, it is especially fitting that we should show the Bernard H. Breslauer Collection here. In offering this exhibition, we are continuing our practice of occasionally presenting outstanding collections in private hands, thus making these materials available for the education and pleasure of all.

We are indebted to William Voelkle and Roger Wieck, Curator and Associate Curator of Medieval and Renaissance Manuscripts, who prepared the catalogue with the assistance of Maria Saffiotti. They in turn are grateful for numerous opinions offered by many of their colleagues on the localization, attribution, and dating of the leaves: Jonathan J. G. Alexander, François Avril, Lynette M. F. Bosch, Vittore Branca, Bodo Brinkmann, Barbara Butz, Walter Cahn, Mirella Levi D'Ancona, Peter Dreyer, Stephen Fliegel, Günther Glück, Jörn Günther, Michael Gullick, Christopher de Hamel, Reinhard Heydenreuter, Julia Bolton Holloway, Laurence B. Kanter, Thomas Forest Kelly, Elizabeth Klemm, Willi Korte, Albinia de la Mare, James Marrow, Hope Mayo, Anna Melograni, John H. Plummer, Lilian M. C. Randall, Sheryl E. Reiss, Lucy Sandler, Kathleen Scott, Maurits Smeyers, Frauke Steenbock, Alison Stones, Robert Suckale, Judith Anne Testa, and Gyöngyi Török. Other assistance was provided by Starr Figuera, Sue Reed, and Roberta Waddell. From the Library staff we should also like to thank David A. Loggie, who, assisted by Edward J. Sowinski, photographed the collection; Elizabeth O'Keefe, Head of Cataloguing, who prepared the indices and checked the bibliographic citations, and David W. Wright, Registrar. In addition, we are grateful for the assistance of Inge Dupont, Mimi Hollanda, Maria Oldal, Sandy Opatow, Carol Wenzel-Rideout, and members of the conservation staff, Patricia Reyes, Timothy Herstein, Nancy D. Seaton, and Holley White.

We are especially pleased to acknowledge the contribution that Mr. T. Kimball Brooker has made in partial support of this catalogue's publication.

Charles E. Pierce, Jr.
Director

BERNARD H. BRESLAUER

Photograph by Margery Schab, 1992.

THE GENESIS OF A COLLECTION

LOOKING BACK over a professional life that spans more than half a century and coincided with horrendous historical events which decisively influenced its course, I consider myself fortunate in many ways, not least in my encounters, especially in my younger years, with men from whom I learned a great deal; they taught me how to look at books, and especially book illuminations, with an informed eye—a way of judging artifacts called, not always approvingly in academic circles, connoisseurship.

I was born into the world of books. My father, Martin Breslauer, one of the leading rare bookdealers of his day, carefully planted and fostered in me from early youth a fascination with books; whenever he had acquired a new collection or group of books or an outstanding manuscript, he would call me to his office and explain to me with unflagging enthusiasm its interest and merit. Small wonder, then, that I too became a bookseller, working with him in Berlin for almost two years, until he was forced to close his business, and from 1937 onwards in London, where he had succeeded in establishing himself and his family. But his escape from almost certain death proved to be of short duration; in 1940 a German bomb ended his life. When I returned from war service in the British army five years later, I was faced, at the age of twenty-seven, with the difficult task of restoring his firm to its former eminence. But luck favored me in adversity, for a number of collectors and librarians in Europe and the United States gave me their confidence and support; among them was a highly knowledgeable collector of early books and manuscripts, and a man of almost saintly human qualities, Wilfred Merton (1889–1957), who soon became a great personal friend. As a student at the University of Cambridge, Merton had come under the influence of Sydney Cockerell (1867–1962), the erstwhile secretary of William Morris and director of the Fitzwilliam Museum at Cambridge, who with small means but a legendary eye for quality and extramurally acquired scholarship had made a collection of medieval illuminated and other manuscripts of extraordinary interest. I was invited to visit Sir Sydney in the early fifties at his house near the Botanical Gardens at Kew. By that time, after an accident, he had permanently taken to his bed, devotedly looked after by relays of very English maiden ladies, one of whom, at his command, fetched several illuminated manuscripts to his bedside to be examined by me under his almost preternaturally bright gaze; but obviously dissatisfied with my cursory way of looking at them, he suddenly admonished me in a stentorian voice: "Look at them properly, you aren't looking at them closely enough"—a lesson I have never forgotten. I did not realize at the time that he was on the warpath: he had decided to sell his manuscripts, which I could not have afforded in any case, and he soon afterwards disposed of them by private treaty and public auction.

Wilfred Merton—whose collections I was to acquire after his death, in accordance with his testamentary dispositions, and record in several catalogues—was an intimate friend of Dr. Eric Millar (1887–1966), the retired keeper of manuscripts in the British Museum, and one of the foremost English authorities on illuminated manuscripts. Merton and Millar would almost invariably lunch on Tuesdays, Wednesdays, and Thursdays,—for the "long weekends" Merton buried himself in the library of his house in the country—and soon I was not infrequently asked to join them, thus learning a great deal from their conversations. Millar, blessed with modest means, had also been influenced by Sir Sydney Cockerell, and had formed, aided by an equally superb eye and knowledge, a perhaps even more outstanding collection. I shall forever be grateful to this kindhearted and ebullient man of vast learning who took an ever youthful delight in showing his treasures. The hours I spent with him in his library were veritable seminars. He left his collections to the British Museum (they are now in the British Library), among them *La Somme le Roy,* one of the principal works illuminated by that great Parisian late thirteenth-century artist Maître Honoré, and the coeval great illuminated York Psalter, both of which I repeatedly held in my hands. An exquisite early fifteenth-century Parisian Book of Hours, illuminated by the Master of the Maréchal de Boucicaut, circumstances forced him to entrust to me for sale, and I described it in one of my catalogues. Through Millar I came to know Francis Wormald (1904–72), at that time professor of paleography at the University of London, later director of its Institute of Historical Research, and a former colleague of Millar's at the British Museum, a delightful though fastidious person with a quiet sense of humor and immense knowledge lightly borne. From him, too, I learned much over the years. I vividly remember a visit to his large paneled office at the Institute in order to show him a miniature of the Calling of St. Matthew which had been offered to me as having been part of a fourteenth-century Perugian *matricola* and which I suspected of being a clever fake. He glanced at it and then virtuously averted his eyes, as if offended by an indecent image, and handed it back to me murmuring, "Don't like it a bit, don't like it a bit," and strode straight to a hidden panel, which to my surprise revealed a well-stocked bar, and poured us both a strong drink, as if to counteract an ingested poison.

Since those days, great illuminated manuscripts have passed through my hands, finding a permanent or at least a long-lasting resting place in the great institutions and private collections of two continents. What I have learned from my mentors—not only those whom I have just mentioned, but others too—is, as I have said in the beginning, connoisseurship. Sir John Pope-Hennessy, one of the eminent art historians of our time, has devoted a fascinating, albeit slightly ambiguous essay to this subject (in *The Study and Criticism of Italian Sculpture*, New York, Metropolitan Museum of Art, 1980)—slightly ambiguous, as he also reveals the lapses from infallibility of such exemplars of his as Berenson, Longhi, Offner, and himself. Sir John's point of departure is Jonathan Richardson the Elder's astonishing treatise of 1719, "The Connoisseur; an Essay on the Whole Art of Criticism," which he summarizes in his inimitable way: "The book rests on two assumptions, the ultimate importance of which Richardson could hardly have foreseen. First, that connoisseurship has a special significance for collectors, and is therefore indissociable from the purchase and sale of works of art. Second, that the form of judgment it implies can be exercised with reasonable success by nonprofessionals. . . ." If by nonprofessional, Sir John means nonacademic, as I assume he does, his summary almost amounts to an "Apologia pro vita sua" of myself. A little further on in his essay he pronounces another word of wisdom: "attribution is or should be a slow process." As an instance of a flash of recognition resulting in an unexpectedly happy outcome when followed by "the slow process of attribution," Annunciation and Brigittine Nuns (No. 75) may serve. This leaf was offered in 1985 in one of Christie's London book sales. Its catalogue illustration set off a whole glockenspiel of recognitions and memories in my head. It was obviously painted by a Florentine artist of the

first class (I thought—not entirely wrongly—of Lorenzo Monaco), and most desirable; but what excited me even more was the lower half, depicting the patron saint of Sweden, St. Bridget, her head surrounded by a halo. As she was canonized in 1391, this had to be a very early representation of her as a saint. Now I had heard in my youth a great deal about St. Bridget, having spent many happy months in Sweden with one of the foremost authorities on St. Bridget, Dr. Isak Collijn (1875–1949), Chief Librarian of the Royal Library in Stockholm, a position with which goes the resounding title of "Riksbibliotekarie," i.e. Imperial Librarian. He and his wife were close friends of my family. I had been familiar with the extensive Brigittine section of Dr. Collijn's large, beautifully bound private library, which, of course, included his voluminous edition of her *Revelations*. It goes without saying that I had to make this leaf my own and achieved this after a long bidding battle over the transatlantic telephone. Seven years later Laurence Kanter recognized it as the only surviving book illumination by Bicci di Lorenzo, the Florentine quattrocento painter who was influenced by Lorenzo Monaco. Attributions, I may add, must often be left to the specialist in a particular field, period, or artist. This process is brilliantly demonstrated by Bill Voelkle and Roger Wieck in the following catalogue, a monument to their learning, expertise, and painstaking research.

I became a collector of book illuminations by chance. Outstanding illuminated manuscripts had begun to play an important role in my professional activities, but it had never occurred to me to keep any of them for myself. Quite apart from the fact that I could hardly have afforded such a luxury, the experiences of my youth had instilled in me a vision of the impermanence of valuable possessions. I had witnessed in those terrible times too many instances of such possessions becoming a ballast that dragged their owners down to perdition or from which they could only free themselves at great sacrifice. One such instance had been my own father's bibliographical library of some twenty thousand volumes, which he considered his life's work: as he could not take it out of Germany, it had to be sold off piecemeal at tremendous loss, both emotional and material.

It so happened that sometime in 1966 I had the dining room of my London apartment redecorated; the resultant rearrangement produced a big empty space on one of its walls. One day I bought at Sotheby's a large leaf from an Antiphonary illuminated soon after 1350 by the famous Bolognese artist Niccolò da Bologna (No. 70). It occurred to me that, when framed, it would beautifully fill that empty space—and it did. Looking at it every day, I soon began to realize how spectacularly such medieval and Renaissance paintings on vellum would decorate other walls of my apartment—and they could still be had at prices that were derisory in comparison with those of other coeval artifacts. (If that situation has now radically changed, I must plead guilty to being an accessory to it.) The early history of painting is largely to be found in illuminated manuscripts. If I could not afford collecting such entire manuscripts (and competing with my clientèle), I could at least afford a group of single leaves which had been separated from manuscripts of high quality, creating a small gallery of medieval and later art "in miniature." Appetite comes with eating, as Rabelais observed, and my collection kept growing in many directions. I had sold a number of single leaves before I had become a collector of them, which I now regretted. Two of them nearest to my heart I was only recently able to reacquire, thanks to the accommodating generosity of the original purchaser (Nos. 3 and 22). I also discovered that my youthful phobia of personal possessions had been assuaged—with a vengeance. There was also a golden rule I discovered: once a dealer decides to form a personal collection on a special subject, he must dig an unbridgeable moat between it and his stock-in-trade, which no temptation, no favorable offer for this or that single item must ever violate.

When fifteen years ago—at an age when many people start contemplating retirement and cherish the prospect of cultivating their gardens or playing endless rounds of golf—I began a *Vita Nova* in this hospitable city which has become my home, my collecting passions, far from abating with increasing age, were re-energized, along with my professional activities, by the vitality pulsating through this—for me—doubly New World.

My principal aim became rounding off the collection in depth and circumference, making it as representative as possible of the trends and developments in the principal countries in which the art of illumination flourished.

My collection has been favored by lucky chances and coincidences. Perhaps a benign fairy had deposited in my cradle a grain of serendipity, the gift for making happy and unexpected finds by accident, as Horace Walpole, that great eighteenth-century English collector, author, and wit, called this faculty after three legendary princes of Serendip, the Sri Lanka of today. Thus, I was able to reunite four of eight surviving masterpieces by the French court painter Jean Bourdichon from the Book of Hours of Henry VII of England, which turned up in three different places within a few months (Nos. 8–11), and two *membra disjecta* of an Antiphonary from the Hospital of Santa Maria della Scala in Siena, illuminated by an outstanding artist of that city, Pellegrino di Mariano (Nos. 83–84). Equally lucky I consider the acquisition, in two fell swoops, at an interval of twenty-three years, of six chefs-d'oeuvre by the celebrated Flemish artist Simon Bening (Nos. 22–27).

Without the unerring judgment and persevering enthusiasm of Dr. Charles E. Pierce, Jr., Director of the Pierpont Morgan Library, this exhibition would never have taken place. If my collection will give even a fraction of the pleasure it has afforded me over the years, to the public to whom it is now unveiled, I shall feel richly rewarded.

Bernard H. Breslauer

New York

Petrus Christus, *Portrait of a Young Man*, ca. 1450, panel. London, National Gallery.

INTRODUCTION

IN ONE WAY the collecting of single illuminated manuscript leaves—a pursuit distinguished here from collecting complete manuscripts—can be traced back at least to the fifteenth century. We know this because fifteenth-century Netherlandish illuminators painted miniatures on single leaves for insertion into manuscripts, especially Books of Hours. The production of such single miniatures was voluminous, to judge from the numbers of them found in manuscripts of the period, and from the fact that their production caused friction between rival centers. In a dispute in 1426, for example, between the Bruges guild of painters and that of book producers, the painters complained that images made in Utrecht and elsewhere were sold both in books and by themselves, a practice that was putting them out of work. Further testimony to the large market for single leaves is the 1463 decree in Ghent which forbade single miniatures to be brought into the city except during fairs. These single pictures were sought after by booksellers who would interleave them in Books of Hours to make these manuscripts more desirable. But some of the pictures also made their way onto people's walls, as devotional images and aids for meditation and prayer or, like today, as decorations. And, indeed, single leaves can be spotted, attached to interior walls of chapels or middle-class houses, in fifteenth- and early-sixteenth-century panel paintings. A wonderful example is Petrus Christus's *Portrait of a Young Man* in London's National Gallery. Carefully tacked to the wall behind the sitter is a single leaf whose prayer has been so meticulously painted that it can easily be read. The words belong to the "Salve sancta facies" (Hail, holy face), a prayer to the face of Christ imprinted miraculously onto Veronica's veil. Very popular in the fifteenth century, especially in Flanders, the prayer was often accompanied by a picture because indulgences could be gained by the person who recited it while looking at an image of Christ's face. A documented early purchase of a single leaf involves the German Renaissance artist Albrecht Dürer. He recorded in his travel diary to the Netherlands that on 21 May 1521 he bought a miniature of Christ as Savior from the illuminator Susanna Horenbout (1503–45), daughter of the artist Gerard, commenting that "It is a miracle that a woman should do so well."

Another documented, though unusual, instance of early single-leaf collecting involves a theft. Bona of Savoy, widow of Duke Galeazzo Maria Sforza of Milan, commissioned a Book of Hours about 1490 from the artist Giovanni Pietro Birago. While part of the manuscript was finished and delivered to its patron, a major section was stolen from Birago's workshop by a certain Fra Gian Jacopo. The artist sought compensation—he valued the stolen section at the high sum of over 500 ducats—and Jacopo was imprisoned. The purloined leaves were, however, never returned, and they soon came into the possession of Giovanni Maria Sforzino, bastard half-brother of Galeazzo Sforza. To date, only three of the pilfered leaves from Bona's Hours have come to light; the Breslauer calendar miniature of a hawking scene (No. 86) is one. Bona's book was the object of a theft because it contained valuable pictures. The secular, aristocratic subject matter of the twelve calendar illustrations would have been especially attractive to a Renaissance audience. These full-page pictures, when framed, could take on the appearance of small panel paintings or, when glazed (as is the Breslauer example), of painted enamels.

In the sixteenth and early seventeenth centuries some artists were famous for their single leaves, most notably Giulio Clovio (1498–1578). Vasari's assessment of him as the "most excellent illuminator" no doubt contributed to the subsequent cult of Clovio, which, from the mid-sixteenth to our own century, has caused many works in similar styles to be wrongly attributed to him (such as No. 93). Although earlier illumination was generally regarded as barbaric, Italian Renaissance illumination was not, which explains why it was favored by many early collectors.

The situation dramatically changed, however, with the French Revolution, the ramifications of which were as great for the collecting of medieval art as they were for politics. The ensuing secularization of monasteries flooded the book market with medieval manuscripts, which were often sold by weight. The dealer Peter Birmann (1758–1844) specialized in medieval miniatures and, beginning in 1795, assembled some 475 of them in an album that he sold to Daniel Burckhardt-Wildt (1759–1819), a minor artist and manufacturer of silk ribbon in Basel. This collector's taste was amazingly catholic for a time in which much illumination was considered the product of crude and unlettered artists. The album remained the property of Burck-hardt-Wildt's descendants until 25 April 1983, when its contents were removed and sold in London by Sotheby's in a sale whose appropriate code word was "scissors." The insertion of miniatures and cuttings into an album calls to mind the related practice of "grangerization" (named for a practice popularized by James Granger in 1769), adding extra illustrations to a book, usually those cut from other books.

Birmann was not the only dealer to take advantage of troubled times. The abbot turned dealer, Luigi Celotti (ca. 1768–ca. 1846), acquired from Napoleon's soldiers a large number of service books that they had looted from the Sistine Chapel in 1798; these he dismembered and profitably sold as fragments at Christie's in London on 26 May 1825. Not content with merely cutting up manuscripts—thus avoiding English import tariffs on bound volumes—Celotti also arranged bits and pieces into clever montages, the better to make them look like pictures and to conceal their bookish sources. Breslauer's Birth of John the Baptist (No. 90) was lot 70 of the landmark Celotti sale, the first devoted entirely to single leaves. Celotti employed William Young Ottley (1771–1836), art historian, collector of single leaves, and later keeper of prints at the British Museum, to catalogue the ninety-seven lots for his sale. "These specimens are," Ottley writes in the sale catalogue's introduction, "in many cases, found in a more perfect state of preservation than the frescoes and other large works of painting remaining to us of the same periods. To this it may be added, that the processes which were resorted to by the ancient Illuminists, in preparing and laying on the different metals used in decorating their paintings, and in mixing their colours, have long ceased to be remembered; so that whatever performances of this kind now remain to us, merit also our regard as the *monuments of a lost Art.*" What we would today call miniatures (from the Latin, *miniare*, to color with red lead), cuttings, or single leaves, had to be sold as "Illumined Miniature Paintings," in other words, as illuminated paintings that happen to be small. Ottley's curiosity about medieval art was wide-ranging enough for him to think of studying illumination for depictions of costumes that might be useful in dating blockbooks. His collection is mentioned in Thomas Frognall Dibdin's 1817 *Bibliographical Decameron*, which includes an early, if rambling, appreciation of illumination. Ottley's own leaves and cuttings were sold, also as "Miniature Paintings," in 244 lots at Sotheby's on 11 May 1838, a sale that further served to heighten interest in the collecting of single leaves.

Another early collector of single leaves was James Dennistoun of Dennistoun (1803–55). This Scottish antiquary went abroad in 1825 and 1826, and, beginning in 1836, stayed in Italy for twelve years collecting material—including single leaves—for a projected study on the history of medieval Italian art. Although the study was never completed, Dennistoun did publish the three-volume *Memoirs of the Dukes of Urbino, Illustrating the Arms, Arts & Literature of Italy, 1440–1630* in 1851. While most of his collection was sold at auction after his death in 1855, Dennistoun's album of cuttings passed to his granddaughter, who sold it to Kenneth Clark in 1930. At the Clark sale in 1984, the album was broken up, and the miniatures were either sold separately or in groups. The three cuttings now in the Breslauer Collection had originally been purchased by Dennistoun directly from the Charterhouse of Lucca in 1838 (Nos. 67–69).

Throughout the course of the nineteenth century the appreciation of medieval art and single leaves increased as an integral part of the Gothic revival. "Cut missal up in evening—hard work," wrote John Ruskin (1819–1900) in a diary entry of 1854. Ruskin, author, critic, social theorist, the first professor of art in England, was himself the owner of nearly one hundred medieval manuscripts. Dismembering an illuminated manuscript was seen as analogous to releasing innocent victims from their prison, a book. William Blades, who in his *Enemies of Books* rails against the choirboys of Lincoln who amused themselves by cutting out with their penknives illuminated initials from the cathedral's service books, could not himself resist the attraction of collecting. In the same book Blades confesses, "Many years since I purchased at Messrs. Sotheby's a large lot of MS. leaves on vellum, some being whole sections of a book, but mostly single leaves. Many were so mutilated by the excision of initials as to be worthless, but those with poor initials or with none were quite good, and when sorted out I found I had got large portions of nearly twenty different MSS . . . . I had each sort bound separately, and they now form an interesting collection."

There were, of course, other European collectors of leaves. It was probably Sir Richard Wallace (1819–90) who assembled the small but fine group of thirty-two examples in the Wallace Collection; these are mostly Italian, which was often the case with early collections. The artist and collector Charles Fairfax Murray (1849–1919), who may have owned No. 86, assembled over seventy leaves and cuttings from Italian manuscripts; these subsequently were owned by the publisher and dealer Ulrico Hoepli (1847–1935) of Milan, and are now part of the Cini Foundation Collection in Venice. By the end of the nineteenth century, the demand for "liberated" illuminations made their faking a lucrative enterprise. The Spanish Forger, working around the turn of the century, probably in Paris, supplied this hungry market with a prodigious number of single leaves with apparent factory-like efficiency; nearly 175 examples of his illuminations have been identified, two of which are in the Breslauer Collection (Nos. 14 and 15).

Our own century has witnessed the flowering of appreciation for the single illuminated leaf. Edouard Kann assembled over fifty examples, including some specimens of Near Eastern illumination. The collection, which was published in a luxurious catalogue in Paris in 1926, was dispersed, and Breslauer's calendar page from the Arenberg Psalter (No. 34) was Kann's most important leaf. Daniel Wildenstein (1917–), whose father, Georges (1892–1963), was one of the founders of the Société Française de Reproductions de Manuscrits à Peintures, collected over two hundred examples and donated them to the Musée Marmottan in Paris. In this country, one thinks of the small but fine selection bought over the years by Philip Hofer (1898–1984), founder of the Department of Printing and Graphic Arts of Harvard's Houghton Library; the over fifty miniatures and leaves assembled by the great collector of rare books and graphic arts Lessing J. Rosenwald (1891–1979) and given to the National Gallery of Art in Washington; the over two hundred miniatures collected by Robert Lehman (1892–1969), some of which are now part of the Lehman Collection at the Metropolitan Museum of Art in New York; and the some three thousand cuttings given by John Frederick Lewis (1860–1932) to the Free Library of Philadelphia, a rich storehouse of material that remains largely unexplored by art historians. J. Pierpont Morgan (1837–1913), of course, collected single leaves as well as codices.

Another person too often ignored in the world of single leaves—and who represents, perhaps, a uniquely American approach to the field—is Otto F. Ege (1888–1951), a Cleveland art educator and designer. Unable to afford perfect manuscripts and printed books, Ege collected damaged and fragmentary codices and single leaves. "For more than twenty-five years, I have been one of those 'strange, eccentric, book-tearers'," Ege wrote in an article, "I Am a Biblioclast," which appeared in the March 1938 issue of *Avocations: A Magazine of Hobbies and Leisure*. He includes in this piece what could be called his five commandments for an honest book breaker: (1) Never take apart a museum piece or unique copy; (2) Make leaves available to schools, libraries, and individuals; (3) Circulate exhibitions supplemented with lectures and slides to foster an interest in fine books; (4) Offer inspiration through leaves to modern calligraphers and private presses; and (5) Build up a personal collection to illustrate the history of the book from its very beginnings. To fulfill some of these commandments Ege assembled and sold portfolios from his leaves and printed sheets: "Original Leaves from Famous Bibles: Nine Centuries, 1121–1935 A. D.," which included four manuscript leaves, and "Original Leaves from Famous Books: Eight Centuries, 1240 A. D.–1923 A. D.," which included three. Two more sets, solely of manuscripts, appeared shortly after Ege's death: "Fifteen Original Oriental Manuscripts" and "Fifty Original Leaves from Medieval Manuscripts: Western Europe, XII–XVI Century."

Special mention should also be made of Mortimer Brandt (1905–). An art dealer in New York from the 1930s to the 1960s, he assembled a collection of twenty-nine illuminations, one of the most important of which is the German Gothic Last Judgment now in the Breslauer Collection (No. 33). Accompanied by a catalogue written by Harry Bober, professor at New York University's Institute of Fine Arts, the collection began a road tour of the United States that started in 1964 at the Cummer Gallery of Art in Jacksonville, Florida, and ended in 1986 at Williams College in Williamstown, Massachusetts—seventeen stops in all.

Although Bernard Breslauer began collecting single leaves only in 1967, when he purchased the large Three Marys at the Tomb by Niccolò da Bologna (No. 70), he has been able, through patience and perspicacity, to assemble one of the finest collections in private hands today. Given his initial predilection for Italian illumination, which links him with some of the collectors mentioned above, it is not surprising that nearly half of his miniatures are Italian. In addition to a second leaf by Niccolò da Bologna (No. 71), there are major examples by the Master of the Dominican Effigies (No. 66), Don Simone Camaldolese (Nos. 72 and 73, the latter signed and dated), Lorenzo Monaco (No. 74), Bicci di Lorenzo (No. 75, the only illumination known by this artist), Pellegrino di Mariano (Nos. 83

and 84), Franco dei Russi (No. 79), and Giovanni Pietro Birago (No. 86, one of the long lost pages discussed above).

After the Italian miniatures, the twenty-four German leaves form the second-largest group, with examples ranging in date from the thirteenth to the sixteenth centuries. Particularly noteworthy are the early-thirteenth-century Death of the Virgin (No. 31), the richly illuminated calendar page from the Arenberg Psalter of about 1238 (No. 34), and a charming late-thirteenth-century Nativity of Swiss origin (No. 38). Although the French section, with fifteen leaves, is smaller than the two schools just mentioned, it contains some highly important works. These include a very rare eleventh-century Lectionary leaf from Jumièges (No. 1), an early-fourteenth-century Crucifixion made for Narbonne Cathedral (No. 4), four superb miniatures by Jean Bourdichon from the so-called Hours of Henry VII (Nos. 8–11), and an Allegory of Peace by Bernard Picart, dated 1715, that was originally part of a manuscript recounting the history of the Peace of Utrecht (No. 13).

Among the ten Netherlandish miniatures are an important Adoration of the Magi by the Master of the Older Prayer Book of Maximilian I (No. 21) and six miniatures by Simon Bening (Nos. 22–27), including what is perhaps his last and most poetic landscape. The most important of the three English miniatures is a rare work, made in London about 1420, representing a murder scene, perhaps Joab killing Abner (No. 18). The two examples from Spain are both noteworthy: the first (No. 29) is from an early-thirteenth-century Beatus Apocalypse made in Castile about 1200, the parent manuscript of which is now in the Bibliothèque Nationale in Paris, and the second (No. 30) is a huge folio from a fifteenth-century Antiphonary made for Cardinal Pedro Gonzales de Mendoza.

We bring this collection to the public not only as a record of Mr. Breslauer's achievement but to share the fruits of his discerning eye. It is our hope that by documenting these miniatures through description and illustration, we will advance knowledge and appreciation about them. We have attempted to reconstruct their original, often liturgical, context by identifying, where possible, the type of manuscript from which the leaves originally came, sister leaves (that is, folios, miniatures, or cuttings coming from the same manuscript), and parent manuscripts (those codices from which the leaves strayed). It is our hope, too, that the present volume will be useful to others facing the often frustrating challenge of cataloguing single leaves and cuttings. Recognizing that our entries and attributions often represent the first investigation of this collection, we invite those who own or are aware of related leaves to bring them to our attention. By learning more about the original context of these leaves, our understanding and appreciation of them will transcend the pleasure experienced in viewing them merely as "miniature paintings."

W. M. V.
R. S. W.

ihm qui crucifixus est queritis. Non est hic.
surrexit enim. sicut dixit. Uenite &ui
dete locum: ubi positus erat dominus.
Et cito euntes dicite discipulis eius: quia
precedet uos ingalileam. Ibi eum uide
bitis ecce predixi uobis.

No. 1. Three Marys at the Tomb, France, Jumièges, late 11th century.

Qð ds cum sit in oniub; reb; cetualit n tn
coinqnat sordib; reru suec tpr mouet.

Cu ds sit ubiqz. æ sep. n tn local. nec loco

Quib; mus aliqd dicat locale. l ecu septibile.

Quid sit mutari secdm tep.

Utru spc creati sit locales. l ecu septibiles.

Qð ds e ubiqz. sine locali motu

An scia. l pscia di sit ca reru. l e conuso.

Utrum pscia di possit falli.   l mutari.

Utru scia di possit augi. l minui. l aliq m

An ds possit nouit. l ex tpr scret l pscire aliqd.

Utru ds possit pla scire quam scit.

Qð ds æ semp. æ simul scit omia.   l saluari.

An aliqs pdestinat possit dapnari. l reprbus

Quid sit reprbatio di. æ in qib; considat. l qs
sit pdestinationis effectus.

Utru aliqd sit iuitu obdurationis l misedie.

De varijs sup hoc carnaliu oppositionib;.

An ea q semel scit ds. l pscit. sep sciat. l p
sciat. l sep scierit. l pscierit.   l facit.

De oipotentia di. quare dicat oips. cu nos
multa possim. que ipse n pot. n qd uult

Quom dicat ds omia posse.

Quod oipotentia di secdm duo considet.
iuiectio cont illos q dicunt dm nil posse
nisi qd uult. æ fac.   l meliori in.

An ds possit fac aliqd meli q fac. l alio.

Utrum ds possit semp omie qd potuit.

De uoluntate di que essentia di e. l de sig
nis eius.

Qð licet idem sit ds uelle qd ee n tam pot
dici. dm omia ee que uult.

De intelligentia haru loqutionu. ds scit
ds uult. ds scit omia. l uult aliquid.

Qð di uoluntas suine bona causa e oiuium.
q natali sit. eu sca n e qrenda. qz pma e. l
summa causa omniu.

Quib; muis accipit dei uoluntas.

Qð pceptio. phibitio. pmissio. consiliu. opa
cio noie uoluntatis intdu accipiunt.

Utru ds uelit ab oib; fieri ea q pcipit. l n
fieri ea que phibet.   l potest.

Qð uoluntas di q ipse e in nullo caissari

Quom intelligendu sit illud. uolui cogre
gare filios tuos. l noluisti. Et illd qd uult

omnes homines saluos fieri.   l fieri boni.

Utru mala deo uolente. l nolente fiant.

Quom intelligendu sit illud augustini. mala

De multiplici acceptione boni.

Qð mala uniusitati ualent.

Qð in deo n e causa. ut fiat ho decior.

Quom uoluntas di de hoie implet qcq; se uitat.

Ex q sensu qdam dnr fieri cont di uoluntate.

Quare pcepit ds omia bona facere. l mala ui
tare. s; n id ab omib; uult impleri.

Qð ho aliqn bona uoluntate aliud uult q ds. l mala ide qð sc.

Qð dei uoluntas p malas hoiu uoluntates iplet.

Utru placuerit iuris scis qd xpc moreret. æ
pateretur.

Utrum passiones scorum debeamus uelle.

ac noue le
gis cotineo
tiam dilige
ti indagine.
etia atqz. æ
considantib;
nob; puta di
gracia inno
tuit. sacre
pagine tra
tatum. circa
res. l signa

pcipue usari. Ut enim egregi doctor aug
uinus ait. in libro de doctrina xpiana. Omis
doctrina. l reru est. l signoru. S; res. æ p
signa discunt. ipe aut hic res appellantur. q
n ad significandum aliqd adhibent. Signa
u. quorum usus e in significando. Eoru aut
aliqua sunt. quoz omis usus e in significa
do. n in iustificando. i. qb; n utimn. i aliq
significandi gra. ut aliq sacramta legalia.
alia que non solum significant. s; cofert
qd in adiuuet. sic euuglica sacramta. Ex
quo apte intelligit. que hic appellent sig
na. res ille uidelicet. q ad significandu aliqd
adhibent. Omie q signu. æ res aliq e. Quod
eni nulla res e. ut in eodem aug. ait. oino
nil e. Hon aut e conuso. omis res signu e. qz

No. 2. Saint Writing, Central France or Paris, ca. 1180.

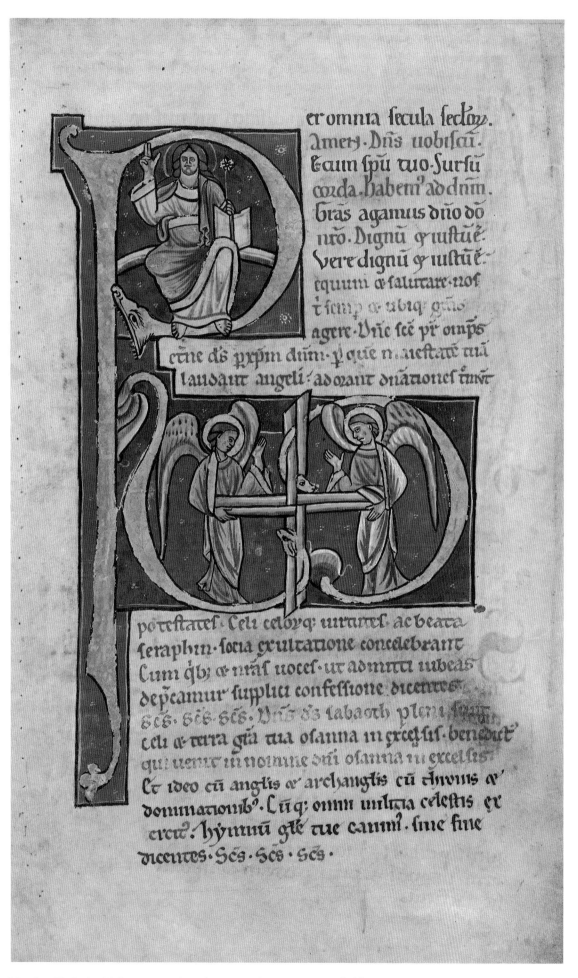

er omnia secula seclo͛z.
Amen. Dns uobiscu.
Et cum spu tuo. Sursu
corda. habem͛ ad dnm.
Gras agamus dno do
nro. Dignu͛ & iustu͛ e.
Vere dignu͛ & iustu͛ e.
equum & salutare. nos
t semp & ubiq͛ gͥͣs
agere. Dͥͤne see pr omps
etne ds pxpm dnm. y qͥe m͛ aiestate tuͣ
laudant angeli: adozant dnͣationes tͥmͤt

potestates. Celi celo͛zq͛ uirtutes. ac beata
seraphin. socia exultatione concelebrant
Cum q͛bᵈ & nͣraſ uoces. ut admitti iubeas
deͥpcamur supplici confessione dicentes.
sc̄s. sc̄s. sc̄s. Dn͛s ds ſabaoth pleni ſunt
celi & terra gͥͣ tua osanna in excelsiſ. benedict͛
qui uenit in nomine dn̄i osanna in excelsiſ.
Et ideo cu͛ anglis & archanglis cu͛ thͥonis &͛
dominationib͛. Et tͥq͛ omni militia celestis ex
ercit͛. Hymnu͛ glͤe tue canim͛. sine fine
dicentes. Sc̄s. Sc̄s. Sc̄s.

No. 3. Christ in Majesty; Two Angels Supporting a Cross, probably France, late 12th century.

No. 4. Crucifixion, France, probably Narbonne, late 13th century.

No. 5. Emperor Heraclius Expounding His Heresies,
France, Loire valley, ca. 1470.

No. 6. The Sultan Receiving the Emperor Diogenes,
France, Loire valley, ca. 1470.

No. 7. Boccaccio Addressing the Philosophers,
France, Loire valley, ca. 1470.

No. 8. Adoration of the Magi, by Jean Bourdichon, France, Tours, ca. 1500.

No. 11. Bathsheba Bathing, by Jean Bourdichon, France, Tours, ca. 1500.

No. 17. St. Saturninus, England, late 14th century.

No. 18. Joab Killing Abner or Amasa, by the Master of
Trinity College B. 11. 7, England, London, ca. 1420.

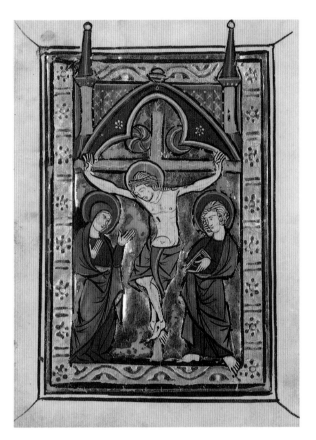

No. 19. Crucifixion, Belgium, probably Bruges or Ghent, ca. 1265–75.

No. 20. Pentecost, Belgium, probably Bruges or Ghent, ca. 1265–75.

No. 21. Adoration of the Magi, by the Master of the Older
Prayer Book of Maximilian I, Belgium, probably Ghent,
ca. 1490.

No. 22. Arrest of Christ, by Simon Bening,
Belgium, Bruges, ca. 1530.

No. 27. Rest on the Flight into Egypt, by Simon Bening,
Belgium, Bruges, 1540s.

No. 28. Tower of Babel, by Jacob van der Ulft, The Netherlands, second half of the 17th century.

No. 29. The Lamb Defeating the Ten Kings, Spain, region of Burgos, first third of the 13th century.

No. 30. Ascension, Spain, probably Toledo, ca. 1482–95 (detail).

No. 31. Death of the Virgin, Germany or Austria, ca. 1200.

No. 33. Last Judgment, Germany, Augsburg, ca. 1235–50.

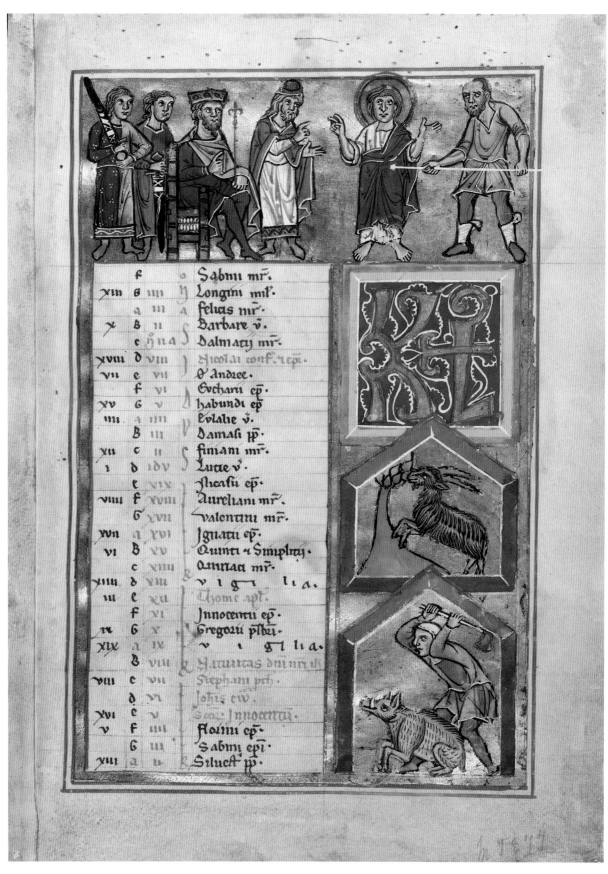

No. 34. Martyrdom of St. Thomas; Capricorn; Butchering a Hog, Germany, diocese of Hildesheim, probably Braunschweig, ca. 1238/39 (recto).

No. 34. Annunciation, Visitation, Nativity, Germany,
diocese of Hildesheim, probably Braunschweig, ca. 1238/39 (verso).

No. 38. Nativity, Switzerland, Lake Constance area, late 13th century.

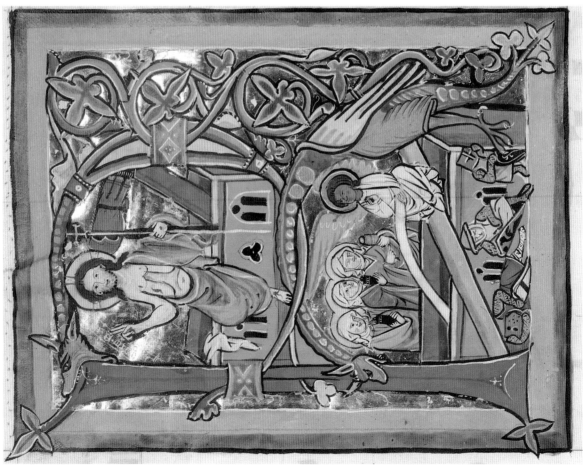

No. 35. Resurrection and Three Marys at the Tomb, Germany, Regensburg, late 13th century (detail).

No. 39. Christ Instructing Two Apostles, in the style of Johannes von Valkenburg, Germany, Cologne, early 14th century.

No. 44. Resurrection, by Conrad Wagner, Germany, Augsburg, ca. 1485–89.

No. 47. Last Supper, by Joannes Zmilely de Pisek or workshop, Czechoslovakia, Prague, ca. 1500 (detail).

No. 46. Christ Appearing to the Three Marys, and John and Peter Arriving at the Tomb, Germany, possibly Augsburg, late 15th century (detail).

No. 48. Coronation of the Virgin, Germany, Bavaria, dated 1504.

No. 49. St. Michael Weighing a Soul, Germany, Nuremberg, ca. 1520.

No. 62. All Saints, Italy, Genoa?, second quarter of the 14th century.

No. 63. Presentation in the Temple, by the workshop of Marino di Perugia, Italy, Perugia, 1320s.

SPIRITOSANTOGLORIO

No. 66. Pentecost, by the Master of the Dominican Effigies, Italy, Florence, ca. 1340.

No. 67. Resurrection, possibly by Martino di Bartolomeo, Italy, Tuscany, probably Lucca, late 14th century.

No. 71. St. Dominic, by Niccolò da Bologna, Italy, Bologna, ca. 1386 (detail).

No. 70. Three Marys at the Tomb, by Niccolò da Bologna, Italy, Bologna, ca. 1365 (detail).

No. 72. Adoration of the Magi, by Don Simone Camaldolese and workshop, Italy, Florence, late 1380s (detail).

No. 74. Ascension, designed by Lorenzo Monaco but completed by Bartolomeo da Fruosino and, possibly, Fra Angelico, Italy, Florence, ca. 1423–24.

No. 75. Annunciation and Brigittine Nuns at Choir, by Bicci di Lorenzo, Italy, Florence, ca. 1435.

No. 78. Ducal Privilege, by the Hippolyta Master,
Italy, Milan, dated 29 September 1462 (detail).

No. 77. Circumcision, by the Master of the
Vitae Imperatorum, Italy, Milan, 1430s.

No. 79. Adoration of the Magi, by Franco dei Russi, Italy, Veneto, 1470s.

No. 81. God the Father Blessing, by Francesco d'Antonio del Chierico, Italy, Florence, early 1460s (detail).

No. 82. Two Male Saints, by Ricciardo di Nanni, Italy, Florence, early 1460s (detail).

No. 83. Christ Calling St. Peter, by Pellegrino di Mariano, Italy, Siena, dated 1471 (detail).

No. 84. Three Marys at the Tomb, by Pellegrino di Mariano, Italy, Siena, datable to 1471 (detail).

No. 86. Hawking, by Giovanni Pietro Birago, Italy, Milan, ca. 1490.

No. 88. Crucifixion, Italy, possibly Lombardy or Naples, late 15th century.

No. 89. Penitent David, Italy, Florence, ca. 1500.

No. 90. Birth of John the Baptist, by Vincent Raymond, Italy, Rome, ca. 1523.

No. 91. Crucifixion, by Vincent Raymond, Italy, Rome, ca. 1545.

No. 92. Adoration of the Shepherds, Italy, Rome, mid-16th century.

No. 93. Presentation in the Temple, Italy, probably Rome, last quarter of the 16th century.

No. 95. Adoration of the Magi.

No. 95. Presentation in the Temple (verso).

No. 96. Betrayal (verso).

No. 97. Christ Crowned by Thorns.

No. 97. Flagellation (verso).

No. 98. Ecce Homo.

No. 98. Way of the Cross (verso).

No. 99. Deposition (verso).

No. 101. St. Catherine.

Italy, probably Rome, late 16th century.

No. 104. Lamentation, by Francesco Grigiotti, Italy, Rome, first third of the 17th century.

CATALOGUE

1 Three Marys at the Tomb

Leaf from a Gospel Lectionary with a miniature. France, Jumièges, late 11th century. Vellum, 275 x 183 (195 x 113) mm, 1 column of 24 lines; the miniature is on a recto.

MICHAEL GULLICK observed, in conversation with us, that the tall, narrow display capitals with pronounced serifs, some finished with dots, used on this leaf and the sister leaf in the Morgan Library are very much like those employed by Hugo, who signed himself *pictor*, the painter, the best known Jumièges artist-scribe from the late eleventh century. (The manuscripts written and/or decorated by Hugo are enumerated by Michael Gullick, "The Scribe of the Carilef Bible: A New Look at Some Late-Eleventh-Century Durham Cathedral Manuscripts," *Medieval Book Production: Assessing the Evidence*, Linda L. Brownrigg, ed., Los Altos Hills, Calif., 1990, 75.) Hugo is best known for the signed self-portrait he added to his manuscript of Jerome's Commentary on Isaiah (Oxford, Bodleian Library, MS Bodley 717, fol. 287v; reproduced, along with a second self-portrait, in Otto Pächt, "Hugo Pictor," *Bodleian Library Record*, III, 1950–51, pls. Va and c). In his manuscript of Jerome on Isaiah, Hugo employs the attenuated capitals seen on the Breslauer and Morgan leaves; and in both is found another of his idiosyncrasies, making the letters *O, E,* and *I* small and then suspending or floating them among the taller letters (compare Christopher de Hamel, *A History of Illuminated Manuscripts,* Boston, 1986, pl. 81). Gullick, however, does not think the Breslauer and Morgan leaves are the work of Hugo, but rather of an artist who could have been trained in Jumièges or encountered Hugo's script elsewhere in Normandy.

Gullick's association of the Breslauer and Morgan leaves with Jumièges can be supported by the stylistic similarity of their drawings to the work of another artist, apparently also working in Jumièges, to whom two manuscripts have been attributed by François Avril: Augustine's Commentary on the Psalms and a Gospel Book (Rouen, Bibliothèque Municipale, MS 459, and London, British Library, Add. MS 17739; see the third chapter of Avril's thesis, *La décoration des manuscrits dans les abbayes bénédictines de Normandie aux XIe et XIIe siècles,* a summary of which is provided in *Ecole nationale des chartes: Positions des thèses,* Paris, 1963, 21–28). This second Jumièges artist gives his figures somewhat chinless heads perched on stretched, taut necks, and has a penchant for softening the normally jagged, English-inspired edges of his drapery, into kidney-shaped forms. These features can be seen in the Rouen Augustine (Avril, *Manuscrits normands, XI–XIIème siècles,* Rouen, 1975, 53, no. 47, illus.) and even more so in the London Gospels (Hanns Swarzenski, *Monuments of Romanesque Art: The Art of Church Treasures in North-Western Europe,* Chicago, 1967, figs. 197 and 198; and Elżbieta Temple, *Anglo-Saxon Manuscripts, 900–1066,* London, 1976, fig. 50). The Morgan leaf, furthermore, has a large initial constructed of two parallel bars with intertwining foliate tendrils terminating in biting lions' heads. Similar constructions can be found in the Rouen and London manuscripts. While it is not possible for us to attribute the Breslauer and Morgan leaves to this second Jumièges artist on the basis of photographic comparison, they may indeed turn out to be by this artist or a third Jumièges illuminator working in a related style.

TEXT: "In die s[an]c[t]o Pasche seque[n]tia s[an]c[t]i evangelii s[e]c[un]d[um] Marcu[m]" (On the day of holy Easter, the reading of the holy Gospel according to Mark) is the rubric for the Gospel from Mark 16:1–7 for Easter, which begins on the verso, "In illo tempore Maria Magdalene et Maria Jacobi et Salome emerunt aromata . . . " (At that time, Mary Magdalene, Mary the mother of James, and Salome bought sweet spices . . .). This is followed by the beginning of the Gospel reading for Monday ("F[e]r[ia] ii") of Easter week. The text at the top of the recto of the leaf, "Ih[esu]m qui crucifixus est . . . ," is the end of the Gospel reading for Holy Saturday (Matthew 28:1–7).

SISTER LEAVES: New York, Pierpont Morgan Library, MS M. 1037 (Pentecost, on a bifolio).

PROVENANCE: Bought from Bernard M. Rosenthal, San Francisco, in 1985.

iħm qui crucifixarus est querras. Non est hic.
surrexit enim. sicut dixit. Uenite drui
dete locum. ubi positus erat dominus.
Et cito euntes dicite discipulis eius. quia
precedet uos in galileam. Ibi eum uide
bitis ecce predixi uobis.

1 Three Marys at the Tomb (color plate p. 17).

2 Saint Writing

Leaf from Peter Lombard, *Liber Sententiarum,* with a historiated initial V. Central France or Paris, ca. 1180. Vellum, 318 x 234 (245 x 154) mm, 2 columns of 45 lines; the initial is on a verso.

PETER LOMBARD'S *Liber Sententiarum (Book of Sentences)*, Jacqueline Turcheck has written, "is the crowning achievement of centuries of scholarly endeavors to systematize the large body of Christian doctrine that had accumulated over the years" ("A Neglected Manuscript of Peter Lombard's *Liber Sententiarum* and Parisian Illumination of the Late Twelfth Century," *Journal of the Walters Art Gallery,* XLIV, 1986, 48–69). Born near Novara in Lombardy, Peter (ca. 1100–60) began his influential teaching career at the Cathedral School of Paris soon after 1134. He wrote his monumental *Sententiarum libri quattuor* from about 1155 to 1158, was appointed bishop of Paris in 1159, and died the following year. Arranged in four major parts, the *Book of Sentences* offers lengthy theological discussions on the Trinity, the Creation and Sin, the Incarnation and the Virtues, and the Sacraments and the Four Last Things. Although after Peter's death certain of his teachings were violently attacked, the *Book of Sentences* emerged unscathed from the Fourth Lateran Council in 1215, which pronounced the text orthodox. Thereafter it became the standard textbook for theology during the Middle Ages. The work's success is to be found not in its originality, but in its comprehensiveness and accessible arrangement. Frequent commentaries appeared after its completion in 1158, the latest in 1635.

The seated saint writing on a scroll in the initial has the stylized drapery and is set within the foliate and animal forms typical of French Romanesque art in the last quarter of the twelfth century. The identification of this figure, however, presents something of a puzzle. Like the manuscript from which this leaf came, a number of manuscripts of the *Book of Sentences*, produced within the first ten or twenty years following Peter's death, include an author portrait at the start of Book I. Usually shown seated and busy writing his text, Peter can be identified, even in the rather generic portraits typical of the late twelfth century, by his maturity, his episcopal garments, and his lack of a halo. The Breslauer figure, however, is clearly a young man, does not wear contemporaneous ecclesiastical garb, and is a saint. St. Augustine comes to mind as a possible identification because this Church Father is the first authority cited in red just below and to the right of the historiated initial and he is the most frequently cited authority in Peter's text. This saint, however, is always depicted as an older man and dressed as a bishop. John the Evangelist is a better candidate, since he is typically depicted as a beardless youth. The reference to the New Testament in the text's opening lines also supports this identification, as does the scroll with which John is often supplied to distinguish him from the other evangelists.

TEXT: "Veteris ac nove legis . . . " (Of the old and new law . . .) is the beginning of Book I ("Incip[it] [pr]i[mus] liber") of Peter Lombard's *Liber Sententiarum.*

SISTER LEAVES: London, Victoria and Albert Museum, MS L. 19-1983 (London, Sotheby's, 25 April 1983, lot 15, illus. [opening leaf with foliate initial]).

PROVENANCE: The parent manuscript: Gilles Robert; given by him to the Jesuit Collège de Clermont (later known as the Collège de Louis-le-Grand) in Paris in 1567 (their no. 152); possibly Gerard Meerman (1722–71), who acquired most of the manuscripts from the Collège after its suppression in 1764 (Meerman's manuscripts passed to his son, Jean, whose estate was sold at The Hague in 1824; many manuscripts went to Sir Thomas Phillipps); possibly the Bibliothèque Impériale, France. This leaf: bought in London, Sotheby's, 5 December 1989, lot 15, illus.

Qd̃ dꝭ cum ſit in onĩb; reb; ēentalit n̄ tñ
coinꝗnat ſordib; reꝝ ſue tpͬ mouet.

Cu̅ dꝭ ſit ubiꝗ; .& ſep.n̄ tñ local. nec loco

Quib; unꝭ aliꝗd dicat̃ locale. l̃ ecuiſcriptibile.

Quo ſit mutari ſedm̄ tēp.

Vͭru ſpē creati ſtͭ locales. ꝛ ecuiſcriptibiles.

Qd̃ dꝭ ē ubiꝗ; ſine locali motu

An ſcīa. l̃ pſcīa dī ſit cā reꝝ. l̃ e conūſo.

Vͭru̅ pſcīa dī poſſit falli. Jmutari

Vͭru̅ ſcīa dī poſſit augͥ.l̃ mĩnui. l̃ aliꝗ m̄

An dꝭ poſſit nouit̃.l̃ ex tpͬ ſciret̃ pſcͥraliꝗd.

Vͭru dꝭ poſſit plͣ ſcire quam ſcit.

Qd̃ dꝭ ꝇ ſemp. ꝙ ſimul ſcit omͥa. Jſaluari

An aliꝗꝭ pd̃eſtinat̃ poſſit dãpnari. l̃ repꝛbus

Quo ſit repꝛbatio dī. ꝙ in ꝗb; conſidat̃.ꝛ ꝗꝭ
ſit pd̃eſtinationis effectus.

Vͭru aliꝗd ſit mͥtͥ obdurationis l̃ miſc̃die.

De uarꝭys ſup hoc carnaluı̄ oppoſiti oͥnib;.

An ea ꝗ ſemel ſcit dꝭ.l̃ pſcit.ſep ſciat̃.ꝛ p
ſciat̃.ꝛ ſep ſcieͭt.ꝛ pſcieͭt. Jſacͭ.

De oͥnipotentia dī. quare dicat̃ opꝭ. cu̅ nos
multa poſſim̃.que ipſe n̄ pot̃.n̄ ꝙd uult

Quo̅ dicat̃ dꝭ omͥa poſſe.

Quod oͥnipotentia dī ſedm̄ duo conſidͤt̃.
mͥectio conͭ illos ꝗ dicunt dm̄ nıl poſſe
niſi ꝙ uult. ꝙ faꝫ. Jmeliori m̄.

An dꝭ poſſit faꝫ aliꝗd melͥ q̃ faꝫ. l̃ alio. l̃

Vͭrum dꝭ poſſit ſemp omē ꝙd potuıt.

De uoluntate dī que eſſentia dī ē ꝛ de ſig
nıſ eıus.

Qd̃ licet idem ſit dꝭ uelle ꝙ ēē n̄ tam̃ pot̃
dicı. dm̄ omͥa ēē que uult.

De mͥtelligentia harͥ loquͥtionu̅.dꝭ ſcit̃
dꝭ uult. dꝭ ſcit omͥa. l̃ uult aliꝗd.

Qd̃ dī uoluntaſ ſu̅me bona cauſa ē omͥum.
ꝗ natͣlit̃ ſt.cauſa n̄ ē ꝗ̃renda.qͭ pͥma ē ꝛ
ſu̅ma cauſa omͥu̅.

Quib; mͥſ accipit̃ deı uoluntaſ.

Qd̃ pc̃eptͥo.ꝓhibͥtͥo.pͥmiſſio.conſiliu̅.opͣ
cıo noͥe uoluntatıſ muͭdu̅ accipıu̅t̃.

Vͭru dꝭ uelıt ab oͥb; fieri ea ꝗ̃ pc̃pͥt.l̃ n̄
fieri ea que ꝓhibet. Jpoteſt.

Qd̃ uoluntaſ dī ꝗ ipſe ē in nullo cauſſari

Quo̅ mͥtelligendu̅ ſit illud.uoluı cõgre
gare filios tuos.ꝛnoluıſtı. Ɇ illud ꝙd uult

omneſ homıneſ ſaluos fieri. Jfieri bonͥ.

Vͭru mala deo uolente.l̃ nolente fiant.

Quo̅ mͥtelligendu̅ ſit illud auguſtinͥ. mala

De multiplıcı acceptione bonͥ.

Qd̃ mala unıͥſıtatı ualent.

Qd̃ in deo n̄ ē cauſa.uͭ fıat hō dectͥor.

Quo̅ uolu̅taſ dī de hoͥe implet̃ ꝙꝗ ſe uͭtat̃.

Ɇ x̃ ꝗ ſenſu ꝙdam dm̄ fieri conͭ dī uoluntate̅.

Quare pc̃pͥt dꝭ omͥa bona facͭe.ꝛ mala mͥ
tare.ſ; n̄ ıd ab oͥnıb; uult ımplerı.

Qd̃ hō aliꝗn bona uoluntate aliud uult q̃ dꝭ.ꝛ mala ıdē ꝙ ſe

Qd̃ deı uoluntaſ p malaſ hoͥu̅ uoluntateſ ıpͥlet̃.

Vͭru placuerıt uirıſ ſcīs ꝙd x̃pē moꝛeretͭ. ꝛ
pateretur.

Vͭrum paſſiones ſecu̅dum debeamus uelle.

pc̃pue uſarı. Vͭ eͭ egregͥ doctoꝛ aug̃
tınuſ aıt.ın libro de doctrina x̃pıana. Omͥſ
doctrına.l̃ reru̅ eſt.l̃ ſıgnoꝛum.S; res̃ ꝗ̃ p
ſıgna diſcuͭt̃.ıp̃e auͭ hͣe reſ appellaͭtur.ꝗ
n̄ ad ſıgnıficandum alıꝙd adhıbenͭ.Sıgna
ñ.quorum uſus ē ın ſıgnıficando.Eoꝝ auͭ
aliꝗ ſunt.quoꝝ omnıs uſus ē ın ſıgnıficaͭ
do.n̄ ın ıuſtıficando.ı.ꝗb; n̄ utͥmͥ.n̄ alıꝙd
ſıgnıficandı grͣ .uͭ alıꝗ ſacraͭnta legalıa.
alıa.que non ſolum ſıgnıficant.ſ; cõferͭ
ꝙd uͭ admͥuet.ſıc eu̅glıca ſacraͭnta. Ɇ
quo apͭe mͥtellıgıͭ.que hͣe appellenͭ ſıg
na.res̃ ılle ındelıcet̃.ad ſıgnıficandu̅ alıꝙd.
adhıbenͭ.Omͥe ꝗ ſıgnı.l̃ res̃ alıꝗ ē.Qͣuod
ecͥ nulla res̃ ē.uͭ ın eodem aug̃.aıt.oͥno
nıl ē.Hon auͭ e conūſo.omͥſ res̃ ſıgnu̅ ē.ꝗ

2 Saint Writing (color plate p. 18).

3   Christ in Majesty; Two Angels Supporting a Cross

Leaf from a Missal with historiated initials P and V+D. Probably France, late 12th century.
Vellum, 289 x 209 (212 x 122) mm, 1 column of 28 lines; the initials are on the verso.

THE Preface of the Mass is introduced by the versicle "Per omnia secula seculorum, Amen" (Forever and ever, Amen), whose large P contains an example of the iconographic type called a Christ in Majesty. The Savior is seated on a rainbow, raises his right hand in blessing, and holds a scepter and book in his left. In a tradition that began at least as early as the ninth century and lasted until the early thirteenth, it was customary to mark the beginning of the Preface in Missals or Sacramentaries with such an image. It was no doubt inspired by the text's reference to Christ's majesty and by the words of the Sanctus, "Holy, holy, holy, Lord God of Hosts. Heaven and earth are filled with your glory. Hosanna in the highest. Blessed is he who comes in the name of the Lord. Hosanna in the highest." It was also traditional to mark the beginning of the text proper of the Preface by enlarging or decorating the monogram, V+D. These letters, joined by a cross, stand for the unchanging words that start all Prefaces, "Vere dignum et justum est" (It is fitting indeed and just). Here the monogram has been placed, for decorative purposes, at the center of the leaf; the actual start of the text can be spotted six lines above. In this V+D two angels support and adore the large cross joining the initials. Angels, the various choirs of which are mentioned in the text of the Preface, frequently accompany Christ in his Majesty.

In *The Year 1200: A Background Survey,* the volume of essays published in 1970 to accompany the Metropolitan Museum of Art's exhibition "The Year 1200," Derek Turner remarked how much more work needed to be done on illumination dating to about 1200. "It is the mutation from Romanesque to Gothic," he wrote, "which particularly calls for investigation, for the progress of research is making abundantly clear how decisive an event this was and, further, that it gave rise to something which was a style in its own right, not just a postlude to Romanesque or a prelude to Gothic." Twenty-two years have passed and Turner's statement still holds true. The decoration of this late-twelfth-century leaf partakes neither of the hard-lined abstractions of Romanesque art, nor yet of the naturalistic fluidity of the Gothic. (A similar ambiguity surrounds the German Death of the Virgin, No. 31.) The painting of the initials has been thought to be German, English, or French. The last seems at this point the most convincing. The thick-set Christ and slow moving angels, for example, share some general similarities with the sluggish figures in the *Life of St. Amand,* painted in St.-Amand in the second half of the twelfth century (Valenciennes, Bibliothèque Municipale, MS 500; Jean Porcher, *French Miniatures from Illuminated Manuscripts,* London, 1960, fig. 38 and pl. XXXII) and, as pointed out by Walter Cahn, with those in the Saint-Fuscien Psalter at Amiens (Bibliothèque Municipale, MS 19; V. Leroquais, *Les psautiers manuscrits latins des bibliothèques publiques de France,* Mâcon, 1940–41, pl. xiv). As Cahn and J. J. G. Alexander observed to us, rather inelegant figures—with thick drapery and somewhat mean-looking facial expressions—resembling those in the Breslauer leaf can be found in the illuminations painted by the "Principal Hand" in the Giffard Bible in Oxford (Jennifer M. Sheppard, *The Giffard Bible: Bodleian Library MS Laud misc. 752,* New York, 1986, 62–69, numerous plates). Traditionally localized to England, the Giffard Bible is given to France in the early 1170s by Sheppard, who says, however, that the artist was English or, at least, trained there. The style of the Breslauer leaf, with its softer drapery folds, seems a little later than that of the Bible. These comparisons are presented for their general shared similarities; a final localization for this leaf cannot be offered here.

TEXT: "Per omnia secula sec[u]lorum . . . " (Forever and ever . . .) introduces the Common Preface and Sanctus. On the recto of the leaf are parts from the Ordinary of the Mass; in the margins, written in a later hand, are variations and additions to the Ordinary.

PROVENANCE: London, Martin Breslauer, Catalogue 94 (*A Miscellany of Manuscripts, Autographs & Printed Books from the 11th to the Present Century . . .*), 1961, 14, no. 37, cover illus.; bought in 1992.

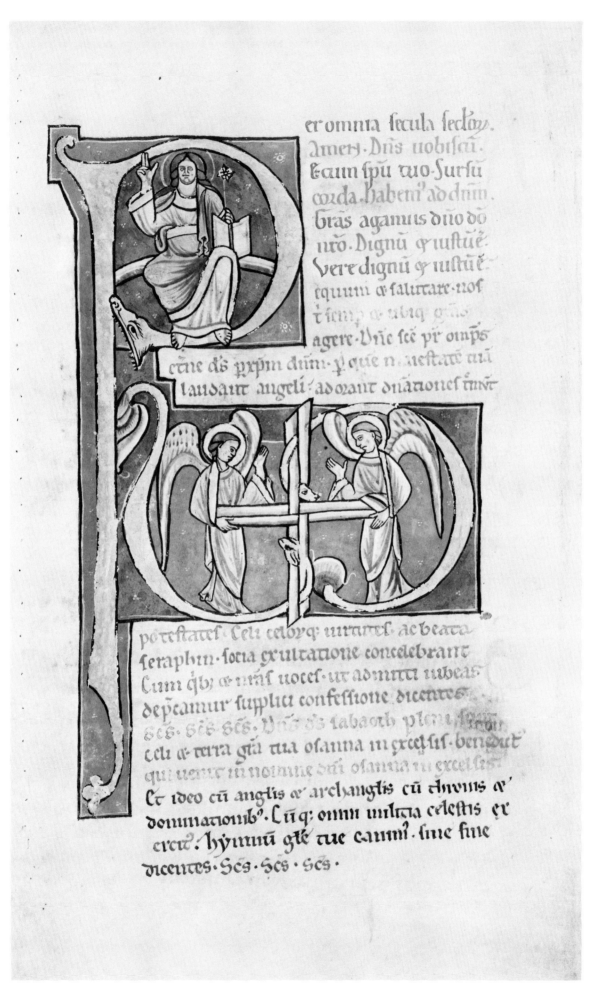

er omnia secula seclox.
Amen. Dns uobiscu.
Et cum spu tuo. Sursu
corda. Habem' ad dnm.
Gras agamus dno do
nro. Dignu & iustue.
Vere dignu & iustue.
equum & salutare. nos
ti semp & ubiq gras
agere. Dnce sce pr omps
etne ds xpm dnm. p que n. uestate tua
laudant angeli. adorant dnationes tint

poteftates. Celi celoxq; uirtutes. ac beata
feraphin focia exultatione concelebrant
Cum qb; & nras uoces. ut admitti iubeas
depcamur fuppliti confeffione dicentes.
Scs. Scs. Scs. Dns ds fabaoth pleni funt
celi & terra gra tua ofanna in excelfif. benedct
qui uenit in noie dni ofanna in excelfif.
Et ideo cu anglis & archanglis cu thronis &
dominationib'. Cu q; omni militia celeftis ex
ercit. Hymnu gte tue canim. fine fine
dicentes. Scs. Scs. Scs.

3 Christ in Majesty; Two Angels Supporting a Cross (color plate p. 19).

71

4 Crucifixion

Miniature from a Missal. France, probably Narbonne, late 13th century.
Vellum, 233 x 161 mm; the miniature is probably on a verso.

WHEN this Crucifixion first appeared on the market it was hailed as a notable unrecorded English Gothic miniature related to that in the Psalter of Robert de Lisle (London, British Library, Arundel MS 83, fol. 132), but more recently it has been assigned to southern France by Alison Stones, who suggested a localization around Toulouse. Now, in addition, it can be connected with the nearby cathedral of Narbonne. The telling clues are the two highly unusual male saints flanking John, identified by the scrolls as Justus and Pastor, the patron saints of that cathedral. Their presence makes it probable that the Missal was commissioned for the cathedral itself, the construction of which was begun under Pierre de Montbrun, archbishop of Narbonne from 1272 to 1286. Since work proceeded slowly on the cathedral, the Missal could also have been commissioned by his successor, Gilles Aycelin, archbishop from 1290 to 1311 and in 1309 appointed chancellor of France. The Crucifixion is also unusual in two other ways: Christ grits his teeth, and, amidst all of the sorrowing figures, the moon smiles, having been permitted to shine unexpectedly from the sixth to the ninth hour, when the sun was darkened. Christopher de Hamel has suggested that Christ's smudged loincloth resulted from repeated osculation, the kissing of the Missal by the priest during Mass.

This Crucifixion, following a long practice, marked the beginning of the Canon of the Mass, the text for which began with the words, "Te igitur." The letter *T*, of course, is a cross, and the text that follows includes the consecration of the bread and wine, symbolizing the body and blood of Christ.

Because the manuscripts produced in southern France have not been well published or studied, it is difficult to determine if the Crucifixion was painted in Narbonne or Toulouse. For a somewhat similar Crucifixion made in Toulouse, also with unusual saints, see the Missal of the Jacobins (Toulouse, Bibliothèque Municipale, MS 103; reproduced by A. Auriol, "Le Missel des Jacobins: Manuscrit de la Bibliothèque de Toulouse," *Les trésors des bibliothèques de France,* Paris, 1935, V, pl. XIX).

PROVENANCE: Bought in London, Sotheby's, 11 December 1979, lot 6, illus.

4 Crucifixion (color plate p. 20).

5 Emperor Heraclius Expounding His Heresies
6 The Sultan Receiving the Emperor Diogenes
7 Boccaccio Addressing the Philosophers Theodorus, Anaxarchus, and Scaevola

Three miniatures from Boccaccio, *Des cas des nobles hommes et femmes*. France, Loire valley, ca. 1470. Vellum, 100 x 79, 115 x 81, and 113 x 76 mm; all the miniatures are on rectos.

IN 1400 Laurent de Premierfait completed his first translation of Boccaccio's *De casibus virorum illustrium;* stiltedly close to the original Latin and in infelicitous French, it was not a success. Premierfait's second translation, finished in 1409 and dedicated to Jean, duc de Berry (for whom Premierfait worked as secretary), was considerably different, included a number of amplifications, and met with approval. Two nearly identical copies of the newly translated text, both with about 150 illustrations, were prepared. One was presented to the duc de Berry as a New Year's gift in 1411 by the archbishop of Chartres (Geneva, Bibliothèque Publique et Universitaire, MS fr. 190), and the other was for his brother John the Fearless, duke of Burgundy (Paris, Bibliothèque de l'Arsenal, MS 5193; for both manuscripts see Millard Meiss, *French Painting in the Time of Jean de Berry: The Limbourgs and Their Contemporaries,* New York, 1974, 283–87). Illustrated copies of Boccaccio's text continued to be popular throughout the fifteenth century, and early printed editions were brought out by Colard Mansion, in 1476, and by Antoine Vérard, in 1494 (see Bibliothèque Nationale, *Boccace en France: De l'humanisme à l'érotisme,* Paris, 1975, 66–72).

The parent manuscript from which these three miniatures and their sisters come was a lavishly illustrated volume of Premierfait's second translation. The surviving fragments indicate that the original manuscript probably had a large, half-page miniature introducing each of the nine books and small, single-column miniatures for many, if not each, of the chapters, totaling, possibly, as many as 176 miniatures. The Breslauer pictures are all from Book IX. In the first, Emperor Heraclius, shown at the right, is promoting the heresies for which he was later to meet his unfortunate end. The second miniature depicts the Turkish sultan, at the left, receiving the defeated emperor of Constantinople, Diogenes. In the third, Boccaccio, in contemporaneous clothing, addresses the philosophers Theodorus, Anaxarchus, and Scaevola. The man singled out in the middle is probably Theodorus, who was brutally killed for refusing to name his fellow conspirators in the slaying of the tyrant Hiero.

The Breslauer miniatures have not been attributed to a known hand. Their style is similar to illumination of the third quarter of the fifteenth century from the Loire valley. Indeed, on the basis of style and costume they can be dated to about 1470. Except for the small sister miniatures listed below, other work by this hand has not yet been found. The problem of attribution is complicated by the fragmentary survival of the original manuscript and the fact that, since the larger miniatures from the manuscript are more accomplished, there was more than one artist at work.

TEXT: All three miniatures contain fragments from Book IX of Boccaccio's *Des cas des nobles hommes et femmes:* No. 5: "il nen distribueroit nulles a ces chie[n]s . . . " is from Chapter 2; No. 6: "et la gloire de dyogenes qui fut grant . . . " is from Chapter 9; and No. 7: "certains moyans & consentement . . . " is from Chapter 22.

SISTER LEAVES: London, Sotheby's, 11 April 1961, lot 96, illus. (large miniature: Samuel Anointing Saul and Boccaccio Writing His Text); London, Sotheby's, 29 November 1990, lots 35–37, illus. (three small miniatures: Death of Laodamia in the Temple of Diana; Andriscus, Imposter King of Macedon, Placed in Stocks; and Execution of Demetrius Nicator, King of Syria); New York,

Pierpont Morgan Library, MS M. 1057 (large miniature: Seleucus Callinicus and Antiochus Hierax Before Boccaccio); Paris, Les Enluminures, Le Louvre des Antiquaires (small miniature: Murder of the Children of Arsinoë II Philadelphus; ex-London, Sotheby's, 10 July 1967, lot 9, illus.); Paris, private collection (large miniature: subject unknown); and probably London, Christie's, 8 December 1981, lot 98, illus. (two small miniatures, subjects undetermined).

PROVENANCE: Bought from H. P. Kraus, New York, about 1970.

BIBLIOGRAPHY: Vittore Branca, ed., *Boccaccio Visualizzato,* Turin, forthcoming in 1993.

5 Emperor Heraclius Expounding His Heresies
(color plate p. 21).

6 The Sultan Receiving the Emperor Diogenes
(color plate p. 21).

7 Boccaccio Addressing the Philosophers
(color plate p. 21).

Four miniatures, from a Book of Hours, illuminated by Jean Bourdichon. France, Tours, ca. 1500. Vellum, 243 x 170 (130 x 81) mm, 1 column of 18 lines; nos. 8, 10, and 11 are on rectos; no. 9 is on a verso.

IN a little over three months during the spring and early summer of 1974, Bernard Breslauer was able to collect these four important miniatures by Jean Bourdichon from the so-called Hours of Henry VII. In the previous fall, Breslauer had read Janet Backhouse's article in the *British Museum Quarterly* (see below) on the fragments of the manuscript housed in the British Library. In March of 1974, he bought the Presentation from H. P. Kraus, and in July he quickly secured the other three in sales at Christie's and Sotheby's in London.

The traditional connection of the parent manuscript with Henry VII of England (1457–1509) is tantalizing, though unproven. The association with the king comes from the spine of the nineteenth-century British Museum binding that houses fifty-two text leaves of the manuscript; the binding's inscription apparently repeats that of an earlier, but now lost, cover. In his 1817 *Bibliographical Decameron,* Dibdin, who saw the book in its earlier binding, mentions Henry's ownership; also, the book came to the British Museum with royal manuscripts. Its leaves, however, lack any signs of English royal ownership, and there is evidence that another king might have commissioned the book. A miniature of Louis XII of France accompanied by his patron saints is thought to come from this manuscript. If so, this would point to the French monarch as the first owner (perhaps around the time of his succession in 1498), but the present location of this miniature is unknown. Thus the issue remains unresolved.

No matter who commissioned or first owned the manuscript, its surviving miniatures rank among the most important by Jean Bourdichon. Working for a succession of France's monarchs—Louis XI, Charles VIII, Louis XII, and Francis I—from the early 1480s until his death in 1520/21, Bourdichon was a versatile court artist who also painted panels, decorated statues, made maps and death masks, and designed tents, banners, and heraldic devices. He headed a large workshop, but it is clear that the miniatures from the Hours of Henry VII were painted by Bourdichon himself. His works for prestigious patrons include the Hours of Charles d'Angoulême, the Hours of Frédéric III d'Aragon, the Hours of Charles VIII, and the Hours of Anne de Bretagne (Paris, Bibliothèque Nationale, MSS lat. 1173, 10532, 1370, and 9474). Of this group, it is to Anne's *Grandes Heures,* the artist's undisputed masterpiece for which he was paid the astounding sum of 1,050 *livres tournois* in 1508, that the Hours of Henry VII is most comparable. Both are large-scale manuscripts, with majestic compositions inhabited by large figures close to the picture plane and set in simple trompe-l'oeil gold frames with epigraphic inscriptions set against a dark, marble background. The absence of the Italianate frames found in Bourdichon's slightly later Books of Hours, such as the *Grandes Heures,* and the conservative treatment of the foliage and flowers painted by an assistant on the backs of the Breslauer leaves support Janet Backhouse's dating of about 1500 for the Hours of Henry VII.

Of the four Breslauer miniatures, the three of the early life of Christ depict scenes that traditionally accompanied the Hours of the Virgin since the late-thirteenth-century inception of the Book of Hours. Bathsheba Bathing as an illustration for the Penitential Psalms was a late French development, replacing the more customary image of the penitent King David, the traditional author of the Psalms. Remarkable, however, is the blatantly seductive attitude assumed by the Breslauer Bathsheba. She more than coyly eyes the king, who peeps at her from his palace window, and shamelessly reveals her anatomically correct genitalia—a highly unusual feature in manuscript illumination. Tiny waves, originally painted silver but now turned black, once highlighted rather than concealed her charms.

TEXT: Adoration of the Magi: "Deus i[n] adiutoriu[m] meu[m] i[n]tende . . . " (O God, come to my aid . . .) is the beginning of Sext of the Hours of the Virgin. Presentation in the Temple: "Deus i[n] adiutoriu[m] meu[m] i[n]tende . . . " is the beginning of None ("Ad Nonam" on the recto of the leaf) of the Hours of the Virgin. Flight into Egypt: "Deus i[n] adiutoriu[m] meu[m] i[n]tende . . . " is the beginning of Vespers of the Hours of the Virgin.

8 Adoration of the Magi (color plate p. 22).

Bathsheba Bathing: "D[omi]ne ne i[n] furore . . . " (O Lord, rebuke me not in thy indignation . . .) is the beginning of the Penitential Psalms.

PARENT MANUSCRIPT: Much of the surviving manuscript is in the British Library: 53 text leaves (Royal MS 2 D. XL, and one stray is in Harley MS 5966, fol. 9) and 3 miniatures: Add. MS 35254, fols. T (Job on the Dung Heap), U (Pentecost), V (Virgin Annunciate).

SISTER LEAVES: Cambridge, Magdalene College, Pepys' Calligraphical Coll., I, p. 13 (text leaf); Edinburgh, National Library of Scotland, MS 8999 (Luke). Two other miniatures, present whereabouts unknown, might also be sisters (King Louis XII of France with Sts. Michael, Charlemagne, Louis, and Denis; and a Nativity).

PROVENANCE: Parent manuscript: possibly King Henry VII of England; probably broken up in England shortly before 1700. Adoration of the Magi: bought in London, Christie's, 11 July 1974, lot 6, illus. Presentation: bought from H. P. Kraus, New York, in March 1974. Flight into Egypt: Sir Tom Hickinbotham; bought at his sale in London, Sotheby's, 8 July 1974, lot 25. Bathsheba: D. E. Schwabach; bought in London, Christie's, 11 July 1974, lot 7, illus.

BIBLIOGRAPHY: Janet Backhouse, "Bourdichon's 'Hours of Henry VII'," *British Museum Quarterly,* XXXVII, 1973, 95–102, pls. XXXVIII, XLII; and "Hours of Henry VII," in *Renaissance Painting in Manuscripts: Treasures from the British Library,* Thomas Kren, ed., New York, 1983, 163–68, figs. 21b, 21c; Eberhard König, *Das Vatikanische Stundenbuch Jean Bourdichons: Cod. Vat. Lat. 3781,* Zurich, 1984, 86, 88, 132 n. 113, Abb. 10; Jane E. Rosenthal, *The Vatican Book of Hours from the Circle of Jean Bourdichon: Cod. Vat. Lat. 3781,* Yorktown Heights, N.Y., 1989, 39, 56, 76, 90 n. 47.

9 Presentation in the Temple.

10 Flight into Egypt.

11 Bathsheba Bathing (color plate p. 23).

12 Entry into Jerusalem

Historiated initial D, from a Gradual, illuminated by the workshop of the Master of Morgan 85. France, probably Rouen, ca. 1520. Vellum, 170 x 175 mm, 1 column with staves of 4 red lines; the initial is on a recto.

WHILE the production of large choir books is normally associated with medieval and Renaissance Italy, Spain, and Germany—as the numerous specimens in the Breslauer Collection testify—late‑fifteenth‑ and early‑sixteenth‑century France seems to have witnessed a sudden interest in this type of liturgical service book. Four large historiated initials survive, for example, from a monumental choir book that, according to its coat‑of‑ arms, was possibly made for the eldest son of King Charles VIII and Anne of Brittany, the Dauphin Charles‑ Orland, who lived only from 1492 to 1495 (the fragments were sold in London, Sotheby's, 8 July 1974, lots 26– 29, illus.). Anne was later involved in the commission of another monumental Gradual, while married to Louis XII (from 1499 until her death in 1514). This choir book, which contains their initials and arms, also survives in fragmentary form (Akron, Ohio, Bruce P. Ferrini Rare Books, Catalogue 1 [*Important Western Medieval Illuminated Manuscripts and Illuminated Leaves*], 1987, no. 64 [where other fragments are cited], illus., and Ulrich Finke, *Katalog der mittelalterlichen Handschriften und Einzelblätter in der Kunstbibliothek,* Berlin, n.d., 42–45, no. 62, figs. 18, 19). Another example is the large multivolume Gradual divided between Cambridge (Harvard University, Houghton Library, pfMS Lat 186), Baltimore (Walters Art Gallery, MS W. 460), Claremont (Scripps College, Denison Library, MS Perkins 4), and Berlin (Staatsbibliothek Preussischer Kulturbesitz, MS lat. fol. 830). Produced in Rouen in the first quarter of the sixteenth century, it is the type of manuscript from which the Breslauer cutting originally came (Lilian M. C. Randall, *Medieval and Renaissance Manuscripts in the Walters Art Gallery, II: France, 1420–1540,* Baltimore, 1992, no. 201). These four hefty volumes comprise the texts for Holy Thursday through the Twenty‑third Sunday after Pentecost, the Common of Saints, and at least part of the Sanctorale (feasts of major saints); lacking are the volumes containing the feasts of Advent, Christmastide, and Lent. Thus it is possible, considering the similar size, style, and script of the Breslauer initial, that it is from a dismembered volume of this broken‑up set.

The Breslauer initial—like those in the Gradual volumes just discussed—can be attributed to the workshop of the Master of Morgan 85, named after a Book of Hours in the Morgan Library (MS M. 85). The artist was trained in Tours, where he sometimes collaborated with one of its leading painters, Jean Bourdichon (see Nos. 8–11). Stylistically, however, the Morgan 85 Master is closer to, and probably trained under, a follower of Bourdichon known as the Master of Petrarch's Triumphs, after Louis XII's manuscript of that text (Paris, Bibliothèque Nationale, MS fr. 594). In the early years of the sixteenth century, both the Master of Morgan 85 and the Master of Petrarch's Triumphs moved from Tours to Rouen, possibly attracted by potential commissions from Cardinal Georges d'Amboise, archbishop of Rouen and an active patron of manuscript illumination. The move was successful, for the cardinal employed the Petrarch Master and his associates on more than one commission. Thus it was probably in Rouen that the Breslauer miniature and the four stylistically related Gradual volumes were painted.

There are, in public collections and on the art market, a number of large historiated initials that could be sisters to the Breslauer cutting: a Presentation in the Temple sold in London (Schuster Gallery, *Illuminated Manuscripts,* 1987, 19, no. 30, illus.); a Nativity sold in New York (H. P. Kraus, Catalogue 172 [*Illuminations . . .],* 1985, 84, no. 24, illus.; this initial had been sold in London, Sotheby's, 25 April 1983, lot 208, where other cuttings are mentioned); and another Nativity in Toledo (Museum of Art, acc. no. 23.3203). A study of these and similar cuttings needs to be undertaken to determine if they come from the same manuscript or set of manuscripts.

TEXT: D begins the Introit for Palm Sunday, "D[omine ne longe facias . . .]" (O Lord, be not far . . .), which continues on the verso, "[m]ea[m]. p[salmus]. Deus de[us . . . m]e qua[re]. me derel[iquisti.]"

PROVENANCE: Bought in London, Sotheby's, 11 De‑ cember 1972, lot 7.

12 Entry into Jerusalem.

13 Allegory of Peace

Leaf, from a manuscript by Don Luis d'Acuña on the War of the Spanish Succession and the peace concluded at Utrecht, illuminated by Bernard Picart. The Netherlands, Amsterdam, dated 1715. Vellum, 365 x 246 mm; the back is blank.

BERNARD PICART was undoubtedly one of the most important and prolific book illustrators of the first third of the eighteenth century. He was born in Paris in 1673, where he studied under his father, Etienne, and Benoit Audran. Later, after he entered the Académie Royale de Peinture et de Sculpture in 1689, he was taught by Sébastien Leclerc. He was encouraged by Charles Le Brun, who, however, died in 1690, too soon to have had much influence on him. Working in the Netherlands by the end of the century, he took up residence in Amsterdam in 1711, where he married, in 1712, Anne Vincent, the daughter of Ysbrand Vincent, a paper merchant. Picart remained in that city until his death in 1733. He is best known for his biblical vignettes in *Marck's Bible* (*Figures de la Bible*) and his illustrations for the nine-volume *Cérémonies et coutumes religieuses de tous les peuples du monde* (1723–43), Ovid's *Métamorphoses* (1732), and *Le temple des Muses* (1733). Given Picart's importance, it is surprising that no comprehensive study has been devoted to him. Consequently, the fundamental catalogues of his works remain those published by his widow in 1734 (see Bibliography) and Charles Le Blanc in 1888 (*Manuel de l'amateur d'estampes*, Paris, 1888, III, 490–96).

Although it would be natural to assume that the present Allegory of Peace was a study for an engraving, it was not. Picart must have regarded it as one of his most original and important works, for it was discussed in the biography published by his widow the year after his death. Indeed, not only are the circumstances regarding the commission given, but also a description of its complex iconography. According to the biography, Picart prepared three highly finished allegorical title pages for three manuscripts Don Luis d'Acuña, the Portuguese ambassador in the Netherlands, had written regarding the War of the Spanish Succession and the peace concluded at Utrecht. Since d'Acuña had then given them to the king of Portugal, it was thought that a short description of the unique pieces would give pleasure to the public. The first two allegories represented War and the Tower of Babel. The third, the Breslauer leaf, gives a general idea of the Peace of Utrecht, and represents the portal of the Temple of Janus. On the pediment is a Janus-headed bust with portraits of Bernard Picart and his father, Stephanus. Hanging over the closed door is a tapestry, where, on a cloud, Peace has been pulled from her carriage, inscribed "PAX," by Force. Discord pulls Peace with a chain, Treachery pushes her, and Poverty embraces her leg. They are compelled to descend to the earth, followed by Abundance, Justice, and Religion. (Peace does not come easily or willingly: she must be fought for, if not abducted. The Peace of Utrecht was achieved in many stages and over a period of years.) In the foreground, warriors react differently to Peace's descent: some hasten to arms; and one waves a standard in the air, as if to assemble the troops; but another breaks his weapon in anger. In the background, men, women, and children all rejoice by dancing, playing, and embracing, while others are busy with the harvest and grape picking; the ship signifies the freedom of commerce. The two cartouches to either side at the bottom offer biblical parallels: one includes the Sacrifice of Noah after the Flood and the Rainbow Signifying the Covenant of God with Man (Genesis 8:20, 9:13–16); the other, Abraham and Lot Dividing the Land of Canaan (Genesis 13:10–14). At the top, flanking the busts of the Picarts, hang festoons composed of scientific instruments, while on the sides festoons are composed of implements representing the arts, which also flourish during peace. On the left are the tools of painting, sculpture, and architecture; on the right, various musical instruments and music. Further down, on either side and protruding from behind the two cartouches, are navigational devices, while at the bottom, are the tools of agriculture and containers full of fruits and grains, the result of a successful harvest.

A more detailed account of the iconography probably accompanied the manuscript, for that given in the *Eloge historique* was itself characterized as cursory; various personifications, for example, were not described, and the women in the right middle ground are not even mentioned—they represent painting, sculpture, architecture, and so on. Nor are we told that the closed doors of the Temple of Janus, also inaccessible because of the tapestry, signify a time of peace, as did the closed doors of the ancient Temple of Janus in Rome. Picart may have gotten the idea from engravings after Rubens's decorations for the triumphal entry of King Ferdinand into Antwerp in 1634, which included a Temple of Janus (John Rupert Martin, *The Decorations for the Pompa Introitus Ferdinandi*, London, 1972, 162–75, pls. 82–87). The two-faced aspect of Janus who holds a knife behind his back was also used for Treachery.

13 Allegory of Peace.

Force is Hercules, and Discord, one of the furies, is depicted with her hair bristling with snakes, a detail derived from Virgil. Abundance carries her cornucopia and Justice her scales under her arm, not quite ready for use. Religion carries the Tablets of the Law, and a flame is above her head. The meaning of the chariot driven by swans, usually reserved for Venus, is not explained. At the end of the volume, according to the biography, Picart depicted a tranquil sea, with a halcyon building its nest on the waves, and a rainbow in the sky.

There were three more drawings in the manuscripts, but these were of contemporaneous historical events relating to the Treaty of Utrecht itself. One represented the arrival of the ambassadors at the town hall of Utrecht, where the conference was held, while the second depicted the signing of the peace between the Spanish and Portuguese ambassadors at the mall of Utrecht. The third represented the exchange of ratifications on the street in Utrecht known as Porte Blanche, where the two coaches of the ambassadors evidently met.

SISTER LEAVES: Paris, Hôtel Drouot, salle no. 8, 5 December 1950, lot 3 (Allegory of War).

PROVENANCE: King John V of Portugal; possibly John Postle Heseltine collection, London; Paris, Hôtel Drouot, salle no. 8, 5 December 1950, lot 3; bought in Monte Carlo, Sotheby's, 13 June 1982, lot 126.

BIBLIOGRAPHY: Bernard Picart, *Impostures innocentes, ou,* *Recueil d'estampes d'après divers peintres illustres, tels que Rafael, le Guide, Carlo Maratti, le Poussin, Rembrandt, &c., gravées à leur imitation, & selon le gout particulier de chacun d'eux, & accompagnées d'un Discours sur les préjugés de certains curieux touchant la gravure. Par Bernard Picart, dessinateur et graveur: avec son Eloge historique, et le Catalogue de ses ouvrages,* Amsterdam, 1734, 6– 8. (William Voelkle is preparing a study on this leaf.)

14 Making and Tasting Wine
15 Annunciation

Two leaves from a 14th-century Italian Antiphonary with miniatures illuminated by the Spanish Forger. France, probably Paris, early 20th century. Vellum, 475 x 357 and 475 x 362 mm, each 1 column with 7 staves of 4 red lines; both miniatures are on rectos.

THE Spanish Forger was one of the most skillful, successful, and prolific forgers of all time. Until recently his numerous manuscripts, panels, and leaves were appreciated and admired as genuine fifteenth- and sixteenth-century works. Now they are sold and collected as works by the Spanish Forger. He has been known as the Spanish Forger since about 1930, when Belle da Costa Greene, then the director of the Morgan Library, so christened him. She did so after having exposed, as a fake, a panel of the *Betrothal of St. Ursula* that had been attributed to Maestro Jorge Inglès, an artist active in Spain about 1450. After she debunked the panel (which was later given to the Morgan Library), she began to keep a record of the Forger's works, especially since he also faked manuscript illuminations. Her original list, which contained only fourteen items, subsequently grew to nearly 150, all of which were reproduced in the catalogue raisonné published by the Library in 1978. Since then over one hundred more have appeared.

Although the Spanish Forger's name is often taken to mean that he was Spanish, there is no convincing evidence that he was. He was probably active in Paris at the end of the nineteenth and beginning of the twentieth centuries, for most of his works were acquired in Paris or France, and nineteenth-century illustrated Parisian publications, especially those of Paul Lacroix, were his chief compositional, thematic, and, to some extent, stylistic sources.

These large folio illuminations and borders are among the Forger's most ambitious, and they exhibit all the characteristics of his easily recognizable style: overly sweet faces, daring décolletage, page costumes, stock figures, theatrical postures and hand gestures, tapestry-like foliage, and stage-set architecture. To aid the deception the Spanish Forger always used genuine but unillustrated leaves from choir books. In the rare case of this Annunciation, the miniature correctly illustrates the text, which is for that feast. The architectural setting and especially the pose and drapery of the standing Virgin are inspired by Alessio Baldovinetti's *Annunciation* in the Uffizi (reproduced in Bernard Berenson, *Italian Pictures of the Renaissance: Florentine School,* London, 1963, II, pl. 794). In the wine scenes, however, the Forger gives himself away because there is no liturgical feast that would call for this subject. Indeed, the verso of the leaf contains the music for the second feria (day) after the first Sunday after the octave of the feast of Epiphany, a feast that is never illustrated. The miniature, moreover, does not even occur at the beginning of the office. Some details of the wine-making scene are derived from the chromolithograph of Benozzo Gozzoli's fresco of the Drunkenness of Noah (Pisa, Camposanto), which was published by Paul Mantz, *Les chefs-d'oeuvre de la peinture italienne,* Paris, 1870, opp. 107.

TEXT: Making and Tasting Wine: "Sana a[n]i[m]am mea[m] q[ui]a peccavi tibi . . . " (Heal my soul, for I have sinned against you . . .) is the Prime response for Monday after the first Sunday after the Octave of Epiphany. Annunciation: "Quomodo fiet istud angele Dei . . . " (How shall this happen, angel of God . . .) is the Benedictus antiphon ("Ad b[e]n[edictus] a[n]t[iphona]") for the feast of the Annunciation (March 25).

PROVENANCE: Said to have been found, along with six other leaves by the Spanish Forger, in an attic in the Neuilly section of Paris; Librairie Lardanchet, Paris; Jean-François Vilain, New York; bought in 1978.

BIBLIOGRAPHY: William Voelkle, assisted by Roger S. Wieck, *The Spanish Forger,* New York, 1978, 52–53, nos. L50 and L52, figs. 166 and 148.

14 Making and Tasting Wine.

15 Annunciation.

16 Bishop Accused of Simony by Two Fornicators

Miniature, from a *Decretum Gratiani*, illuminated by an artist of the Milemete group. England, 1320s. Vellum, 67 x 66 mm, 2 columns; the miniature is on a verso.

THE twelfth-century Camaldolese monk Gratian is called the father of canon law. He was the author of the *Concordantia discordantium canonum* (Concordance of Discordant Canons), later known as the *Decretum Gratiani*. Dealing with the inconsistencies of nearly four thousand citations from papal decretals (letters), council decrees, and the writings of Church Fathers touching on all aspects of Church discipline, Gratian designed a clear and logical framework for these disparate sources. The first part of his *Decretum* consists of 101 *Distinctiones* that discuss the sources of canon law, the clergy, and their offices. The second part contains thirty-six *Causae*, that is, difficult hypothetical juridical cases. The third part, *De consecratione*, provides the laws relating to the rituals and sacraments of the Church. Soon after publication, Gratian's Decretals became the basic medieval text on canon law, not just in Bologna, where Gratian taught, but also in Paris, Oxford, and other European universities. It remained the foundation of canon law until the promulgation of the Church's new *Codex iuris canonici* in 1917.

Medieval manuscripts of the Decretals were written in two columns (to accommodate a great deal of text) and, when illuminated, often had miniatures decorating the following textual divisions: the beginning of the *Distinctiones*, each of the thirty-six *Causae*, and *De consecratione*. (See Anthony Melnikas's three-volume *Corpus of the Miniatures in the Manuscripts of Decretum Gratiani*, Rome, 1975, 14–19.) While the miniature for the *Distinctiones* was sometimes a large one, spreading across both columns, the numerous illustrations of the *Causae* were smaller, single-column pictures.

The Breslauer miniature originally introduced *Causa* VI, which discusses the case of a bishop accused by two fornicators of simony, the buying or selling of Church offices. The two fornicators in the center, in lay dress, gesture accusingly toward the seated bishop, who raises his hands in defensive argument, and toward the monk on the right to whom they apparently make their accusation. Gratian's text emphasizes that while accusations made by men of dubious morals should be treated cautiously, the accused is still compelled to prove his innocence.

As Lucy Sandler has kindly pointed out, the style of the Breslauer miniature is related to that of a group of artists who illuminated the Treatise of Walter Milemete compiled in London in 1326–27 (Oxford, Christ Church, MS 92; most recently published by Sandler, *Gothic Manuscripts, 1285–1385,* London, 1986, II, 91–93, no. 84). Lucy Sandler finds the work of five different artists within the Milemete Treatise, and the Breslauer miniature is very close to, if not by, her Hand IV. The figures by Hand IV have a gentle Gothic sway, and their faces are delicately drawn and do not bear the harsh features favored by other artists of the Milemete group. The artists of the Milemete group seem to have specialized in illuminated texts for the university market, including Oxford and Paris. Surviving manuscripts include the Decretals of Pope Boniface VIII and an Apparatus on them (Oxford, Bodleian Library, MSS e. Mus. 60 and Lat. misc. b. 16, respectively).

TEXT: On the recto of the miniature is a fragment from the end of *Causa* V of the *Decretum Gratiani*, "li[abc]t in corpore q[uod] velit occultari . . . si de cibo securus iusticia[m]."

PROVENANCE: Bought from Bernard M. Rosenthal, San Francisco, in 1985.

16 Bishop Accused of Simony.

17 St. Saturninus

Miniature from a Book of Hours. England, late 14th century. Vellum, 200 x 135 (150 x 81) mm, 1 column of 23 lines; the miniature is on a recto.

THIS St. Saturninus is the finest of the full-page miniatures (originally numbering thirty-two) that have been located since the Book of Hours to which they belonged was broken up. The miniatures, listed in the Quaritch catalogue cited below, all depict saints and originally accompanied Suffrages that followed the Matins and Lauds portion of the Hours of the Virgin. Although it is unusual to find pictures of Saturninus (Sernin), the first bishop of Toulouse, in English Books of Hours, his name occurs in some Sarum calendars. He was dragged to death by a bull after he refused to offer sacrifice to pagan gods. His feast day is November 29.

It is not certain whether the letters that occur in some of the borders of the other miniatures (k, n, e, y, f, t) are meant to represent a name (possibly a form of Knyvett) or a motto. "Thys is mystrys marys boke, G." is inscribed on a flyleaf, but since the textual portions of the manuscript have not been located, it is not possible to determine if the flyleaf was integral. The Suffrage section of the manuscript contained six miniatures relating to Mary Magdalene. The other important texts—Hours of the Virgin, Seven Penitential Psalms, Office of the Dead— must also have had large miniatures.

Although the miniatures are full-page, it is curious that the figures only occupy the upper part of the page. It is not clear if this resulted from a change in format (perhaps text was to occupy the lower part) or a possible misunderstanding of a prototype where the lower portion was intended to represent a floor. The love of such extravagantly diapered backgrounds can also be found in a geomancy manuscript in Oxford (Bodleian Library, MS Bodley 581) compiled for Richard II in 1391 (various miniatures are reproduced in Amanda Simpson, *The Connections between English and Bohemian Painting during the Second Half of the Fourteenth Century,* New York, 1984, figs. 255–57; and Otto Pächt and J. J. G. Alexander, *Illuminated Manuscripts in the Bodleian Library, Oxford,* Oxford, 1973, III, no. 673, pl. LXX). For reproductions of other works of the same period see Margaret Rickert, *Painting in Britain: The Middle Ages,* London, 1954, especially chapter 7.

TEXT: On the verso is the Suffrage for St. Saturninus, "De sancto saturnino m[a]r[tyr]e. Ant[iphona]. Saturninus martir . . . . "

PARENT MANUSCRIPT: Book of Hours offered by Bernard Quaritch in 1931 (see Provenance).

SISTER LEAVES: Los Angeles County Museum of Art, acc. no. M. 74.100 (3 leaves: text [1], St. Andrew [2v], St. Thomas Beckett [3]); New York, private collection, 2 miniatures (St. Edmund, Raising of Lazarus); London, Sotheby's, 9 February 1948, lots 215 (St. Matthias?) and 216 (St. Margaret).

PROVENANCE: Thomas Boycott, 1761 (bookplate); London, Bernard Quaritch, *A Catalogue of Illuminated and Other Manuscripts, Together with Some Works on Palaeography,* 1931, no. 56, 2 pls. (St. George, St. John the Baptist); bought from Quaritch by H. P. Kraus in 1941; bought from Kraus in the early 1950s by Rudolf Wien, who apparently broke up the manuscript (five leaves were subsequently repurchased by Kraus—see Kraus Catalogue 80, 1956, nos. 16a–e, pl. with St. Nicholas; St. Saturninus was bought from Wien by Eric Korner (his no. 20) in 1952; his sale, London, Sotheby's, 19 June 1990, lot 32; bought from the buyer after the sale.

17 St. Saturninus (color plate p. 24).

18   Joab Killing Abner or Amasa

Miniature, possibly from a Psalter or Book of Hours, illuminated by the Master of Trinity College B. 11. 7. England, London, ca. 1420. Vellum, 142 x 90 mm; the back is blank.

ALTHOUGH this large miniature was thought to represent the murder of Darius or Julius Caesar, its format and lack of text on the back make it less likely that it was once part of an English Alexander romance or *Histoire ancienne.* Two Old Testament scenes, however, both involving murders by Joab, may be more attractive candidates; both were used typologically to prefigure the betrayal of Christ by Judas. In the first, Joab takes Abner aside to speak to him treacherously and then stabs him in the groin to avenge the death of Asael, his brother (2 Kings 3:27). The two soldiers may represent Joab's army. The man behind Abner expresses horror. In the second scene, Joab takes Amasa by the chin with his right hand as if to kiss him, but stabs him in the side, telling him "God save thee, my brother" (2 Kings 20:8 –10). The killing of Abner was used in the *Biblia pauperum,* whereas that of Amasa was used in the *Speculum humanae salvationis.* "O Mors" (O Death) is written on the garment of the victim. The miniature may have been part of an Old Testament cycle in a Psalter or used typologically as the Matins illustration (usually the Betrayal) of the Hours of the Passion in a Book of Hours. Evidence to support the latter can be found in a recently discovered miniature depicting Jacob and Rachel Lamenting their Son Joseph, which, in the *Speculum humanae salvationis,* is a type for the Deposition, the usual Vespers illustration for the Hours of the Passion. Rachel's inclusion further strengthens the typological connection, as the *Speculum* text specifically compares her sorrow with that of the Virgin Mary. Although the new miniature is smaller than the Breslauer leaf, and by a different hand, it may have been part of our Passion cycle; the difference in size and hand could be explained by the fact that the full-page Breslauer leaf, which began the cycle, would have been illuminated by the best artist, while the smaller miniatures for the other hours would be by an assistant.

The miniature has been compared with the work of the illuminator Johannes, active in the first quarter of the fifteenth century: he signed the famous Marco Polo manuscript *(Li livres du Graunt Caam)* in Oxford (Bodleian Library, MS Bodley 264) and also worked on the Hours of Elizabeth the Queen (London, British Library, Add. MS 50001). The former is dated about 1400 (Otto Pächt and J. J. G. Alexander, *Illuminated Manuscripts in the Bodleian Library, Oxford,* Oxford, 1973, III, no. 792, pl. 164a) and the latter from about 1420 to 1430 (Richard Marks and Nigel Morgan, *The Golden Age of English Manuscript Painting, 1200 –1500,* New York, 1981, pls. 35 and 36). This miniature, however, has now been attributed by Kathleen Scott to the Master of Trinity College B. 11. 7, named after the manuscript in Cambridge (in *Later Gothic Manuscripts,* London, forthcoming in 1992). The comparison with the donor before the Virgin and Child in the Trinity College Book of Hours (reproduced by Eric G. Millar, *English Illuminated Manuscripts of the XIVth and XVth Centuries,* Paris, 1928, pl. 92) is particularly striking, and the penwork designs surrounding the inscriptions (Maria) on the Virgin's robe are nearly identical to those found on the robe of the stabbed man in this miniature.

SISTER LEAVES: Possibly Paris, Les Enluminures, Le Louvre des Antiquaires (Jacob and Rachael Lamenting their Son Joseph).

PROVENANCE: Bought in London, Sotheby's, 19 June 1990, lot 53, illus.

18 Joab Killing Abner or Amasa (color plate p. 25).

19 Crucifixion
20 Pentecost

Two miniatures, probably from a Psalter, illuminated by the Ghent/Bruges "Second Group."
Belgium, probably Bruges or Ghent, ca. 1265–75. Vellum, 119 x 88 and 115 x 88 mm;
the backs are blank.

FLEMISH Psalters of the thirteenth century often contained, as their primary pictorial element, cycles of full-page miniatures illustrating the life of Christ. Part of these miniatures often formed a prefatory series while others marked textual divisions within the Psalms. This Crucifixion and Pentecost came from such a series, with the Crucifixion probably as one of the prefatory miniatures and the Pentecost contained within the text. The somewhat short, almost stocky figures with rugged features and crisp, simple drapery with folds drawn in thick black lines are typical of those painted in the third quarter of the thirteenth century in Flanders, especially in Bruges and Ghent. While Flemish and nearby Mosan art of the Romanesque era was primarily Germanic in style, during the course of the thirteenth century Belgian illumination fell increasingly under the sway of the courtlier French Gothic style. These two miniatures can be compared with those in a Psalter produced in Bruges's Groot Seminarie about 1260–65 and still in that institution (MS 55/171; see Gruuthusemuseum, *Vlaamse kunst op perkament: Handschriften en miniaturen te Brugge van de 12de tot de 16de eeuw,* Bruges, 1981, 141–75, no. 74). Maurits Smeyers (in conversation) compared the Breslauer miniatures to an illustrated *Life of St. Lutgarde* produced in the Abbey of Afflighem about 1274 (Copenhagen, Royal Library, Ny kgl. Saml. 168, quarto; published in Sint-Truiden, Provinciaal Museum voor Religieuze Kunst, *Handschriften uit de abdij van Sint-Truiden,* Louvain, 1986, 278–84, no. 65). Both of these manuscripts belong to Kerstin Carlvant's "Tweede Groep," the "Second Group" of artists working in similar styles, first mainly in Bruges and then in Ghent, from the 1260s to the 1280s ("Thirteenth-Century Illumination in Bruges and Ghent," Ph.D. diss., Columbia University, 1978). One of the principal characteristics of these artists is their use of canopies. As can be seen in the Breslauer miniatures, they consist of trefoil gables surmounted by architectural members and framed on four sides by colored and decorated borders.

While Flemish illumination had declined by the end of the twelfth century, by the middle of the thirteenth century a new era had begun. Liège was an important center, as Judith Oliver has demonstrated (*Gothic Manuscript Illumination in the Diocese of Liège, c. 1250 – c. 1330,* Louvain, 1988), as were the cities of Ghent and Bruges, as Carlvant has written. For the next eighty years both areas became important for the production of illuminated Psalters and Psalter-Hours. This new interest in private prayer books resulted from two important factors. The first was the establishment in the Mosan region of the mendicant orders, the Franciscans and the Dominicans. The second was the lay religious movement for women, the Beguines. Although some *béguinages,* the clusters of houses in which the Beguines lived, were already established in the late twelfth century, most in the diocese of Liège were founded between 1240 and 1260, just at the beginning of the period under discussion. From Liège the movement spread to Bruges and Ghent. Beguines were pious widows and virgins who lived together and led a religious life, but did not enter a monastic order. They were known for their pious reading, and many of the prayer books of the second half of the thirteenth and first third of the fourteenth centuries seem to have been made for and used by these women.

PROVENANCE: Bought in Paris, Hôtel Drouot, 15
November 1971, lot 99, illus.

19 Crucifixion (color plate p. 26).   20 Pentecost (color plate p. 26).

21 Adoration of the Magi

Miniature, from a Book of Hours, illuminated by the Master of the Older Prayer Book of Maximilian I. Belgium, probably Ghent, ca. 1490. Vellum, 170 x 90 mm; the miniature is on a verso, the recto blank.

THIS Adoration of the Magi and its sister miniatures have been attributed to an artist called the Master of the Older Prayer Book of Maximilian I after a manuscript made for the Holy Roman Emperor shortly after 1486 (Vienna, Österreichische Nationalbibliothek, cod. 1907; published in facsimile by Wolfgang Hilger, *Das ältere Gebetbuch Maximilians I,* Graz, 1973). The Maximilian Master was one of the major figures of late Flemish illumination; active mainly in Ghent, he was a prolific artist whose career spanned nearly fifty years. Because his career coincides in time and place with that of the illuminator Alexander Bening (active 1469–1519), some scholars have—with reason—identified the Maximilian Master with Alexander, father of the famous Simon Bening (see Nos. 22–27).

As Patrick De Winter has demonstrated, the Maximilian Master was often influenced by such Flemish artists of his day as Gerard David, Joos van Gent, Dieric Bouts, and especially the Ghent painter Hugo van der Goes. He also, as this Adoration makes clear, incorporated the style and compositions of a slightly older contemporary illuminator, Simon Marmion. As De Winter and others have observed, the Breslauer miniature is quite close to Marmion's Adoration in a Book of Hours in Naples, called "La Flora" because of its many floral borders (Biblioteca Nazionale, MS I B 51, fol. 125v; see De Winter, fig. 90). The Maximilian Master saw Marmion's version among the large collection of that illuminator's miniatures when he was called in to help complete the "La Flora" Hours, possibly after the death of Marmion. While the Maximilian Master attenuated Marmion's composition, replaced the gold sky with a blue one, and gave the Virgin his typically broad cheeks, he retained the physiognomic types of Marmion's Magi, especially that of the eldest Magus at the front of the picture. From Marmion, too, the Master borrowed the idea of the dramatic closeup, the placement of the dramatis personae of the miniature close to the picture plane. The Maximilian Master held Marmion's composition of the Adoration in high esteem; he repeated it a few years later in the Hours of Isabella the Catholic of about 1492 (Cleveland Museum of Art, acc. no. 63.256, fol. 136v; see De Winter, cover illus.) and in two Books of Hours, of about 1497–98 and 1508, respectively, in Munich (Bayerische Staatsbibliothek, Clm 28345, fol. 56v; and Clm 28346, fol. 78v).

This miniature is one of a group of six that were once part of a Book of Hours; it most probably marked Sext of the Hours of the Virgin. The sister leaf with the unusual subject of the Elevation of the Host, which may have introduced a Mass or the Thursday Hours of the Blessed Sacrament (two texts that only occasionally appear in Books of Hours), indicates that the original manuscript was probably richly illustrated.

SISTER LEAVES: Belgium, private collection (Elevation of the Host; London, Christie's, 6 December 1989, lot 6, illus., which was lot 11 of the 1928 Sotheby sale cited below); London, Sotheby's, 21 May 1928, lot 10 (Rest on the Flight into Egypt); London, Sotheby's, 28 June 1962, lot 52, illus. (Crucifixion); New York, Pierpont Morgan Library, MS G. 10 (Visitation, which was lot 8 of the 1928 Sotheby sale cited above); Paris, Mr. and Mrs. Frederick B. Adams, Jr. (Annunciation to the Shepherds; which was lot 9 of the 1928 Sotheby sale cited above).

PROVENANCE: Charles Scarisbrick (1801–60), high sheriff of Scarisbrick Hall and Wrightington, Lancaster County (his mark on recto, Lugt 522); the painter Jean François Gigoux, Paris (1806–94; his mark on recto, Lugt 1164); bought in London, Sotheby's, 11 December 1972, lot 9, illus.

BIBLIOGRAPHY: Patrick M. De Winter, "A Book of Hours of Queen Isabel la Católica," *Bulletin of the Cleveland Museum of Art,* LXVII, 1981, 413, fig. 91 (as whereabouts unknown); Dagmar Thoss, *Flämische Buchmalerei: Handschriftenschätze aus dem Burgunderreich,* Graz, 1987, 111 (as Privatbesitz); *Twenty-first Report to the Fellows of the Pierpont Morgan Library, 1984–1986,* New York, 1989, 52; Bodo Brinkmann and Eberhard König, *Simon Bening: Le livre d'heures aux fleurs, Clm 23637, Bayerische Staatsbibliothek München,* Lucerne, 1991, 361 (as collection privée).

21 Adoration of the Magi (color plate p. 27).

22 Arrest of Christ

Miniature, from a prayer book or Book of Hours, illuminated by Simon Bening. Belgium, Bruges, ca. 1530. Vellum, 132 x 89 (89 x 61) mm, 1 column of 15 lines; the miniature is on a verso.

WORKING in Bruges in the early sixteenth century, Simon Bening (ca. 1483–1561) was both the son and the father of an illuminator. His father, Alexander, was one of the leading illuminators in Flanders in the late fifteenth century. He can probably be identified with the Master of the Older Prayer Book of Maximilian I, who painted the Breslauer Adoration of the Magi (No. 21). One of Simon's five daughters, Lavinia, was to take her skills as a portrait miniaturist to the court of King Henry VIII of England in the mid-sixteenth century. Of this family of painters, however, Simon's fame is the most enduring, and he is rightly regarded as the last great Flemish illuminator. (See Bodo Brinkmann and Eberhard König, *Simon Bening: Le livre d'heures aux fleurs. Clm 23637, Bayerische Staatsbibliothek München,* Lucerne, 1991, 241–55.) We are fortunate to possess a great deal of information on the life and career of Bening. A document of 1500 tells us that he was required, with other illuminators, to register at the Painters' Hall in Bruges the mark (alas, not identified) with which he signed his miniatures. In 1508 he joined Bruges's guild of St. John and St. Luke, to which illustrators, binders, and engravers belonged. Bening's name appears regularly from 1516 on in the accounts of the Bruges stationers' guild, of which he was dean in 1524, 1536, and 1546. There are also dated, signed, and documented works, as well as two self-portraits (see Georges Dogaer, *Flemish Miniature Painting in the 15th and 16th Centuries,* Amsterdam, 1987, 171–77).

This miniature combines the Agony in the Garden with the Arrest. In the dark background, Christ kneels before a radiant angel who proffers him the chalice symbolizing the passion he is about to endure. Nearby, unable to stay awake and pray, sleep three apostles. In the foreground, his eyes still swollen and red from prayer, the Savior stands quiet and resigned amid the surrounding tumult. Judas, shown at the left in nefarious profile, rushes away with his payment in a bag; he has just identified Christ by a kiss. In his futile attempt to defend Christ, Peter has unsheathed his sword and is about to slice off the ear of Malchus, who lies sprawled on the ground. Jostling and shouting, the soldiers encircling Christ begin to lead him away.

Part of Bening's inspiration for this composition derives from a print of the Arrest by the German artist Martin Schongauer. The print obviously struck a chord with Bening, for he also used it as a source for a miniature in the Prayer Book of Albrecht of Brandenburg (Malibu, J. Paul Getty Museum, MS Ludwig IX.19). The Malibu version is a bit stiffer, with nearly all the soldiers' heads on the same level and most of the spears held at parallel angles, and Christ's drapery follows the Schongauer print more closely than it does in the Breslauer version (Anton von Euw and Joachim M. Plotzek, *Die Handschriften der Sammlung Ludwig,* Cologne, 1982, II, fig. 503). For these reasons, it makes sense to follow Plotzek's dating of the Breslauer miniature to about 1530, that is, just after the Malibu prayer book.

We have been unable to identify the textual fragment on the recto of the miniature. A prayer, it would probably have once been part of a Book of Hours or, more likely, a prayer book, possibly of the type called a "Rosarium," a collection of miscellaneous devotions to the Virgin. Bening provided miniatures for a number of prayer books, of which the better known are the Prayer Book of Albrecht of Brandenburg, mentioned above, and the Beatty Rosarium in Dublin (Chester Beatty Library, MS W.99). Both of these manuscripts contain a long series of miniatures illustrating the Passion of Christ.

TEXT: "sui eum non receperunt . . . Deo gratias" is the end of a prayer.

PROVENANCE: London, Sotheby's, 6 July 1964, lot 225; London, Martin Breslauer, Catalogue 99 *(Books, Manuscripts, Autograph Letters from the Renaissance to the Present Time),* 9–10, no. 13, illus. front cover, and Catalogue 100 *(Books, Manuscripts, Autograph Letters, Bindings from the Ninth to the Present Century),* 46–47, no. 26, illus.; bought in 1992.

BIBLIOGRAPHY: Joachim M. Plotzek, *Andachtsbücher des Mittelalters aus Privatbesitz,* Cologne, 1987, 232–33, no. 77, illus.

22 Arrest of Christ (color plate p. 28).

23 Visitation
24 Annunciation to the Shepherds
25 Flight into Egypt
26 Pentecost

Four miniatures, probably from a Book of Hours, illuminated by Simon Bening. Belgium, Bruges, ca. 1540. Vellum, 75 x 48, 74 x 47, 73 x 46, and 75 x 47 mm; the miniatures are on versos.

AS much as Simon Bening is known for the elaborate Passion cycles he created, as exemplified in the previous entry, his greatest claim to fame is considered to be the cycles of full-page miniatures he painted for the calendars in Books of Hours. These miniatures often featured deep and sensitively rendered landscapes. Bening's keen interest in landscape is evident in three of the four miniatures here. The towering cliffs—complete with a castle—in the Visitation seem especially distant and emphasize the Virgin's long journey to visit her cousin Elizabeth. In the Flight into Egypt, the background hill includes Herod's soldiers questioning farmers who, while working in their fields, might have seen the Holy Family who passes in the foreground. The fourth Breslauer miniature, the Pentecost, exemplifies another technique which Bening used successfully: the dramatic closeup. In a spatially compact stage set, Bening's typically expressive figures are half-length and placed close to the picture plane.

As Thomas Kren has observed (*Simon Bening: Flemish Calendar, Clm 23638, Bayerische Staatsbibliothek München*, Lucerne, 1988, 203–64), Bening's landscapes after 1530 are painted in tiny, fleck-like brush strokes that give the miniatures a velvety texture and a heightened sense of atmosphere. At the same time, Bening diminished the relative sizes of his figures, and the landscapes became more important. The Breslauer miniatures typify Bening's new approach to illumination in the later years of his career. The landscapes, for example, have a depth and painterly softness similar to those in the Munich Calendar discussed by Kren. Since the Calendar dates to about 1540, these four miniatures probably date about the same time, or shortly before, since they are not quite as sophisticated and do not yet reflect the keen interest in atmosphere or weather conditions as the Munich manuscript does. Bening's Rest on the Flight into Egypt, described in the next entry, represents another and more advanced stage in the artist's fascination with the natural world.

These four miniatures most likely came from a Book of Hours. Three would have appeared in the Hours of the Virgin: the Visitation at Lauds, the Annunciation to the Shepherds at Tierce, and the Flight into Egypt at Vespers. The Pentecost would have been placed at the beginning of the Hours of the Holy Spirit.

PROVENANCE: Bought in London, Sotheby's, 10 December 1969, lot 20, illus.

BIBLIOGRAPHY: Judith Anne Testa, "Fragments of a Spanish Prayer Book with Miniatures by Simon Bening," *Oud Holland*, CV, 1991, 112 n. 5.

23 Visitation.

24 Annunciation to the Shepherds.

25 Flight into Egypt.

26 Pentecost.

27 Rest on the Flight into Egypt

Miniature illuminated by Simon Bening. Belgium, Bruges, 1540s. Vellum, 122 x 87 mm; the miniature is glued to wood.

SIMON BENING'S keen interest in landscape, as discussed in the preceding entry, reaches a climactic triumph in this masterful miniature. The foreground vegetation is painted with such care that the leaves seem to grow as we look at them. The leaves of the middle ground are smaller but still retain their individuality, while the foliage of the background seems to dissolve into a lacy, atmospheric mass in which, however, individual trees can still be picked out. Our eye is led into the depth of this landscape via a winding path that climbs to the top of a vertiginous mountain. A sense of ascending and descending space is further enhanced by Bening's placement of the viewer at a bird's-eye perspective. From this high vantage point we peer into the miniature, looking first down upon the Holy Family and the clearing they inhabit, and then up, to the top of the summit. The miniature is a tour-de-force, and in his virtuosity Bening surpasses the achievement of his Munich Calendar, considered by some to be his finest accomplishment in landscape painting (see the preceding entry). The twisting, verdant mountain, its juxtaposition to the distant valley below, the at times almost ethereal foliage, and the microscopic soldiers go beyond Bening's previous handling of landscapes and figures in them. Here, as in no other painting, he has broken away from self-imposed Renaissance concepts and entered a mannerist phase.

Along the road up the mountain, soldiers are seen walking or riding; other members of this military party can be spotted engaging in some activity in the fields that lie before the distant town. These are Herod's soldiers, who pursue the Holy Family. This vignette, also found in Bening's Flight into Egypt (No. 25), illustrates the miracle of the harvest. In their flight the Holy Family passed farmers who were sowing wheat. Overnight the wheat miraculously grew so that when Herod's soldiers the next day asked the peasants when the fugitives had passed by, they were able in all honesty to answer, "When we were sowing our wheat." In the foreground Joseph walks toward the Virgin and Child, his hat filled with fruit. The fruit alludes to another miracle associated with the Flight into Egypt, that of the palm tree. According to legend, when the Virgin and Joseph were unable to pick the fruit of a palm tree that grew too high, Christ ordered the tree to bend down so his parents could reach its boughs.

The Rest on the Flight into Egypt, as a variation on the theme of the Flight itself, became especially popular in the Netherlands in the early sixteenth century. Joachim Patinir, who worked in the first quarter of the sixteenth century in Antwerp, where Bening often visited, painted the subject frequently. Gerard David, active in late-fifteenth- and early-sixteenth-century Bruges, where Bening lived, also did many paintings of the Rest on the Flight. It seems clear that the Davidesque elements in the miniature—the Virgin's drapery, her placement within the landscape, and the still-life elements at her feet, especially the meticulously rendered woven basket—are a reference, if not a tribute, from Bening to Gerard David, his fellow Bruges painter.

PROVENANCE: Bought in 1992.

27 Rest on the Flight into Egypt (color plate p. 28).

28 Tower of Babel

Gouache by Jacob van der Ulft. The Netherlands, second half of the 17th century.
Vellum, 352 x 478 mm.

ALTHOUGH manuscript illumination ceased to be a viable art about the middle of the sixteenth century, vellum continued to be used by artists, and not just for portrait miniatures. Some artists, such as Hans Bol, were especially known for their works on this support. The Tower of Babel, which is signed by van der Ulft (1627–89), as well as his Russian Delegation Visiting the Townhall of Gorkum (Gorinchem), are both on vellum. The latter, in the collection of the Institut Néerlandais (Paris, inv. no. 5719), is reproduced in the 1974 catalogue cited below (pl. 64).

Van der Ulft, who was born in Gorinchem, assumed various civic positions there beginning in 1661, including those of mayor and tax collector. He seems to have been largely self-taught, and is best known for his drawings and watercolors, which are mostly topographical or imaginary. If his numerous Italian scenes are not based on firsthand experience (according to Arnold Houbraken, *De groote Schouburgh der nederlantsche Konstschilders en Schilderessen,* The Hague, 1753, II, 197, van der Ulft never went to Italy), they must depend on engravings and the works of others. The influence of Jan de Bisschop (1628–71) has been observed, both for subject matter, which van der Ulft copied, and style, especially in the use of washes to convey the play of dark and light.

Although representations of the Tower of Babel occur during the Middle Ages (see Helmut Minkowski, *Aus dem Nebel der Vergangenheit steigt der Turm zu Babel: Bilder aus 1000 Jahren,* Berlin, 1960), the subject only became popular as an independent painting during the sixteenth and seventeenth centuries, especially among Flemish and Dutch artists. Pieter Bruegel painted the most famous of these in 1563 (Vienna, Kunsthistorisches Museum). According to Genesis 11:1–9, the tower, whose top was to reach heaven, would make the names of its builders famous. Babel, meaning confusion, became synonymous with the divine punishment for the pride exhibited in the erection of the building—the beginning of different languages. John Calvin dismissed the notion that the tower had been built as a refuge against future deluges and likened the story to the ancient fable of giants who had heaped mountains on mountains in order to drag Jove from his celestial throne. In the fourteenth-century *Speculum humanae salvationis,* the subject was regarded as a type for Pentecost, when the Holy Spirit descended on the apostles (Acts 2:1), permitting them to speak in diverse tongues.

Myriad activities are included in the picture. In the foreground a plan is presented to Nimrod, the legendary builder of the tower, while all around stones are measured, carved, and transported. Closer to the tower are two huge furnaces for making bricks. Tiny figures work on the various levels of the tower itself, which is mostly composed of Roman architectural elements. The signature "J: v: ulft F" (Jacob van der Ulft made this) occurs at the bottom.

PROVENANCE: Pieter Langerhuizen (his mark, Lugt 2095), Crailoo, near Bussum; Amsterdam, Müller, 12 December 1935, lot 905; bought by the firm of Martin Breslauer in London, Sotheby's, 26 November 1970, lot 14, illus.; sold to Martin Bodmer, Geneva-Cologny; bought from Alice Bodmer in 1972.

BIBLIOGRAPHY: Institut Néerlandais, *Dessins flamands et hollandais du dix-septième siècle,* Paris, 1974, 157; Pierpont Morgan Library, *Rembrandt and His Century: Dutch Drawings of the Seventeenth Century from the Collection of Frits Lugt, Institut Néerlandais,* New York, 1978, 161.

28 Tower of Babel (color plate p. 29).

29 The Lamb Defeating the Ten Kings

Miniature from Beatus of Liébana, *Commentarius in Apocalypsim*. Spain, region of Burgos, first third of the 13th century. Vellum, 294 x 235 mm; the miniature is on a verso.

THE Apocalypse, or Book of Revelation, is not only the last Book of the New Testament, but also the most difficult, puzzling, and terrifying. According to the text, it was written on the island of Patmos by a man named John, who, from the second century, was traditionally identified with the "beloved" apostle of Christ and the author of the fourth Gospel. The most extensive, important, and numerous Apocalypse picture cycles, however, do not occur in Bibles, but in commentaries on the Apocalypse itself. In Spain, for example, from the tenth to the thirteenth century, copies of St. Beatus of Liébana's *Commentary on the Apocalypse* (completed about 776), were richly illuminated; some contain over one hundred and ten miniatures. Nearly two dozen illustrated manuscripts survive, and these constitute the greatest achievement of medieval Spanish illumination.

The present cutting is from a manuscript thought to have come from the Cistercian Convent of San Andrés de Arroyo in the province of Castile (there is a fourteenth- or fifteenth-century ex libris on folio 167 of the parent manuscript). The convent was a dependency of the monastery of Las Huelgas. The style of the miniature appears to have developed out of the late-twelfth-century Castilian style exemplified by a Beatus in Madrid (Museo Arqueológico Nacional, MS 2) and a Bible in Burgos (Biblioteca Provincial). Although the parent manuscript has been dated about 1200, John Williams suggests that it could be as late as the second quarter of the thirteenth century because of the hell iconography on folio 160. That iconography, which he feels is due to French influence, includes the damned as high-ranking ecclesiastical and secular figures led by a rope, and the wheel as an instrument of torture (see the fifth volume of his forthcoming *Illustrated Beatus: A Corpus of Illustrations of the Commentary on the Apocalypse*).

In the miniature, one Lamb of God is placed in the sky while a second is shown beheading a group of five kings. This is the Lamb that Beatus's commentary describes as Christ—hence the Lamb's cruciform halo—and the Church combined. At the bottom the first five beheaded kings are consumed by the beast, an event not mentioned in the biblical text or Beatus's commentary. The subject of the miniature, based on Apocalypse 17:12–14, is rarely encountered outside of Spain.

TEXT: The recto of the leaf contains the end of Beatus's commentary on Apocalypse 17:4–13, ("[poste]rea dixit dant . . . patientia confunditur.") followed by the rubrication and text of Apocalypse 17:14–18 ("Incipit de agno et bestia superata. Hii decem reges . . . que h[abe]t regnum su[per reges terrae.]" The verso, with the miniature, begins with the rubrication and commentary for Apocalypse 17:14–18: "Explan[ati]o sup[ra]sc[ri]pte hystorie. Hii de-cem reges cum agno . . . [ec]cl[es]ia unu[m] corpus. Pug-nab[un]t usq[ue] in finem donec regnum omne . . . " (The explanation for the above text. These ten kings with the lamb . . .).

PARENT MANUSCRIPT: Paris, Bibliothèque Nationale, MS nouv. acq. lat. 2290; the leaf originally followed fol. 145.

PROVENANCE: Eugène Rodriguez; his sale, Amsterdam, Müller, 11–13 March 1921, lot 243; Robert von Hirsch,

Basel; bought at his sale in London, Sotheby's, 20 June 1978, lot 4, illus.

BIBLIOGRAPHY: Georg Swarzenski, "Ein Einzelblatt aus einer romanischen Apokalypse," *Städel-Jahrbuch*, II, 1922, 5–10, pl. 1; Georg Swarzenski and Rosy Schilling, *Die illuminierten Handschriften und Einzelminiaturen des Mittelalters und der Renaissance in Frankfurter Besitz*, Frankfurt, 1929, 35, no. 38, pl. XIX; François Avril et al., *Manuscrits enluminés de la péninsule ibérique*, Paris, 1982, 65–66, no. 71 (as Sotheby's, 20 June 1978); Bibliothèque Royale Albert Ier, *Los Beatos*, Brussels, 1985, 120, no. 24; Gertrud Schiller, *Ikonographie der christlichen Kunst, Band V: Die Apokalypse des Johannes*, Gütersloh, 1991, Textteil, 134, no. 6, Bildteil, 142–143, fig. 603 (as Einzelblatt); John Williams, *The Illustrated Beatus: A Corpus of Illustrations of the Commentary on the Apocalypse*, London, V, forthcoming in 1993.

29 The Lamb Defeating the Ten Kings (color plate p. 30).

30 Ascension

Leaf from an Antiphonary, with a historiated initial P, made for Cardinal Pedro Gonzales de Mendoza. Spain, probably Toledo, ca. 1482–95. Vellum, 702 x 475 mm, 1 column with 5 staves of 5 red lines; the initial is on a verso.

THIS Antiphonary leaf, two Passionals, and a Missal dated 1476 (the last three in the Cathedral Library of Toledo) were commissioned by Cardinal Pedro Gonzales de Mendoza (1428–95). All contain his arms, which include the beginning of the Hail Mary, "AVE MARIA GR[ATIA]" (see Jesús Domínguez Bordona, *Manuscritos con pinturas,* Madrid, 1933, II, figs. 585–87). Mendoza, the fourth son of Iñigo Lopez de Mendoza, marquess of Santillana, was also much involved with martial matters—he fought for Isabella at the battle of Toro (1 March 1476) and played an important role in her securing the throne. In his youth he translated Sallust, the *Iliad* of Homer, Virgil, and some poetry of Ovid into Spanish. He was appointed bishop of Calahorra in 1453 and of Siguenza in 1467. In 1473 he was made cardinal-deacon of the titular church of S. Maria in Dominica; in 1474, archbishop of Seville; in 1478, cardinal-priest of Santa Croce in Gerusalemme; and finally, in 1482, archbishop of Toledo and primate of Spain (for Mendoza patronage see Helen Nader, *The Mendoza Family in the Spanish Renaissance, 1350 to 1550,* New Brunswick, N. J., 1979).

For style and border decoration this leaf should be compared with the remaining choir books in Toledo Cathedral, one of which also contains Mendoza's arms (see Bordona, *Spanish Illumination,* New York, 1930, II, 60, pl. 128). Since the leaf was originally the second folio in the Antiphonary (the recto bears that number) and contains Mendoza's arms, it was probably also the first illumination in the volume. Similar paneled borders, which are based on French prototypes, occur in a late-fifteenth-century choir book in the Lázaro collection (see Bordona, *Exposición de códices miniados españoles,* Madrid, 1929, pl. 69). The present leaf probably dates after 1482, when Mendoza became archbishop of Toledo. It should also be remembered that Spanish illuminators at this time were frequently itinerant and open not only to influences from each other but from France, the Netherlands, Germany (via prints), and Italy. The Crucifixion in Mendoza's Missal, for example, is based on an engraving by Martin Schongauer. The distinctive grouping of John and Mary in the Breslauer Ascension, where John is seen from the back and faces Mary, also occurs in an Ascension by Juan Carrión, active in Avila in the 1470s (reproduced by Lynette M. F. Bosch, "Los manuscritos abulenses de Juan de Carrión," *Archivo español de arte,* no. 253, 1991, fig. 8). Although documents name two illuminators who were active in Toledo (Benito de Córdoba and Juan Rodriguez), they cannot yet, unfortunately, be connected with this leaf or other works (Bordona, II, 60).

The Ascension is of the "disappearing Christ" type, in which only his feet are shown beneath the clouds (see Meyer Schapiro, "The Image of the Disappearing Christ: The Ascension in English Art Around the Year 1000," *Gazette des Beaux-Arts,* XXII, 1943, 135–52). The ancient tradition that Christ's footprints were embedded on the spot where he ascended from the Mount of Olives was popularized by the thirteenth-century *Golden Legend* of Jacobus de Voragine. The texts in gold and silver around the P are taken from the day's Office: on the left stem and top, "Ascendens Christus in altum captivam duxit captivitatem, Dedit dona hominibus" (Ascending on high, Christ led captivity captive, He gave gifts to man), is a psalm antiphon; the texts on the right, "Ascendit Deus in iubilatione" (God mounts his throne amid shouts of joy), and bottom, "Dominus in voce tube" (The Lord, amid trumpet blasts), repeat the psalm versicle and response given on the text of the leaf itself. The erased inscription above the versicle, "Ascendit . . . ," and response, alas, does not relate to provenance but was a rubricator's note, for it also contains the same versicle and response. The borders contain at least one classical reference: the man with the lion-headed helmet probably represents Hercules battling the Stymphalian birds. The illusionistically rendered fly on a flower in the lower border was probably inspired by the Ghent-Bruges style of illumination. (Although Vasari credited Giotto with the invention of such trompe-l'oeil insects, their origin may also go back to antiquity. Philostratus the Elder [born A.D. 190], for example, wrote [*Imagines,* I, 23] that there were ancient painters who could depict a bee on a flower in such a way that one could not decide if an actual bee had been deceived by the picture or a painted bee deceived the beholder.)

TEXT: "Post passionem su[am . . .]" (After his passion . . .) is the first Matins response for the feast of the Ascension.

PROVENANCE: Cardinal Pedro Gonzales de Mendoza (1428–95); bought in London, Sotheby's, 6 December 1988, lot 17, illus.

mo celo egressio eius et oc

cursus eius alleluya . ps.

℣. Ascendit Deus in iu
bilatione alleluya. ℟.
Et dñs in voce tube alla.

80

Celi enarrant. primo ℟.

Ost passio

nem su

30 Ascension (color plate p. 31).

31 Death of the Virgin

Leaf from a Psalter-Hours with a historiated initial D. Germany or Austria, ca. 1200. Vellum, 192 x 122 (162 x 101) mm, 1 column of 23 lines; the initial is on a recto.

THE iconography of this Death of the Virgin is based on Byzantine traditions. Mary lies on a soft bed with rounded ends, the upper part of which slopes up to support the top half of her body. Two symmetrical groups of apostles, wearing sorrowful expressions and raising their hands in gestures of grief, stand at the head and foot of the bed. Among them, Peter, with his gray beard and bald pate, can be recognized at the front of the group on the left. In the center stands Christ who, while looking down upon the body of his mother, turns away from the deathbed to cradle in his arms her swaddled soul. The gesture of Christ lifting up the Virgin's soul can be better understood in the context of this scene's iconographic source: in Byzantine depictions of the Death of the Virgin, Christ is often shown raising up Mary's soul to entrust it to angels who, flying above, wait to carry it to heaven. The narrow strips of blue and white clouds above Christ's head in the initial are a remnant of this heavenly sphere. The kind of Byzantine Death of the Virgin that inspired the Breslauer initial can be found, for example, among the twelfth-century mosaics in the Martorana chapel in Palermo (see Otto Demus, *Byzantine Art and the West,* New York, 1970, fig. 174). This type of Death of the Virgin did not remain popular in the West for long, however, because it left open the question of the corruptibility of the Virgin's body. Preferred were images of the Virgin's death combined with her assumption into heaven or coronation, for these reflected the belief that the Virgin, like her Son, entered heaven in both body and soul.

The figure of the crippled archer with the wild, streaming hair at the upper left of the initial is something of a mystery. While he has no connection with the Virgin's death, his body forms the upper part of the letter D, and without him the initial would look like an O. Foliage, battling beasts, and ancillary figures often help compose letter forms on the pages of Romanesque manuscripts.

The style of this initial is enigmatic. The Sotheby sale catalogue compared it to the late-twelfth-century Ingeborg Psalter, a monumental work of the transition from the French Romanesque to the Gothic (Chantilly, Musée Condé, MS 1695). The drapery in the Breslauer initial is not painted with the same curvilinear fluidity as the Ingeborg Psalter, however, and the faces seem much sweeter. The semi-circular pattern of the border surrounding the initial, furthermore, recalls similar patterns to be found in late-twelfth-century enamels from Cologne, such as on the Shrine of St. Benignus today in Sieburg's Church of St. Servatius (see Dietrich Kötzsche, "Zum Stand der Forschung der Goldschmiedekunst des 12. Jahrhunderts im Rhein-Maas-Gebiet," in Schnütgen-Museum, *Rhein und Maas: Kunst und Kultur, 800-1400,* Cologne, 1973, II, 227, fig. 56). And the initial shares some stylistic similarities with a mid-twelfth-century Gospels thought to be Rhenish or northern German (Paris, Bibliothèque Nationale, MS lat. 17325; see François Avril et al., *Le temps des Croisades,* Paris, 1982, fig. 182). Making localization even more confusing is the initial's iconographic similarity to a miniature of the Death of the Virgin on page 379 of the Antiphonary of St. Peter's (Vienna, Österreichische Nationalbibliothek, cod. S.n. 2700), a twelfth-century manuscript produced in Salzburg (Franz Unterkircher and Otto Demus, *Das Antiphonar von St. Peter,* Graz, 1974). The iconographic, as well as some stylistic, similarity of the miniature in the Antiphonary to the Breslauer initial, thus, does not rule out Salzburg as a possible place of production.

The initial began the Hours of the Virgin, a text that was sometimes included in Psalters to form prayer books that are today called Psalter-Hours. While Psalter-Hours were very popular in the mid- and late thirteenth century, examples as early as the manuscript from which this leaf originates are very rare.

TEXT: "Domine labia mea aperies . . . " (Lord, you shall open my lips . . .) is the beginning of Matins of the Hours of the Virgin.

PROVENANCE: Dr. Gert Naundorf; bought at his sale in London, Sotheby's, 5 July 1976, lot 7, illus.

labia mea aperies. Et os meu anuntiabit
laudem tuam. Ds in adiutoriu meu
intende. Dne ad ad adiuuandu. me·f·

n honore beatissime marie uirginis iubilem᷒ dno.
enite exultem᷒ dno iubilem᷒ deo salutari nro
poccupem᷒ facie ei in cofessione a in psalmis iu

31 Death of the Virgin (color plate p. 32).

32 St. Michael Slaying the Dragon

Historiated initial Q from a Psalter. Germany, early 13th century. Vellum, 95 x 85 mm (rectangular field), 1 column; the initial is on a recto.

THE recitation of the 150 Psalms of David formed, for the Middle Ages as well as for today, the core of the daily prayers required by the Church of her clergy and ordained. The Psalter, therefore, developed early on as one of the most important prayer books of the Middle Ages, remaining popular into the fourteenth century, when it was supplanted by the Book of Hours. A number of different traditions developed in dividing the Psalms into groups, with a major initial, sometimes historiated, marking the beginning of each textual division. Psalm LI was a main division when the Psalter was divided into thirds (at Psalms I, LI, and CI), as well as when it was divided into ten sections (Psalms I, XXVI, XXXVIII, LI, LII, LXVIII, LXXX, XCVII, CI, CIX) that combined the tripartite division with the eight-part ferial division, that is, dividing the Psalms according to those recited during the seven days of the week plus Vespers (see V. Leroquais, *Les psautiers manuscrits latins des bibliothèques publiques de France,* Mâcon, 1940–41, lxxxvi–xcix). The tradition in Germany, going back at least to the early eleventh century (to be found in a Psalter in Evreux, Bibliothèque Municipale, MS 78), was to decorate the Q of Psalm LI with an image of Michael Slaying the Dragon. (French Psalters seem to have preferred pictures of David Slaying Goliath for this Psalm.) Thus, by the thirteenth century, St. Michael is found in a large number of Q's for Psalm LI in German Psalters (see Hanns Swarzenski, *Die lateinischen illuminierten Handschriften des XIII. Jahrhunderts in den Ländern an Rhein, Main und Donau,* Berlin, 1936, II, figs. 469, 481a, 516, 523, 646, 714, 715, 722, 821, 909).

Stylistically the Breslauer Michael is hard to localize. The Upper Rhine and South Germany have both been suggested, and the saint's physiognomy is similar to that in an illumination attributed by Swarzenski (fig. 909) to Würzburg.

TEXT: Q begins Psalm LI, "Q [uid gloriaris in malitia . . .]" (Why dost thou glory in malice . . .); on the verso of the cutting are fragments of the end of the Psalm, "Deum adiutorem suum . . . sanctorum tuorum," and the beginning of Psalm LII, "Dixit insipien[s] in corde suo . . . " (The fool said in his heart . . .).

PROVENANCE: Bought from John Fleming, New York, about 1968.

32 St. Michael Slaying the Dragon.

33 Last Judgment

Leaf from a Psalter with a historiated initial D. Germany, Augsburg, ca. 1235–50.
Vellum, 205 x 145 (141 x 91) mm, 1 column of 19 lines; the initial is on a recto.

IN this unusual Last Judgment Christ floats on a blue sponge-like cloud, exposing his bleeding wounds and with the sword of justice in his mouth. The Virgin and John the Baptist, intercessors for the dead rising below, caress the Savior's bleeding feet. Above, two angels hold instruments of Christ's Passion: the cross, the spear, and the crown of thorns. The theme, the iconography of which is inspired by Byzantine art, seems to have been used to mark the opening of Psalm CIX since the text speaks of Christ as judge. As mentioned in the discussion of St. Michael Slaying the Dragon (No. 32), the Psalms of the medieval Psalters could be divided in several different ways. Those that divided the Psalms in eight or ten sections both had Psalm CIX as a major division; this initial would have come from such a manuscript.

The composition as well as the style of this historiated initial, as Harry Bober observed, are similar to one in a Psalter in the Morgan Library (MS M. 280, fol. 13v; reproduced in Hanns Swarzenski, *Die lateinischen illuminierten Handschriften des XIII. Jahrhunderts in den Ländern an Rhein, Main und Donau*, Berlin, 1936, II, fig. 773). In fact, the iconographic and stylistic parallels are so close that the Breslauer leaf and the Morgan Psalter must have originated in the same workshop. Furthermore, the style of the large gilt initial on the back of the Breslauer leaf, set against a solid background and enlivened with white filigree, is also the same in both. Finally, the small gilt initials with alternating blue and red filigree also on the back of the Breslauer leaf are identical to those in another, although fragmentary, Psalter in the Morgan Library (MS M. 275), a manuscript that Elizabeth Klemm attributed, in conversation with us, to the same shop as M. 280. Both Morgan Psalters—and thus the Breslauer leaf—belong to a group of manuscripts made in Augsburg in the second quarter of the thirteenth century (see Meta Harrsen, *Central European Manuscripts in the Pierpont Morgan Library*, New York, 1958, 37, 39, nos. 23 and 25, pls. 41, 43, 44).

Like St. Michael Slaying the Dragon (No. 32) and the leaf from the Arenberg Psalter (No. 34), the illumi-nation of this historiated initial also demonstrates how long the Romanesque style lingered on in Germany. Indeed, until nearly the middle of the thirteenth century, German illumination maintained much of the abstraction, flat framing devices, and two-dimensionality that characterize Romanesque painting of the previous century.

TEXT: "Dixit Dominus . . . " (The Lord said . . .) begins Psalm CIX, the rest of which continues on the verso and is followed by the beginning of Psalm CX, "Confi-tebor tibi. . . . "

PROVENANCE: L. V. Randall, Montreal; Mortimer Brandt, New York (his no. 1298); bought by Sam Fogg and Bruce Ferrini in 1988 as part of the entire Brandt collection of manuscript leaves; bought in November 1988.

BIBLIOGRAPHY: Harry Bober, *The Mortimer Brandt Col-lection of Medieval Manuscript Illuminations*, Hatfield, Herts., 1966, 6–9, no. 1, illus.

33 Last Judgment (color plate p. 33).

34 Martyrdom of St. Thomas; Capricorn; Butchering a Hog; Annunciation, Visitation, Nativity

Leaf from the Arenberg Psalter with a historiated border and full-page miniature. Germany, diocese of Hildesheim, probably Braunschweig, ca. 1238/39. Vellum, 224 x 155 mm; the calendar border is on the recto, the full-page miniature on the verso.

THIS leaf comes from the Arenberg Psalter, a manuscript named after the previous owners, the dukes of Arenberg, but now in the Bibliothèque Nationale in Paris. The original manuscript was richly illuminated. Each calendar page had vignettes depicting the martyrdom of a saint, a zodiacal sign, and a labor of the month; a cycle of four full-page miniatures illustrating the life of Christ preceded the Psalms (the present leaf, Presentation in the Temple and Adoration of the Magi, Entry into Jerusalem and Last Supper, and the Flagellation and Crucifixion). One large and numerous small initials marked the major textual divisions of the Psalter; and the litany was illustrated by two full-page miniatures (Paradise with Christ in the Lap of Abraham and the Resurrection of the Dead) and historiated borders depicting the Deësis (Christ as Judge flanked by the Virgin and John the Baptist), angels, and saints.

At some point in the manuscript's history seven leaves strayed—three with miniatures and four text pages. The locations of four, however, are known. Of the four, the Breslauer leaf is particularly interesting, for it contains an illustration for each of two distinct parts of the manuscript: the last calendar page and the first of the prefatory miniatures preceding the Psalter. As was customary with medieval calendars, this one contains columns listing the Golden Numbers, the Dominical Letters (both used to determine the date of Easter), and the ancient Roman calendar (here in two columns). These were followed by the list of feast days for the month beginning, here, at December first with the martyr St. Sabinus. (The presence of Sabinus and other saints venerated in the bishoprics of Hildesheim and Magdeburg helps localize the Arenberg Psalter.) The top of the leaf illustrates the martyrdom of the apostle Thomas (whose important feast on December 21 is written in red): an executioner spears the saint under the direction of King Mazdai of India (tradition has it that when the apostles divided the world for conversion, India fell to Thomas). At the right, below this scene, are the large gold letters KL, the monogram (which stands for "Kalends," the first of the month) that is to be found, more traditionally at the very top, in all medieval calendars. Below this are the zodiacal sign for December, Capricorn (the goat), and the labor for that month, butchering a hog. On the verso of the leaf is the full-page miniature that originally began the prefatory cycle of the life of Christ; it depicts the Annunciation, Visitation, and the Nativity with the Annunciation to the Shepherds. Scrolls play an important role in the miniature. Gabriel's reads (in Latin), "Hail Mary, full of grace"; while the angel below tells the shepherds, "I bring you news of great joy." Two prophets, pointing to the central figure of the Virgin, bear scrolls quoting prophecies of Isaiah, "Behold, a virgin shall conceive and bear a son," and, "There shall come forth a rod out of the root of Jesse" (Isaiah 7:14 and 11:1).

The Arenberg Psalter is thought to have been commissioned, possibly by Duke Otto of Braunschweig, for the marriage of his daughter Helen to Landgraf Hermann II of Thuringia on 9 October 1239. The back of the sister leaf in Washington contains a copy of a letter from Pope Gregory IX to Hermann II's mother, St. Elizabeth of Hungary, who was canonized in 1235, just four years after her death; the same pope wrote a letter in 1238 to Otto granting dispensation for the marriage of his daughter Helen to Hermann.

The Psalter belongs to what Arthur Haseloff has designated the Saxon-Thuringian school of illumination, and it is especially close to three others, all produced during the fourth decade of the thirteenth century (Berlin, Staatliche Museen Preussischer Kulturbesitz, Kupferstichkabinett, cod. 78 A 7; Wolfenbüttel, Herzog August Bibliothek, cod. Guelf. 515; and Donaueschingen, Fürstlich Fürstenbergische Hofbibliothek, cod. 309). The illumination of this group is painted in the "zackigstil," or jagged style, in which drapery folds appear angular and frozen; this style is one of Germany's contributions to Gothic illumination of the thirteenth century. The curious shape of the miniature seems to have been designed specifically to accommodate the scenes and figures illustrated; uniquely shaped frames are to be found around other miniatures in the Arenberg Psalter, as well as in the three other manuscripts of its group. Finally, one should take note of the tiny holes that perforate the top of the Breslauer leaf. The miniature was originally—or at a very early date—protected by a silk curtain that was once sewn in. Such curtains, used for protective as well as decorative purposes, are still to be found in some medieval manuscripts.

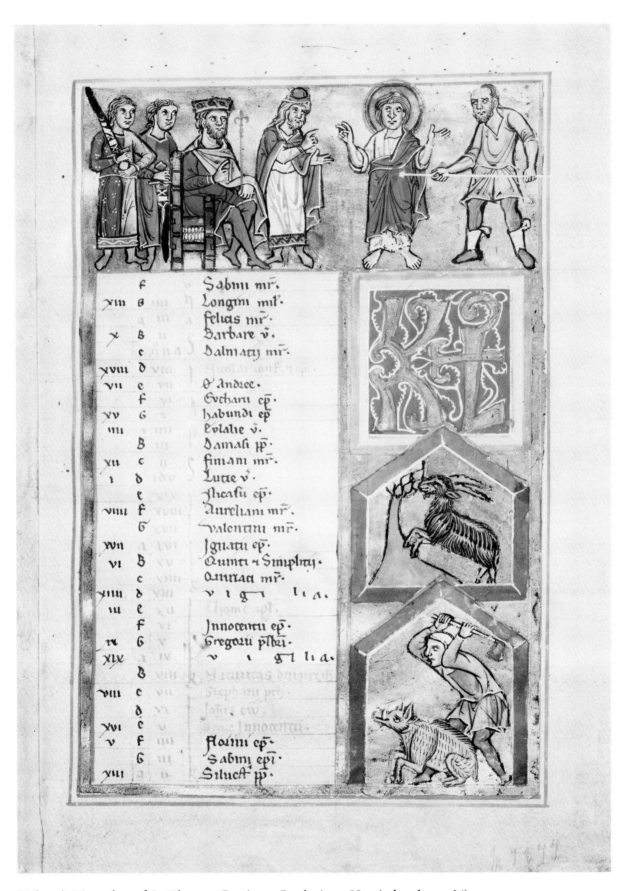

34 (recto) Martyrdom of St. Thomas; Capricorn; Butchering a Hog (color plate p. 34).

34 (verso) Annunciation, Visitation, Nativity (color plate p. 35).

TEXT: "Sabini m[arty]r[is] . . . " ([Feast of] Sabinus, martyr . . .) begins the list of feasts for December.

PARENT MANUSCRIPT: Paris, Bibliothèque Nationale, MS nouv. acq. lat. 3102.

SISTER LEAVES: Berlin, Staatliche Museen Preussischer Kulturbesitz, Kunstbibliothek, 4000-99,332 (leaf with foliate D); Chicago, Art Institute, acc. no. 24.671 (Flagellation and Crucifixion); Washington, National Gallery of Art, Rosenwald Collection, acc. no. 1946. 21.11 (Paradise with Christ in the Lap of Abraham).

PROVENANCE: Parent manuscript: possibly Landgraf Hermann II of Thuringia and his wife, Helen; the manuscript was in Hildesheim in the fourteenth century; dukes of Arenberg (their MS 4); bought from them through Seligmann by Comte Guy de Boisrouvray; given by him to the Bibliothèque Nationale in 1961. This leaf was separated from the parent manuscript by 1904, when it, along with two other leaves from the manuscript, was owned by Dr. Robert Forrer, Strassburg; Edouard Kann, Paris, who owned this single leaf (his no. 68) by 1926; bought by Joel Spitz, Glencoe, Illinois, from Ernest Brummer in 1948; bought in London, Sotheby's, 29 November 1990, lot 6, illus.

BIBLIOGRAPHY: Arthur Haseloff, "Die mittelalterliche Kunst," in *Meisterwerke der Kunst aus Sachsen u. Thüringen . . .*, Oscar Doering, ed., Magdeburg, 1905, 98 (as owned by Dr. Forrer); Amédée Boinet, ed., *La collection de miniatures de M. Edouard Kann,* Paris, 1926, 9–10, no. I, pl. I; Paul Wescher, *Beschreibendes Verzeichnis der Miniaturen—Handschriften und Einzelblätter—des Kupferstichkabinetts der Staatlichen Museen Berlin,* Leipzig, 1931, 15 (as Kann); Walters Art Gallery, *Illuminated Books of the Middle Ages and Renaissance,* Baltimore, 1949, 15 (as one of three leaves . . . separated from a Psalter); Jacques Seligmann & Co., *Illuminated Manuscripts (11th Century through the 16th Century) from the Bibliothèque of Their Highnesses the Dukes d'Arenberg,* New York, 1952, 16 (as collection of Mr. Joel Spitz); Bibliothèque Nationale, *Manuscrits à peintures offerts à la Bibliothèque nationale par le comte Guy du Boisrouvray,* Paris, 1961, 28, 29 (as Spitz); C. U. Faye and W. H. Bond, *Supplement to the Census of Medieval and Renaissance Manuscripts in the United States and Canada,* New York, 1962, 167, no. 9F; Johann-Christian Klamt, "Zum Arenberg-Psalter," *Munuscula Discipulorum: Kunsthistorische Studien, Hans Kauffmann zum 70. Geburtstag, 1966,* Berlin, 1968, 155 (as M. Edouard Kann); Gary Vikan, ed., *Medieval & Renaissance Miniatures from the National Gallery of Art,* Washington, 1975, 119 (as Joel Spitz Collection), fig. 33g; Württembergisches Landesmuseum, *Die Zeit der Staufer: Geschichte, Kunst, Kultur,* Stuttgart, 1977, I, 601 (as Sammlung Joel Spitz); Joachim M. Plotzek, *Andachtsbücher des Mittelalters aus Privatbesitz,* Cologne, 1987, 74 (as zugehörigen Blättern). For additional references to the parent manuscript, see the citations given by Gary Vikan, ed., *Medieval & Renaissance Miniatures* (1975) and in the Sotheby sale catalogue of 29 November 1990.

35 Resurrection and Three Marys at the Tomb
36 Crucifixion

Two leaves from a Gradual with historiated initials R and T. Germany, Regensburg, late 13th century. Vellum, 503 x 341 mm, 1 column of 9 staves of 4 red lines; both initials are on versos.

THE importance of Regensburg as a center of German manuscript illumination was underscored in 1987 by a major exhibition, "Regensburger Buchmalerei," held there and organized by museums in that city and the Bavarian State Library in Munich. Regensburg, the oldest city in Bavaria, had already become its major town by the sixth century. By the eighth century it had its own bishop and school of illumination, and manuscripts of high quality were consistently produced there over the next seven hundred years.

The attribution of these two leaves to Regensburg was first made by Christopher de Hamel in a 1986 Sotheby sale catalogue, an attribution with which Robert Suckale agreed in conversation with us. The drapery and figural style is comparable to work done toward the end of the thirteenth century, such as the illuminated panels sewn into the reliquary casket that is now in Regensburg's Domschatzmuseum (D 1974/66) and a copy of Jacobus de Voragine's *Golden Legend* originally from Regensburg's Monastery of St. Emmeram (Munich, Bayerische Staatsbibliothek, Clm 14034; for both the reliquary and the *Golden Legend,* see Florentine Mütherich and Karl Dachs, eds., *Regensburger Buchmalerei: Von frühkarolingischer Zeit bis zum Ausgang des Mittelalters,* Munich, 1987, 87–88, nos. 67 and 69, pls. 145 and 50). The physiognomies of the figures in the Breslauer leaves, as well as Christ's somewhat peculiar anatomy in both pictures, are not as accomplished as in the comparisons just cited, but it does seem likely that the leaves date to about the same time, the 1290s, because they do not betray the sweeter style and doll-like figures that characterize Regensburg illumination of the early fourteenth century.

Christopher de Hamel (in the same Sotheby sale catalogue) conjectured that the leaves are from a Gradual originally made for the Dominican convent of Heilig Kreuz (Holy Cross) in Regensburg. His theory is based on the rare use of a Crucifixion as the illustration for the feast of the Dedication of a Church. This postulation must be treated with caution, however, for, as Elisabeth Klemm has pointed out to us (in a letter of 17 December 1991), Crucifixions illustrating the feast of a Dedication do occur elsewhere, such as in a Missal from Seitenstetten now in Baltimore (Walters Art Gallery, MS W. 33, fol. 132).

TEXT: "Resurrexi et adhuc tecum sum . . . " (I arose and am still with you . . .) is the Introit for the feast of Easter. "Terribilis est locus iste . . . " (How awesome is this place . . .) is the Introit for the feast of the Dedication of a Church ("In dedicatio[n]e ecclesie. Introitus.").

SISTER LEAVES: Christopher de Hamel has kindly alerted us to five possible sisters sold in Lucerne, H. Gilhofer &

H. Ranschburg, Katalog XIX (*Einzel-Miniaturen des XIII. bis XV. Jahrhunderts von ausgesuchter Qualität . . .*), n.d., nos. 2–6, illus. (Ascension, Nativity, Pentecost, Entry into Jerusalem, and Peter Escaping from Prison).

PROVENANCE: Bought in London, Sotheby's, 24 June 1986, lot 8 (both leaves), illus.

E furrexi et ad huc

tecum sum al le lu ia

po fui fti super me

manum tu am alle

·c·vii·

lu ia mira bilis fca est fci en cia tu

a alle lu ia· al le lu ia· pm̄s Domine pro

bafti me et cognouifti me tu cognouifti feffionē

meam et refurrectio nem meam v̄s Gloria Gr

hec di es quam fecit do mi

35 Resurrection and Three Marys at the Tomb (color plate p. 36).

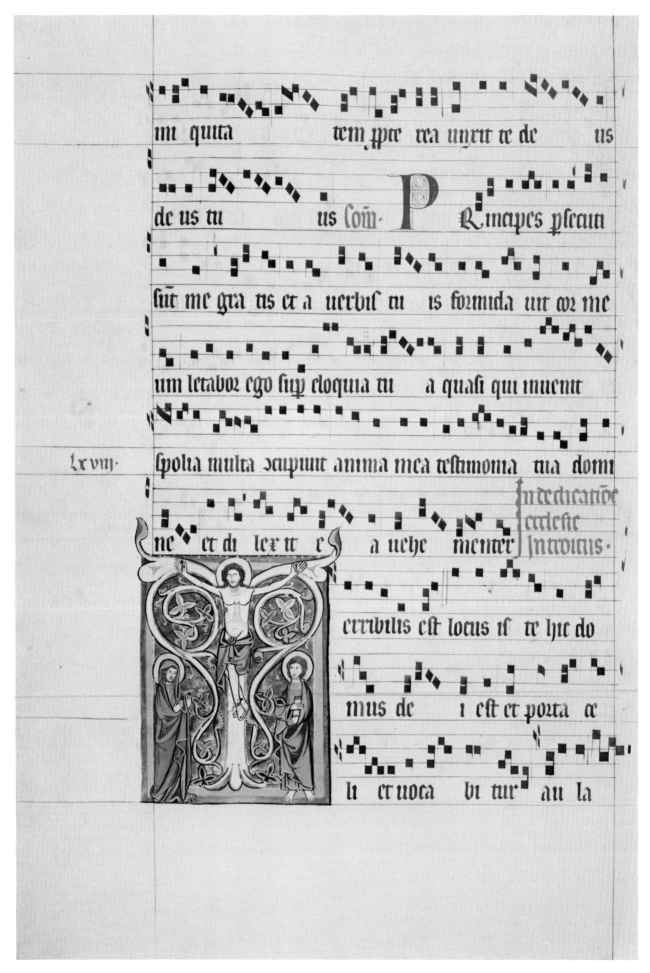

mi quita tem ppe rea unxit te de us

de us tu us com. P Rincipes pfeuiu

fut me gra tis et a uerbif tu is formida uit cor me

um letabor ego sup eloquia tu a quafi qui inuenit

lx vuj. fpolia multa 3cipiunt anima mea teftimonia tua domi

In dedicatoe

fecclefie

ne et di lexit e a uehe menter Introicus.

erribilis eft locus if te hic do

mus de i eft et porta ce

li et uoca bi tur au la

36 Crucifixion.

124

36 (detail) Crucifixion.

37 Harrowing of Hell

Historiated initial S from an Antiphonary. Switzerland, Lake Constance area, late 13th century. Vellum, 110 x 112 mm, 1 column with 3 staves of 4 red lines; the initial is on a recto.

THIS initial, and eleven others, may have come from an elaborately illustrated late-thirteenth-century Antiphonary that can be stylistically connected with the celebrated Gradual of St. Katharinenthal (Zurich, Schweizerisches Landesmuseum, MS LM 26117), a monument of high Gothic book illumination in Switzerland (six initials are reproduced by Rosenthal; three are cited by Hanns Swarzenski, *Die lateinische illuminierten Handschriften des XIII. Jahrhunderts in den Ländern an Rhein, Main und Donau*, Berlin, 1936, 54 n. 1, II, figs. 609–10; three recently were sold at auction). Indeed, Ellen Beer suggests the possibility that the Antiphonary was once in the Dominican convent of St. Katharinenthal itself, for its style represents an important preliminary stage to that found in the Gradual, which is dated about 1312 (*Das Graduale von Sankt Katharinenthal: Kommentar*, Lucerne, 1983, 168–69).

The subject of the miniature, the Harrowing of Hell, is appropriate for Holy Saturday, for it was believed that Christ descended into hell sometime between his entombment on Good Friday and resurrection on Easter Sunday. The scriptural germ for the event can be found in St. Paul's Epistle to the Ephesians (4:9): "Now that he ascended, what is it, but because he also descended first into the lower parts of the earth?" The idea of fetching the dead from the lower regions, of course, recalls stories from classical mythology: Hercules rescuing Alcestis from the underworld, and Orpheus attempting to bring Eurydice back from Hades. In the second century, descriptions of Christ's descent began to appear, and in the fifth-century apocryphal Gospel of Nicodemus a full narrative account is given, which is specifically referred to in Jacobus de Voragine's thirteenth-century *Golden Legend*. In the office for Holy Saturday, the response and versicle for the fourth lesson state that "Today our Savior has broken the bars and the very gates of death" and "He has destroyed the prisons of hell and overthrown the power of the devil." According to the *Golden Legend* and other accounts, Christ broke the doors of hell from their hinges, overcame and bound Satan, and liberated the souls of the Old Testament saints, beginning, as in the upper part of the initial, with Adam. Eve followed. In the lower part of the initial is the bound Satan, along with other Old Testament souls, some of whom have attributes.

TEXT: S begins the first Matins response for Holy Saturday, "Sepulto Domino . . . " (When the Lord had been buried . . .); on the verso of the cutting are the fragments, "[mortu]is, pone[ntes.] . . . et exue te ve[stibus iucundi]tatis in[duere . . .]," the end of the versicle following the first Matins response, and part of the second response, both for Holy Saturday.

SISTER LEAVES: possibly Berlin, Antiquariat Tiedemann (Beheading of St. Catherine); Germany, private collection (St. John and Christ; ex-Bruce Ferrini, Catalogue 1, 1987, no. 2, illus. [where the initials G and R are wrongly cited as part of the Antiphonary; these are from an early-fourteenth-century Dominican Gradual now in Nuremberg, Germanisches Nationalmuseum, MS 21897, for which see Beer, 172]); possibly Munich, Graphische Sammlung, Inv. 40230 (Betrayal of Christ); London, Christie's, 16 December 1991, lot 6, illus. (Baptism of Christ), and lot 7, illus. (Capture of Unicorn); London, Sotheby's, 20 June 1978 (Robert von Hirsch sale), lot 5, illus. (Presentation in the Temple); possibly Stuttgart, H. G. Gutekunst, Auktionskatalog 69, 1911 (four scenes with Christ with Souls in Heaven); Switzerland, private collection (Christ and Isaiah, St. Luke and the Virgin); Switzerland, private collection (Last Supper); Washington, National Gallery of Art, Rosenwald Collection, acc. no. 1959.16.1 (Ecclesia and Christ); location unknown (Martyrdom of St. Lucy and St. Lucy at the Grave of St. Agnes).

PROVENANCE: Bought from John Fleming, New York, in the late 1960s.

BIBLIOGRAPHY: Erwin Rosenthal, "Illuminations from a Dominican Gradual of about 1300," *Zeitschrift für Schweizerische Archäologie und Kunstgeschichte*, XXXIII, 1976, 64, fig. 6; London, Sotheby's, 20 June 1978 (Robert von Hirsch sale), 12; Akron, Ohio, Bruce P. Ferrini Rare Books, Catalogue 1 *(Important Western Medieval Illuminated Manuscripts . . .)*, 1987, 8.

37 Harrowing of Hell.

38 Nativity

Historiated initial H from an Antiphonary. Switzerland, Lake Constance area, late 13th century. Vellum, 156 x 116 mm, 1 column with 4 staves of 4 red lines; the initial is on a recto.

THIS Nativity probably came from the same Antiphonary as the better-known initial depicting John asleep in Christ's bosom, which was formerly in the Robert von Hirsch collection. (For a discussion of the iconography of the Christ-St. John group and its popularity in the Lake Constance region see Ellen J. Beer, *Das Graduale von Sankt Katharinenthal: Kommentar,* Lucerne, 1983, 136–38.) Both historiated initials are by the same artist, exhibit the same broad treatment of folds, are set against a heavily burnished gold field, and have similar frames. Alfred Stange (*Deutsche Malerei der Gotik. I: Die Zeit von 1250 bis 1350,* Berlin, 1934, 58, pl. 61) and Ellen J. Beer (p. 137) date the Christ-St. John initial to the end of the thirteenth century. To this group can now be added the historiated initial in Cleveland (Fig. 1) with which the volume must have begun, the A for the first Matins response ("Aspiciens . . . ") for the first Sunday of Advent; the initial depicts a cleric, probably Isaiah, pointing to the hand of God surrounded by a cruciform halo emerging from the clouds, which is the subject of the first lesson (Isaiah 1:1–3) and part of the response itself, "I see God coming in power, as in a cloud of light."

In the Nativity, the Virgin tenderly touches the Christ Child, whose happiness is shared by the donkey and ox in the upper part of the initial.

TEXT: H begins the first Matins response for Christmas (December 25), "H[odie nobis celorum rex . . .]" (On this day the King of Heaven . . .); on the verso of the cutting are fragments from the second Nocturn of the same feast, "Suscepimus [Deus misericordia]m tuam in medio tem[pli tui. Ps. Magnus] Do[minus] a[ntiphona] Orietur [in] diebus. . . . "

SISTER LEAVES: Cleveland Museum of Art, Otto F. Ege deposit, TR 12828/15 (Cleric pointing to the Hand of God in the Clouds, Fig. 1); Germany, private collection (Christ with St. John the Evangelist Sleeping in his Bosom; ex-London, Sotheby's, 17 December 1991, lot 22, illus.).

PROVENANCE: Dr. Silvain S. Brunschwig; bought from his heirs in 1978.

Fig. 1. Cleric Pointing to the Hand of God. Cleveland, Cleveland Museum of Art, Otto F. Ege deposit, TR 12828/15.

38 Nativity (color plate p. 36).

39 Christ Instructing Two Apostles

Cutting from an Antiphonary with a historiated initial E illuminated in the style of Johannes von Valkenburg. Germany, Cologne, early 14th century. Vellum, 150 x 210 mm, 1 column with staves of 4 lines (3rd is red); the initial is on a verso.

THIS initial was painted in Cologne by an artist working in the style of Johannes von Valkenburg. Von Valkenburg wrote, notated, decorated, and supplied his own portrait to two Graduals in that city in 1299 (Cologne, Erzbischöfliche Diözesanbibliothek, MS 1 B; and Bonn, Universitätsbibliothek, MS 384). He is credited with introducing Gothic illumination to Cologne, drawing inspiration from Flemish and northern French sources, and fostering a generation of illuminators who followed his style until the middle of the fourteenth century. (See Wallraf-Richartz-Museum, *Vor Stefan Lochner: Die kölner Maler von 1300 bis 1430*, Cologne, 1974, 126–32, nos. 69–74, illus.; and Judith Oliver, "The French Gothic Style in Cologne: Manuscripts Before Johannes von Valkenburg," *Miscellanea Neerlandica: Opstellen voor Dr. Jan Deschamps ter gelegenheid van zijn zeventigste verjaardag*, E. Cockx-Indestege et al., eds., Louvain, 1987, I, 381–96, with previous literature.) Von Valkenburg's new elegant style was a change from the mid-thirteenth-century "zackigstil," the jagged style of which the Breslauer leaf from the Arenberg Psalter is such a characteristic example (No. 34).

The initial shows a seated Christ instructing two standing apostles. The two barefoot and bearded apostles have no identifying attributes or physiognomies, but this might be purposeful since the text of the cutting is from the Common of the Apostles, a feast calling for generic rather than particular apostles. One can compare the Breslauer cutting to another in a similar style formerly in the Mortimer Brandt collection (Harry Bober, *The Mortimer Brandt Collection of Medieval Manuscript Illuminations,* Hatfield, Herts., 1966, 9–11, no. 2, illus.; this cutting was recently sold in London, Christie's, 26 June 1991, lot 5, illus.). In the Brandt initial Christ addresses a group of apostles among whom Peter and Paul can be easily identified from their beards and physiognomies. Kneeling outside the Breslauer initial is a Franciscan friar. Ordained figures representing the men and women who paid for and used these choir books make frequent appearances among the leaves of late-thirteenth- and early-fourteenth-century manuscripts produced in northern Europe, and they are often to be found in manuscripts painted by von Valkenburg and his followers.

In addition to the Brandt initial mentioned above, others that may be sisters of the Breslauer cutting have recently been sold (see London, Sotheby's, 19 June 1990 [Korner collection], lots 10 and 11, illus., where other cuttings are cited). Until closer examination of these is made, including the texts and notations, judgment will have to be postponed as to whether or not they come from the same manuscript as the Breslauer cutting.

TEXT: "Ecce ego mitto vos [sicut oves] in medio luporum, [dicit Do]minus, Esto[te ergo pru]dentes sicut serpentes, et simplices si[cut columbae]" (Behold I send you out as sheep in the midst of wolves, says the Lord, so be wise as serpents and innocent as doves) is the first Matins response for the feast of the Common of the Apostles. On the recto of the cutting are other fragments from the First Nocturn of the feast, "ps[almus] Celi enarrant. an[tiphona] Hec [est gen-erat]io querentium Dominum querentium faci[em Dei Jacob. . . .] p[salmus] D[omi]ni est terra. an[tiphona] Verbo Domini. . . . "

PROVENANCE: Siegfried Laemmle; bought in London, Sotheby's, 8 December 1975, lot 9, illus.

BIBLIOGRAPHY: Los Angeles County Museum, *Mediaeval and Renaissance Illuminated Manuscripts: A Loan Exhibition,* Los Angeles, 1953, 17, no. 25, illus.

ce ego mitto uos

in medio luporum

mis Estot

entes sicut serpen tes et simplices si

39 Christ Instructing Two Apostles (color plate p. 37).

40 Christ before the High Priest Annas

Miniature from a Lectionary (Epistles and Gospels), in German. Germany, Swabia, ca. 1470. Paper, 114 x 148 mm, 2 columns (144 mm wide); the miniature is on a recto.

MANUSCRIPTS on paper became increasingly popular in the fifteenth century and were most frequently used for secular or vernacular texts, especially romances and historical chronicles (see Hellmut Lehmann-Haupt, *Schwäbische Federzeichnungen: Studien zur Buchillustration Augsburgs im XV. Jahrhundert,* Berlin, 1929). Lectionaries and other liturgical manuscripts on paper are less usual. To judge by the two pictures that have thus far appeared (the second is Fig. 2), the manuscript from which this miniature comes must have been profusely illustrated. Since paper does not lend itself to heavy illumination, the miniatures usually consisted of watercolors or pen drawings with wash, such as in the present example. An examination of the verso of the sister leaf made it possible to determine that the parent manuscript, written in a Swabian dialect, was not a Bible but a Lectionary, for it contained rubrics for both a Gospel and Epistle reading (for the feasts of St. Stephen and St. John, respectively). The verso of the Breslauer leaf contains a portion of the Gospel reading for Good Friday, the only day of the year for which there is no Mass. The parent manuscript was already broken up by about 1850, for the sister leaf was then in the Museo Cavaleri collection in Milan.

Although the subject of the Breslauer leaf has been identified as Christ before the High Priest Caiaphas, it is more likely Christ before the High Priest Annas. It is sometimes difficult to distinguish between the two events, but according to John 18:22, it was Christ's answer to Annas that caused one of the servants to strike Christ.

TEXT: On the verso: "Ihus und sprach Ich haun offenlich der welt geredet . . . " (Jesus answered him: I have spoken openly to the world . . . ; [John 18:20]) is part of the Gospel reading for Good Friday.

SISTER LEAVES: Dr. Jörn Günther, Hamburg, MS 28 (Stoning of St. Stephen, Fig. 2).

PROVENANCE: Bought in London, Christie's, 11 July 1974, lot 1.

Fig. 2. Stoning of St. Stephen. Hamburg, Dr. Jörn Günther, MS 28.

40 Christ Before the High Priest Annas.

41 Crucifixion

42 Virgin Appearing to a Dying Priest

Two leaves from a *Spiegel menschlicher Behältnis* with miniatures. Southern Germany, third quarter of the 15th century. Paper, 175 x 113 mm, 1 column of 27 lines; both miniatures are on rectos.

THE *Speculum humanae salvationis* (Mirror of Human Salvation), which was written by a Dominican probably in Strassburg between 1309 and 1324, rivaled even the thirteenth-century *Biblia pauperum* in popularity and influence. Though both are profusely illustrated typological compendia, the former has nearly five thousand lines of explanatory Latin verse, three types (prefigurations) for each New Testament scene (the antitype) rather than two, and includes secular as well as Old Testament types. The work contains forty-five chapters: the first two deal with the Old Testament (including the Creation and Fall of Man); the next forty treat, in a typological fashion, events from the lives of Mary and Christ, ending with hell and heaven. The last three, which are not typological, deal with the Hours of the Passion and the Seven Sorrows and Joys of the Virgin Mary. Complete cycles of 192 pictures were evidently planned from the beginning, for the earliest manuscripts have them. According to the prologue the unlearned are taught by pictures, which are the books of the lay people (see Adrian Wilson and Joyce Lancaster Wilson, *A Medieval Mirror: Speculum humanae salvationis, 1324–1500,* Berkeley, 1984, 24).

The *Speculum* appeared in manuscripts, of which almost four hundred survive, blockbooks, and in incunabula. It was translated early on into the major European languages. The Breslauer leaves come from a German version written in verse (J. Lutz and P. Perdrizet, *Speculum humanae salvationis,* Mulhouse, 1907, 104, for example, mention verse translations by Conrad von Helmsdorf and Heinrich von Laufenberg). These two miniatures, and those of the sister leaves mentioned below, are from the final nontypological chapters of the work. The Crucifixion illustrates the sixth Sorrow of the Virgin, which must be a variant, for the Crucifixion is usually the fifth Sorrow. The Virgin Appearing to a Dying Priest precedes the introductory section of the Seven Joys of the Virgin, where, according to the text, the Virgin, attended by angels, appeared to a dying priest in order to comfort him, for he was much oppressed by his sins. Since the priest had often recited her Joys, she promised to bring him to eternal joy.

TEXT: Crucifixion: "Der sechsten ser erman ich dich . . . " (I admonish you of the sixth . . .). Virgin Appearing to a Dying Priest: "Maria muter maget heer . . . " (Mary, mother, elevated handmaiden . . .).

SISTER LEAVES: Cambridge, Mass., Harvard University, Houghton Library, MS Typ 270 (Pietà; Harvard College Library, *Illuminated & Calligraphic Manuscripts,* Cambridge, Mass., 1955, 27, no. 91, pl. 64); Southport, Conn., Laurence Witten, Catalogue 12, 1980, nos. 56 and 57 (Christ Before Pilate and Annunciation).

PROVENANCE: Tomás Harris (his name written on the backs of both leaves); his sale, London, Sotheby's 12 July 1971, lot 3 (containing 4 leaves: Virgin Appearing to a Dying Priest, Annunciation, Christ Before Pilate, and Crucifixion), bought by Bernard Breslauer, who kept the Crucifixion and sold the rest; the Virgin Appearing to a Dying Priest was reacquired in the early 1980s.

Er sechsten er erman ich dich
Do du wert so trauwens reich
Dein hertz in grossem laid versenkt
Do dein sun was gehenkt
An das creutz gar an schult
Dar umb dein hertz gross iamer dult
Das es gar versehret wart
Sein treu er auch an dir mit spart
Do er iohanes bey dir sach
Von krankem leib er zu ir sprach
Euch fraw den sun dein
Der sol nu dein pfleger sein
Und sprach zu deyner schwester sun
Sie sol dein muter wesen nu
Die red dein laid so erbakt

41 Crucifixion.

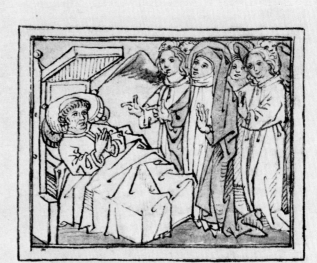

Maria muter maget her
Gib mir die sin und auch die ler.
Das ich die siben fraud von dir
Betichten kum nach meyner gir
Und mit deynen frauden fraud han
Dich deyner fraud ermanen schon
Als ich in aynem buch las
Wie das ain weltlich priester was
Der mit gantzem willen sein
Dich mant der siben fraud dein
Mit fleis all tag sunder bar
Do er das tet vil manig iar
Bis er kam an sein alte tag
Und er an dem tot bet lag
Do gedacht er hin und dacht her

42 Virgin Appearing to a Dying Priest.

43 Virgin and Child in a Garden

Leaf from a Gradual with a historiated initial S. South Germany, probably Augsburg, last quarter of the 15th century. Vellum, 547 x 370 mm, 1 column with 8 staves of 5 red lines; the initial is on a verso.

SINCE no other leaves from the original Gradual have been identified, and the rubric for the Introit for the feast of the Dedication of a Church, which is included on the present leaf, does not include the name of a specific church, there is no liturgical evidence that can be used to localize it. Neither the border ornament nor the form of the musical notation (*Hufnagel* or hobnail) indicates a precise localization. Nevertheless, stylistic affinities can be found in choir books produced in south Germany, especially in Augsburg (see Erich Steingräber, *Die kirchliche Buchmalerei Augsburgs um 1500,* Augsburg, [1956], figs. 2, 19, 20) and in Bamberg (Germanisches Nationalmuseum, *Die Grafen von Schönborn: Kirchenfürsten Sammler Mäzene,* Nuremberg, 1989, 487, no. 372, fig. 372).

In the initial, the Virgin is crowned and offers Christ a piece of red fruit; she is seated in a garden, suggesting the *hortus conclusus* (garden enclosed), one of the types in the *Speculum humanae salvationis* for the annunciation of the birth of the Virgin to Joachim. The type derives from an interpretation of the Song of Songs (4:12–13: "My sister, my spouse, is a garden enclosed, a fountain sealed up. Thy plants are a paradise of pomegranates with the fruits of the orchards") in which the spouse was identified with the Virgin Mary. The enclosed garden thus came to symbolize both her virginity and Immaculate Conception.

TEXT: "Salve sancta parens enixa puerpera re-gem . . . " (Hail holy parent who didst bring forth the king . . .) is the Introit for a Saturday Votive Mass of the Virgin ("De sancta Maria virgine").

PROVENANCE: Bought in Germany about 1975.

a fiait qui inuenit spolia mt

ta concupiuit anima mea testi

monia tua domine et dilex

it e a uehe men ter.

Terribilis est locus.

Dixit dominus ser.

In dedicatione
ecclesie introitus.

quere in tempore
folio. cczu In dedicatione altaris. intro
itus. quere in libro de tpe.
folio. cczu

De sancta
maria uir
gine. Introit.

Al ue sancta

parens e nixa puer

pera regem qui celum terram

43 Virgin and Child in a Garden.

44 Resurrection

Leaf from the Missal of Johannes von Giltlingen with a historiated initial R illuminated by Conrad Wagner. Germany, Augsburg, ca. 1485–89. Vellum, 348 x 262 (235 x 78–19–78) mm, 2 columns of 32 lines; the initial is on a recto; the leaf is backed by a larger piece of vellum and outlined with gold hatching resembling sewing.

JAMES MARROW was the first to connect this leaf, and a second dated 1485, with the sumptuous Missal Conrad Wagner illuminated for Johannes von Giltlingen, abbot of the imperial Monastery of Saints Ulrich and Afra in Augsburg from 1482 to 1496. Wagner, who is mentioned in Frater Wilhelm Wittwer's chronicle of the monastery, compiled from 1493 to 1497, was praised for his skills as an illuminator ("bonus il-luminista"). From the same document we learn that Wagner, who was from Ellingen, was a conventual at the monastery and decorated and illuminated numerous books there, including a Missal completed in 1480, a Gradual finished in 1490, and the Missal of Abbot Johannes von Giltlingen. The appropriate portions of the chronicle have been published by Erich Steingräber, *Die kirchliche Buchmalerei Augsburgs um 1500,* Augsburg, [1956], 46–47. Of these luxury manuscripts, we now have only the Gradual of 1490 (still preserved in Augsburg, Maximilian-museum, but owned by the Diözesanmuseum, Inv.-Nr. DMI 11) and thirteen illuminated leaves from Giltlingen's Missal, one of which we recently identified in the Victoria and Albert Museum (Fig. 3). Marrow has suggested that as many as twenty-one leaves may have survived from the Missal, for that is the largest of the modern arabic numbers appearing on the leaves; consequently as many as eight more remain to be discovered.

Wagner apparently worked on the Missal over a period of four years, because two different dates appear on some of the leaves, 1485 (some have mistakenly read it as 1487) and 1489. One of the leaves, dated 1489, contains the name of Giltlingen and the initials of the artist, C. W. None of the surviving Missal leaves or the Gradual contain full-page miniatures, so his art can only be judged by historiated initials and border decorations. The borders are remarkable for their density, rich coloration, and highly burnished and tooled gold backgrounds. In this leaf the borders are mostly inhabited by birds, including a crowing cock that seems to announce the early hour of Christ's Resurrection, taking place in the initial below. If, as James Marrow has suggested, the Missal consisted of two volumes, this leaf (fol. 107) would have been one of the few from the first, which contained the Temporale (Proper of Time or Season); the second would have contained the Sanctorale (Proper of Saints). Although Wagner died in the same year as Giltlingen, 1496, his distinctive decorative vocabulary found echoes in the works of his successors, such as Jörg and Leonhard Beck and Jörg Gutknecht.

TEXT: "Resurrexi, et adhuc tecum sum . . . " (I arose, and am still with thee . . .) is the Introit for the feast of the Resurrection.

SISTER LEAVES: Germany, private collection (Pentecost; reproduced by Marrow, fig. 4); London, Victoria and Al-bert Museum, 274.2/MS 424 (Adoration of the Magi, Fig. 3); Nuremberg, Germanisches Nationalmuseum, 10 leaves: Mm1 (not historiated, but has the initials of the artist, the name of the patron, and the date 1489); Mm2 (lower margin has an icon of John the Baptist); Mm3 (St. Andrew); Mm4 (St. Simbert); Mm5 (St. Narcissus); Mm6 (Death of the Virgin); Mm7 (St. Afra); Mm8 (Last Judgment); Mm9 (Apocalyptic Madonna and Child); Mm10 (Bishop Con-secrating a Church).

PROVENANCE: Viennese-American collector; bought from him by H. P. Kraus, Ridgefield, Conn., in the early 1960s; bought from his estate in 1990.

BIBLIOGRAPHY: James H. Marrow, "Two Newly Identi-fied Leaves from the Missal of Johannes von Giltlingen: Notes on Late-Fifteenth-Century Manuscript Illumination in Augsburg," *Anzeiger des Germanischen Nationalmuseums,* 1984, 27–31, fig. 3.

44 Resurrection (color plate p. 38).

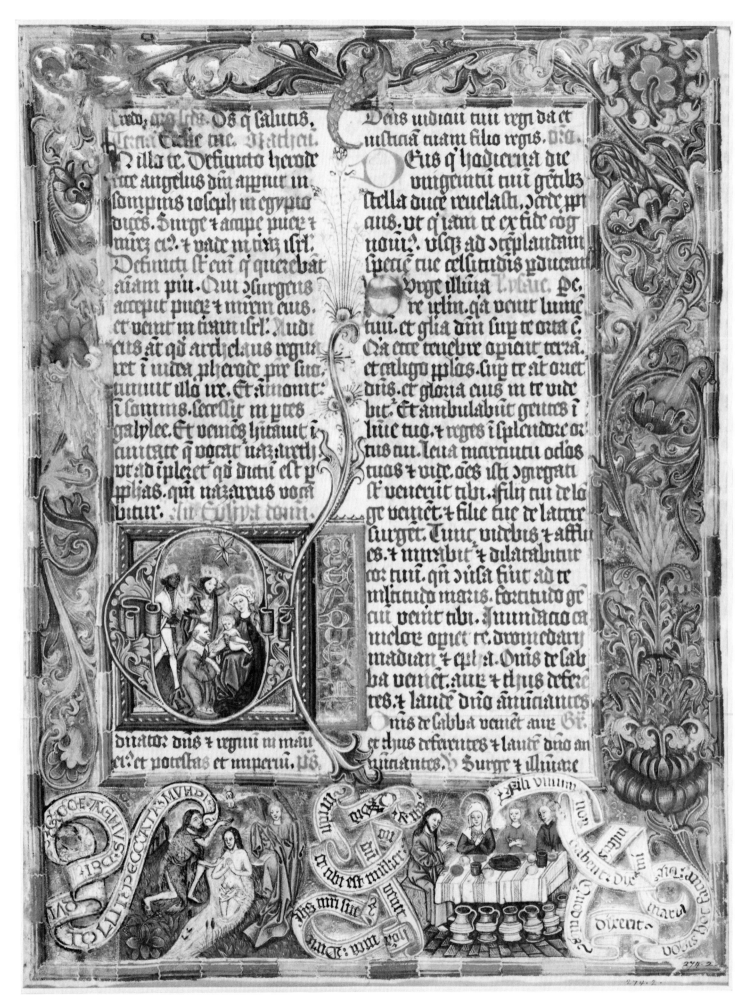

Fig. 3. Adoration of the Magi, Baptism of Christ, and Wedding at Cana, by Conrad Wagner. London, Victoria and Albert Museum, 274.2/MS 424. Courtesy of the Board of Trustees of the Victoria and Albert Museum.

45 Entombment
46 Christ Appearing to the Three Marys, and John and Peter Arriving at the Tomb

Two leaves from an Antiphonary with historiated initials I and A. Germany, possibly Augsburg, late 15th century. Vellum, 580 x 400 and 575 x 394 mm, 1 column with 6 staves of 4 red lines; the initials are on versos.

THESE two leaves, which are nearly identical in size, probably came from the same Antiphonary; their borders are similar, the palette of the two historiated initials is the same, and the color of the gold-tooled background, as well as some of the tooling, matches. The leaves date from fairly late in the fifteenth century because one of them, the Entombment, is based on Martin Schongauer's engraving of that subject, which is dated about 1480.

The historiated initial with Christ Appearing to the Three Marys is larger in size, reflecting the greater liturgical importance of the feast with which it is connected, that of Easter. Iconographically it is also the more interesting, for the artist has conflated several Gospel accounts. Matthew (28:1–10), for example, is unique in describing Christ's appearance and greeting to the Marys, but he mentions only Mary Magdalene and another Mary (not three). According to Jerome, they were the first to hear Christ's "Hail" *(Ave)* that the curse of Eve might be removed in these women: as Rabanus Maurus put it, they bear not the word *Eva,* but *Ave* (Thomas W. Mossman, *The Great Commentary of Cornelius à Lapide, S. Matthew's Gospel,* London, 1883, III, 343). After the greeting, the two Marys came up to him, took hold of his feet, and adored him. St. Peter Chrysologus (the "golden-worded"), argued that "they held his feet to show that the head of Christ is the man, that the woman is in Christ's feet, and that it was given to them, through Christ, not to go before, but to follow the man" (*Catena Aurea: Commentary on the Four Gospels Collected Out of the Works of the Fathers by S. Thomas Aquinas,* Oxford, 1874, II, 982). According to John (20:17), however, Christ told Mary Magdalene not to touch him. Christ then instructed the two Marys (Matthew 28:10) to tell the brethren; and, according to St. John Chrysostom, "because a woman was made the cause of sorrow to man, now women are made the ministers of joy to men." (On the basis of Christ's words to the women, Martin Luther had concluded that women may preach; for this and the Chrysostom reference see Mossman, 344.) John (20:2–4) is also the only evangelist to mention that Mary Magdalene specifically told both Peter and John, the beloved disciple, of the empty tomb, causing them to run to it; as in our initial, John, the younger and more energetic, outran Peter, and was the first to arrive. Curiously, the precise subject matter of the initial is not reflected in the liturgy of Easter. The Gospel reading for the Mass, taken from Mark 16, mentions three women (Mary Magdalene, Mary the mother of James, and Salome) visiting the tomb, but Christ does not appear to them; nor do Peter and John visit the tomb. Mark 16 is also the first lesson for the Office of Easter, but the first Matins response, which our initial begins, is in fact a paraphrase of Matthew's account (28:2–6). The artist has clearly not illustrated the response—which mentions that an angel rolled back the stone, sat on it, and told the women not to be afraid— but has chosen to continue pictorially Matthew's account (28:9–10) by showing Christ appearing to the women in the initial; to this he also added the Peter and John episode (from John 20:2–4), creating a historiated initial that is actually fairly rare.

TEXT: "In pace in idipsum dormiam . . . " (I will lie down in peace . . .) is the first Matins antiphon for Holy Saturday ("Sabbato s[an]cto ad matutinas antiphona . . . "). "Angelus Domini descendit de celo . . . " (An angel of the Lord descended from heaven . . .) is the first Matins response for Easter.

PROVENANCE: Entombment was bought from Kistner in Nuremberg in 1988; Three Marys was bought in London, Sotheby's, 21 June 1988, lot 22, illus.

npa

ce midiplus:

dozmiam et requiescat: ps

Cum muuo · an · Nabita

bit in tabernaculo tuo re

quiescet in monte sancto

45 Entombment.

46 Christ Appearing to the Three Marys (color plate p. 39).

47   Last Supper

Leaf from a Gradual with a historiated initial C illuminated by Joannes Zmilely de Pisek or his workshop. Czechoslovakia, Prague, ca. 1500. Vellum, 610 x 385 mm, 1 column with 9 staves of 5 red lines; the initial is on a recto.

THIS leaf and two others (Figs. 5 and 6) can be compared with a group of choir books illuminated in Prague at the end of the fifteenth and the beginning of the sixteenth century (see Josef Krása, *Ceské iluminované rukopisy 13./16. století,* Prague, 1990, figs. 183–89), and especially to the Wladislaus Gradual (Esztergom, Főszékesegyházi Könyvtár, MS I.3), which was presumably made for the Royal Chapel of Wladislaus II Jagiello, who, succeeding Matthias Corvinus, was king of Hungary from 1490 to 1516. The Gradual and the Breslauer leaf are approximately the same size and have the same tall and narrow text box, an identical number of staves and lines, and similarly trimmed borders on the right and bottom. The Last Supper certainly comes from a luxurious manuscript, for the beginning lines of text for the feast of Corpus Christi are alternately written in blue and red rather than black, and the musical notation is alternately written in gold and silver (now tarnished).

The Office and Mass for Corpus Christi, which celebrates the institution of the Eucharist, was composed by St. Thomas Aquinas. The initial C of the feast's Introit is usually illustrated with a Last Supper, regarded as the first Eucharist. The body of Christ was symbolized by the bread (grain is mentioned in the Introit) and his blood by the wine (clusters of grapes are shown in the border).

The miniature, which in style is more late Gothic than Renaissance, is very close to one in a German private collection. Both depend on the same print, a Last Supper (Fig. 4) in Stefan Fridolin's *Schatzbehalter* (Treasure Chest), published by Anton Koberger in Nuremberg on 8 November 1491, both were made in Prague about the same time, and both share the same foliate forms of the initial. If this artist also worked on the Mladoboleslavsky Gradual (Mladá Boleslav, Okresní Muzeum), he could be identified either as Joannes Zmilely de Pisek, whose name is given in that Gradual, or to an assistant. The Wladislaus Gradual has also been attributed to Zmilely by both Ilona Berkovits, who regarded him as one of the best Bohemian illuminators of his day ("Az Esztergomi Ulászló-Graduale," *Magyar Könyvszemle,* LXV, 1941, 342–53), and Budavári Palota (*Kódexek a közepkori Magyarországon,* Budapest, 1985, no. 180, pls. 87–88). Berkovits also suggested that Zmilely was influenced by German prints and Michael Wolgemut, to whom the *Schatzbehalter* has been attributed.

TEXT: "Cibavit eos ex adipe frumenti . . . " (He fed them with the fat of wheat . . .) is the Introit for the feast of Corpus Christi ("de corpore xpi").

SISTER LEAVES: Bern, Dr. Ernst and Sonya Böhlen (Presentation in the Temple, Fig. 5, also based on the *Schatzbehalter*); New York, private collection (Ascension, Fig. 6).

PROVENANCE: Bought privately in New York in 1979.

Fig. 4. Last Supper, woodcut by Wolgemut's shop, from Stefan Fridolin's *Schatzbehalter.* New York, The Pierpont Morgan Library, PML 178.

ce   li ce cordu omubus unucti

bus confitebimur e   i quia fe

ur nobis   cum mise   ricor

diam   suam   ex corpore xpi

gla uite

os exadi pe

frumen ti a

e   v   ia et dextra melle   ca

bi rauit eos deu iga tu va

47 Last Supper (color plate p. 39).

Fig. 5. Presentation in the Temple, by Joannes Zmilely de Pisek or shop. Bern, Dr. Ernst and Sonya Böhlen.

Fig. 6. Ascension, by Joannes Zmilely de Pisek or shop. New York, private collection.

48 Coronation of the Virgin

Leaf probably from a Missal, with a miniature, commissioned by Abbess Barbara Vetter von Schwenningen for the Cistercian convent at Oberschönenfeld. Germany, Bavaria, dated 1504. Vellum, 380 x 282 mm; the miniature is on a verso.

ACCORDING to the dedicatory inscription beneath the Coronation of the Virgin, "the book was commissioned by the worthy and spiritual lady Barbara Vetter von Schwenningen, abbess of the worthy House of God, for the good of the House of God, so that God would be merciful and compassionate to her; as one counts after the birth of Christ, one thousand, five hundred, and four years." Although the name of the Cistercian convent Oberschönenfeld was not given, it has been kindly established by Dr. Reinhard Heydenreuter (Generaldirektion der Staatlichen Archive Bayerns), who also supplied other information about the abbess and the coats-of-arms on the leaf. Barbara, who was abbess from 1492 to 1508, is dressed in the black Cistercian habit and holds a crosier. Kneeling at the right, she bears a scroll inscribed with a petition to the Virgin: "O mater misericordie ora pro me ut michi misericordia prestetur" (O Mother of Mercy, pray for me that I may obtain forgiveness). The two arms grouped together are those of her parents. Those of her father, Georg Vetter von der Gilgen (*Gilgen* means *lilies*), who was since 1469 the "Herr der Hofmark" of Schwenningen, occur on the heraldic right (three silver lilies against a blue background); the Vetter line ended with the death of Adam Vetter von der Gilgen in 1595. The arms of her mother, Margareta von Schwenningen, occur on the heraldic left (a silver stag antler against a red background); in 1484, with the death of Margareta's brother Hans, this branch of the family came to an end. The arms on the left, with a crosier behind, is that of the Cistercian order, and would here refer to Oberschönenfeld, in the rural district of Dillingen. According to Dr. Heydenreuter, the convent was founded in 1248, secularized in 1803, but renewed in 1836. (For further information see Alfred Schröder, "Schwenningen in Bayern: Geschichte eines schwäbischen Dorfes," *Jahrbuch des historischen Vereins Dillingen A.D.*, XXXVII, 1924, 1–90, L. H. Cottineau, *Répertoire topo-bibliographique des abbayes et prieurés*, Mâcon, 1937, II, 2117, and Edgar Krausen, *Die Klöster des Zisterzienserordens in Bayern*, Munich, 1953.)

Representations of the Coronation of the Virgin, an event not mentioned in the Bible, seem to have originated in the Gothic period, when devotions to the Virgin Mary intensified, and when cathedrals were increasingly dedicated to her. Her crowning is referred to in apocryphal works, various religious writings and commentaries, and in the *Golden Legend* of Jacobus de Voragine. According to the last, Jerome said that Mary ascended into heaven on August 15, and, according to St. Gerardus, was applauded by the Trinity. Depictions of her coronation by the Trinity, however, do not seem to have originated before the early fifteenth century. The Breslauer leaf is of a late type and compositionally close to several panels by Hans Holbein, the Elder, who was active in nearby Augsburg (see Augsburg-Rathaus, *Hans Holbein der Ältere und die Kunst der Spätgotik*, Augsburg, 1965, figs. 4, 62). The leaf differs in that Christ displays his wounds and wears a crown of thorns.

TEXT: "Das buch hat lassen schriben die wirdig und gaystlich fraw. fraw barbara vetterin von Schwenningen eptissen des wirdigen gotezhaus hatt das lassen machen vo[r] des gotezhaus gut der gott genedig und baremherczig sei. als man zalt nach XPI [Christi] geburt M CCCCC und iiii Jar" is the dedicatory inscription below the miniature.

PROVENANCE: Oberschönenfeld; bought in Hamburg, Hauswedell & Nolte, 22 and 23 May 1984, Auktion 251, lot 542, pl. 30.

Das büch hat lassen schuben die wudig vnd gayslich frauw. frauw ...
... aptissen des wurdigen gotz haus
hat das lassen machen vo des gotzhaus gut der gott gened...
vnd barmhertzig si . als man zalt nach xpi gebürt ... cc ...
vnd im jar

48 Coronation of the Virgin (color plate p. 40).

49 St. Michael Weighing a Soul

Historiated initial S from an Antiphonary. Germany, Nuremberg, ca. 1520. Vellum, 130 x 123 mm, 1 column with staves of 4 red lines; the cutting is probably on a recto.

ALTHOUGH the subject of St. Michael weighing souls has a long history and was especially popular in northern Europe during the fifteenth and sixteenth centuries, the idea was never officially promulgated by the Church. The theme probably derived from its counterparts in ancient Egyptian and Greek religions, the weighing of the heart in the former, and the weighing of the soul by Hermes in the latter (see S. G. F. Brandon, *The Judgment of the Dead: The Idea of Life After Death in the Major Religions,* New York, 1969, chapters 1, 4, 5). The weighing is not mentioned in the Mass or Divine Office for the feast of St. Michael (September 29), though his role as the prince and guardian over souls, both in the dreadful judgment and on their journey home, is, in fact, the subject of the antiphon on the back of the leaf itself. In the initial, moreover, Michael seems more concerned with stopping the interference of the devil, who has placed a millstone in the cup and tries to pull his part of the balance down. A millstone is actually mentioned in the Gospel for the day (Matthew 28:6)—as part of the punishment by drowning for those who scandalize believers in Christ. In a late medieval fresco in the Steig-Kirche near Schaffhausen the devil pulling the cup down actually wears a millstone about his neck (reproduced by Leopold Kretzenbacher, *Die Seelenwaage: Zur religiösen Idee vom Jenseitsgericht auf der Schicksalswaage in Hochreligion, Bildkunst und Volksglaube,* Klagenfurt, 1958, fig. 29, who also discusses some German legends about the weighing that help to explain its popularity there). Michael's protective role may also explain why the weighing scene illustrates the Office of the Dead in some Dutch Horae (see James H. Marrow et al., *The Golden Age of Dutch Manuscript Painting,* New York, 1990, 171, pl. VII, 60). In our own day St. Michael has taken on yet another role, for in 1950 Pope Pius XII made him the patron saint of policemen.

The leaf was probably illuminated in Nuremberg about 1520, but has not been attributed to a specific artist. It may be possible to find other works by the same hand when Nuremberg illumination has been more fully studied and published. A similar weighing occurs in the *Allegory of the Papacy* (Berlin-Dahlem, Gemäldegalerie) attributed to Hans Springinklee; indeed, Barbara Butts, who called this painting to our attention, thinks that there may also be a stylistic connection. The subject was also popular in woodcuts: a St. Michael and the devil attributed to the young Albrecht Dürer was published by Anton Koberger in his 1488 edition of the *Passional oder der Heiligen Leben;* and a St. Michael with similarly loose drapery folds was executed by Lucas Cranach the Elder in 1506. Sculptured examples were popular, and the type represented by the statue of about 1470–80 in the Lorenzkirche at Nuremberg, with its loose-fitting drapery and heavy gilding, may well have served as a source of inspiration for the illuminator of this St. Michael. This might explain the yellow color of Michael's robe in the miniature, a curious choice given the gold background. (The statue, attributed to Veit Stoss, is reproduced in Metropolitan Museum of Art, *Gothic and Renaissance Art in Nuremberg, 1300–1550,* New York, 1986, 161, fig. 35.)

TEXT: The S probably begins the antiphon (or response or versicle), "Stetit angelus juxta aram templi . . . " (An Angel stood before the altar of the temple . . .), from the feast of St. Michael the Archangel (September 29); on the back of the cutting is the fragment, "Archa[ngele Michael] constitui te p[ri]n[cipem super omnes animas suscipien-das]" (Archangel Michael, I have appointed you prince and guardian over all souls on their journey home), another antiphon from the same feast.

PROVENANCE: Eric Korner (his no. 48), London; bought at his sale in London, Sotheby's, 19 June 1990, lot 38, illus.

49 St. Michael Weighing a Soul (color plate p. 41).

Historiated initials K, I, S, R, and Q from a Gradual. Germany, second quarter of the 16th century. Vellum, 71 x 67, 71 x 57, 71 x 66, 75 x 71, and 67 x 68 mm.

THE pictorial cycle in most medieval and Renaissance Graduals consisted of a series of large historiated initials marking the Introit, the opening prayer of the Mass (such as Nos. 12, 35, 36, 43, 47, 60, 62, and 72–74). The other chanted prayers in Graduals—the Gradual, Alleluia, Offertory, and Communion—were usually marked with smaller foliate or filigree letters. The Gradual from which these five initials came must have been unusually luxurious, for some of the letters marked, not the Introit, but those prayers that normally did not receive historiated initials. The Q, for example, seems to have marked the Communion prayer from the feast of Corpus Christi, which began "Quotiescumque manducabitis panem hunc" (As often as you shall eat this bread). Our conjecture is based not only on the appropriate iconography of the initial but also on the identification of the tiny textual fragment on the back of the cutting, a mere four letters and a hyphen, "et pa-", that may be from the Offertory of the same feast, "Sacerdotes Domini incensum *et pa*nes offerunt. . . . " Supporting our identification is the fact that music accompanying this fragment is a near match to that for the Offertory prayer found in published Graduals. The K with the seated Christ Child could be the K of the Kyrie eleison. Iconographically this makes sense, since the invocations of the prayer ("Lord, have mercy" and "Christ, have mercy") are addressed to the Savior. On the back of this initial are the letters "x ho-" that could be from the opening words of the Gloria, "Gloria in excelsis Deo. Et in terra pa*x ho*minibus," that is sung immediately after the Kyrie. The music accompanying the "x ho-" fragment also supports this identification, for it, felicitously, is the same as in published Graduals. The other three initials and their textual and musical fragments have, so far, eluded identification.

The inspiration for what would have been a vast number of historiated initials in the original parent Gradual could have come from a printed Missal. There is some similarity in approach, as well as in the foliate forms of the Breslauer initials themselves, to those used in a Missal for the use of Augsburg printed by Sebald Mayers in Dillingen in 1555 (see A. F. Butsch, *Die Bücherornamentik der Hoch- und Spätrenaissance,* Leipzig, 1881, pl. 76).

PROVENANCE: Bought in London, Sotheby's, 13 December 1976, lot 18, illus.

50 Christ Child.

51 Man Clubbing a Dog.

52 A Soul Saved.

53 Vision of Christ as Judge.

54 Family Receiving Communion.

55 Angel of Matthew

Leaf from a Missal with a historiated I. Italy, Puglia, late 11th century. Vellum, 347 x 248 (263 x 81–21–81) mm, 2 columns of 29 lines; the initial is on a verso.

THE large initial I set with interlace panels, decorated with animal-headed terminals, and topped by a bust-length figure of the angel of Matthew, holding what appears to be an elongated book, marks the beginning of the most important reading from the Mass, the Gospel lesson. In a simple program of historiation, the initial is accompanied by the symbol of the evangelist from whose Gospel the reading is extracted. In the sister leaf owned by Martin Schøyen, for instance, the Gospel reading, taken from Luke, is marked by an initial surmounted by an ox. Other parts of the Mass are marked by unhistoriated and smaller initials. A simple two-line S marks the beginning of the Secret and a more elaborate V+D monogram, standing for "Vere dignum" (It is fitting indeed), begins the Preface of the Mass.

The Breslauer leaf, however, is more interesting for its script—Beneventan—than its decoration. Beneventan script is the name given to the peculiar writing that developed and flourished within the ancient duchy of Benevento. Its chief center was the famous Benedictine Monastery of Monte Cassino. One of the most enduring of the national bookhands, Beneventan remained in use from the late eighth to the early sixteenth century in the monasteries and schools throughout southern Italy and extended even across the Adriatic to Dalmatia. The script reached its zenith of clarity and elegance in the second half of the eleventh century, the date of the present leaf. The script has its origins in early medieval cursive forms that remained untouched by the changes wrought over most of Europe by Carolingian calligraphic reforms, which stopped just south of Rome and did not reach southern Italy. (See E. A. Lowe, edited and enlarged by Virginia Brown, *The Beneventan Script: A History of the South Italian Minuscule,* Rome, 1980; additions to Lowe's original list of manuscripts are in his article, "A New List of Beneventan Manuscripts," *Collectanea vaticana in honorem Anselmi M. Card. Albareda a Bibliotheca Apostolica edita,* Vatican City, 1962, II, 211–44; and Virginia Brown, "A Second New List of Beneventan Manuscripts," *Mediaeval Studies,* XL, 1978, 239–89 [part one], and L, 1988, 584–625 [part two].)

Beneventan script has a number of distinguishing features. The first is the unusual form of the *a* and *t;* the first looks like two *c*'s touching each other, and the second looks much the same but with a straighter cross-stroke. The second feature is the distinctive ligatures formed by *ei, fi, gi, li, ri,* and *ti.* The third characteristic is the "*i*-longa," that is, occasionally making the *i* tall, like an *l,* in accordance with certain principles of pronunciation. The fourth feature of the script is the ligature of *t* with the vowels *a, e, i,* and *u,* in which the *t* loses its normal form. Beneventan scribes also employed certain distinctive abbreviations and punctuation marks. The latter include one point plus a semicolon (looking something like .;) that indicated the Beneventan full stop and the point (.) that was the Beneventan equivalent of today's colon. Some of these features can be observed in the Breslauer leaf, and, for the convenience of our readers, we provide a transcription of the opening lines of the text marked by Matthew's angel: "In ill[o] t[em]p[ore]. Dixit Ih[e]s[us] discipulis suis. Cum vos persequentur in civitate una, fugite in alia. Amen dico vobis, non consumabitis . . . " (At that time Jesus said to his disciples, When they shall persecute you in this city flee into another. Amen I say to you, you shall not finish . . .). The writing on the Breslauer leaf is a subspecies of Beneventan script called the Bari type. Characteristics include the distinctly rounded effect of the script as a whole (as opposed to the angular look of the script that flourished at Monte Cassino and the Benevento) and the broken back of the *c,* which makes it look like a majuscule *E.*

Of interest on this leaf, too, are the sung portions of the Mass. These chants, in a smaller script, are accompanied by musical notation typical of the region, written without the aid of staff-lines or clefs.

TEXT: The Gospel reading from Matthew 10:23–32, given above, is for the feast of Sts. Vitus, Modestus, and Crescentia (June 15).

SISTER LEAVES: Cambridge, Mass., Harvard University, Houghton Library, MS Typ 701 (one leaf; ex-Philip Hofer collection); Oslo, Martin Schøyen, MS 63 (two consecu-tive leaves; ex-London, Quaritch, Catalogue 1128, cited below, 22–24, no. 8, illus. and frontispiece).

PROVENANCE: Bought privately in 1972.

BIBLIOGRAPHY: London, Bernard Quaritch, Catalogue 1128 (*Bookhands of the Middle Ages. Part IV: Beneventan Script*), 1990, 24 (as American private collection).

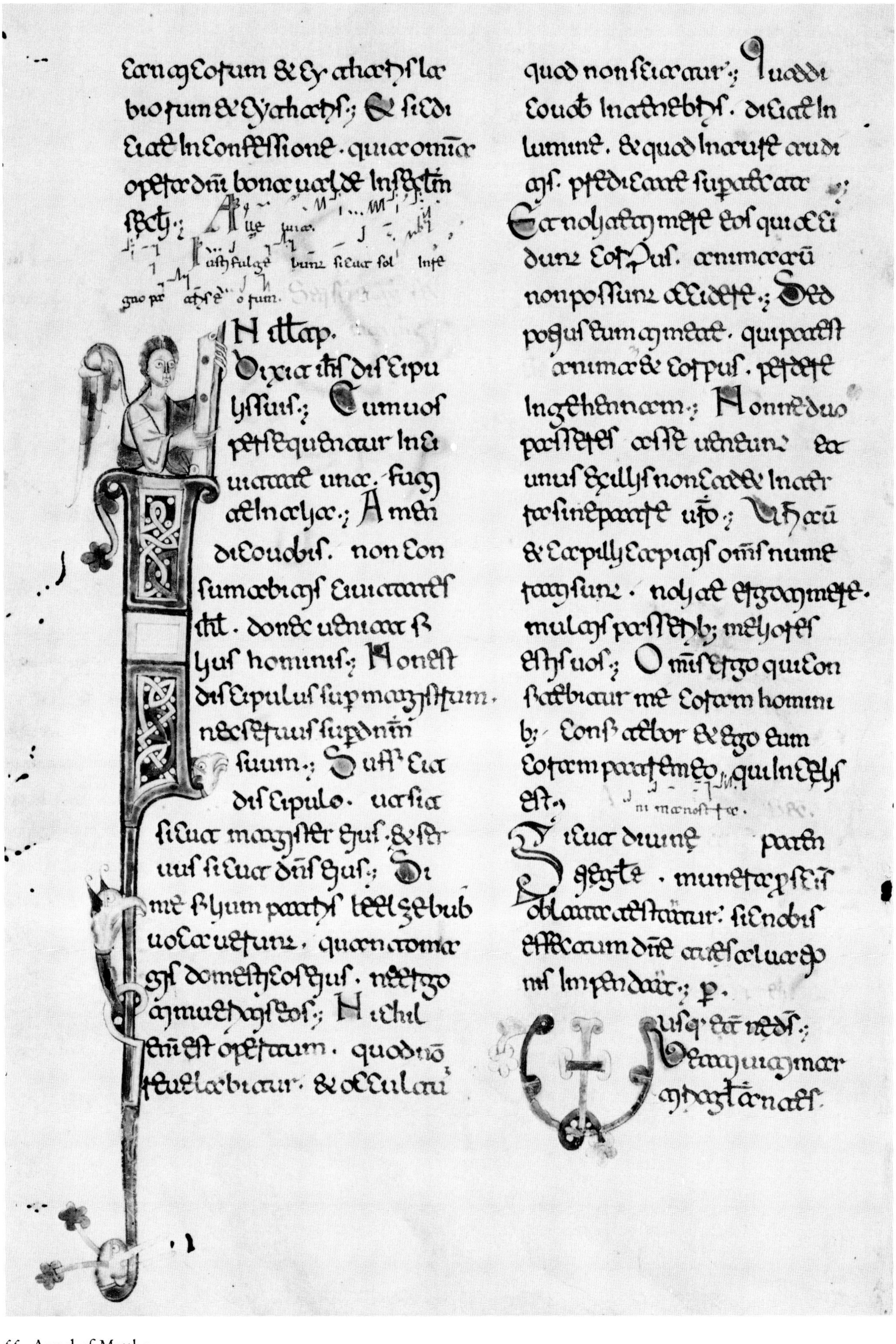

55 Angel of Matthew.

56 St. Paul

Cutting from a Bible with a historiated initial P. Italy, Bologna, ca. 1270. Vellum, 460 x 163 mm, 2 columns (originally) of 41 lines; the initial is on a verso.

IN the middle of the thirteenth century, illumination in Bologna broke from the Romanesque style typical of the twelfth and first half of the thirteenth centuries. In the third quarter of the century, Bolognese illumination began to be influenced by art from north of the Alps, especially French Gothic painting. This early Gothic manner is what art historians call the "First Style" of Bolognese illumination. (See Alessandro Conti, *La miniatura bolognese: scuole e botteghe, 1270–1340,* Bologna, 1981.) The style is characterized by lively figures whose drapery falls in soft, pliant folds. There is also an increased use of foliage, in which curving tendrils often include figures or narrative scenes that enliven the borders. This St. Paul is painted in the Bolognese First Style. The spare palette of orange, gray, and blue is characteristic of the earlier phase, that is, about 1270. The Breslauer Paul can be compared in style to two Bolognese choir books, one in Bologna's Museo Civico Medievale (MS 518, see Conti, figs. 22, 23) and another in Gemona's cathedral (cor. 3; Conti, fig. 58). Iconographically the figure of Paul has the characteristic features always given to this saint by medieval artists: a narrow face, a bulbous forehead, and a long pointed beard.

This large cutting is actually only half of a leaf from a large, two-column Bible, the kind often called a "refectory Bible" because the volumes were read from during meals at a monastery. The chapter divisions of this fragment are not those of the modern Bible, which were only codified in the early thirteenth century, probably by Stephen Langton, who drafted the Magna Carta (see Christopher de Hamel, *A History of Illuminated Manuscripts,* Boston, 1986, 116–17). Until around 1300, "there were also various systems of capitulation, some giving fewer, others many more chapters than our present system" (Beryl Smalley, *The Study of the Bible in the Middle Ages,* Notre Dame, 1964, 221–22). The *tituli* of this fragment, written on the recto, offer thirty chapters for the First Epistle of Paul to Timothy, whereas the modern Bible has only six.

TEXT: "Explicit prologus" (Here ends the prologue) is followed by "Incipit Ep[isto]la ad Timotheum: Paulus [apostulos] Xp[ist]i Ih[es]u secundum i[m]perium Dei . . . " (Here begins the Epistle to Timothy: Paul, an apostle of Jesus Christ, according to the commandment of God . . .), the beginning of the First Epistle of Paul to Timothy. On the recto of the cutting is the end (chapters ix through xxx) of the list of the *tituli* (table of contents) for the Epistle, and the *argumentum* (prologue).

SISTER LEAVES: London, Sotheby's, 25 April 1983, lot 20, illus. (two cuttings, each with an initial of St. Paul); Newton, Mass., Rendells, Catalogue 146 *(The Medieval World, 800 AD – 1450 AD),* 1979, nos. 35 and 36, illus. (St. Paul; and John the Evangelist with an Eagle Head).

PROVENANCE: Bought from Laurence Witten in 1979.

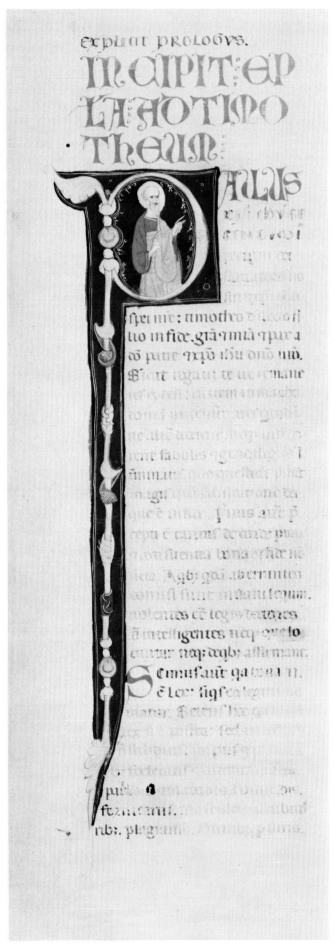

56 St. Paul.

57 Presentation in the Temple

Leaf from an Antiphonary with a historiated A illuminated by Jacobellus of Salerno. Italy, Bologna, ca. 1270. Vellum, 528 x 350 mm, 1 column with 7 staves of 4 red lines; the initial is on a recto.

THIS leaf once belonged to a set of choir books consisting of at least four volumes: a Gradual and a three-volume Antiphonary, of which two survive, the third existing only in a few leaves. The set was written, illuminated, and notated by Jacobellus, known as Muriolus, of Salerno. His unusually specific colophon, in Latin, is found on folio 159v of the Getty Gradual, one of the parent set: "I, Jacobellus, known as 'muriolus' [mini-mouse], of Salerno, wrote, illuminated, and notated this book, which was the first work by my hand" (Anton von Euw and Joachim M. Plotzek, *Die Handschriften der Sammlung Ludwig,* Cologne, 1979, I, 262). Since Jacobellus does not preface his name with "frater" (as we might expect from a monastic scribe in this period), he may have been a lay scribe who, as his name indicates, came from the southern Italian city of Salerno. His manner of painting differs from the Bolognese "First Style," as exemplified in No. 56.

Jacobellus's Presentation of Christ is the traditional illustration for the feast of the Purification of the Virgin celebrated on February 2. The feast commemorates the purification of the Virgin and the presentation of Christ in the Temple that took place forty days after Christ's birth, following Jewish law. (For another Presentation in the Breslauer Collection, also for the feast of the Purification, see No. 63.)

Stylistic elements and motifs employed by Jacobellus in this leaf can be found in the parent manuscripts and sister leaves. The canopy over the figures and the diapered background in the Breslauer initial, for example, are similar to those in a Nativity in the Stockholm Antiphonary (Carl Nordenfalk, *Bokmålningar från medeltid och renässans i Nationalmusei samlingar,* Stockholm, 1979, no. 18, fig. 104). The roundels in the bottom border with busts of Dominican monks and nuns are also to be found in the Stockholm Antiphonary (Nordenfalk, figs. 104 and 107), the Chicago Antiphonary (Nordenfalk, fig. 222), the Getty Gradual (Fig. 7 and see von Euw and Plotzek, pls. 171, 172, and illus. p. 263), and the leaf in a German private collection (see Mickenberg below).

The many roundels of Dominican monks and nuns that occur frequently throughout the original manuscripts, as well as textual elements in the signed Gradual, indicate that the choir books were made for a Dominican institution. Because of the many nuns, von Euw and Plotzek (p. 264) suggested the Convent of San Guglielmo in Bologna. The choir books, however, could have been made for any number of Dominican institutions established during the century following St. Dominic's founding of his popular order in 1216.

TEXT: "Adorna thalamu[m] tuu[m] Syon . . . " (Sion, adorn your dwelling . . .) is the first Matins response for the feast of the Purification of the Virgin (February 2).

PARENT MANUSCRIPT: Originally at least a four-volume set of choir books: Malibu, J. Paul Getty Museum, MS Ludwig VI.1 (signed Gradual, Fig. 7); Stockholm, Nationalmuseum, MS B. 1578 (Antiphonary); Chicago, Art Institute, acc. no. 11.142.B (Antiphonary); the fourth volume, also an Antiphonary, survives in leaves (for which, see below).

SISTER LEAVES: Philadelphia, Museum of Art, acc. no. 62–146–2 (Last Supper); private German collection (Conversion of Saul; ex-Ellin Mitchell, Inc., see David Mickenberg, *Songs of Glory: Medieval Art from 900–1500,* Oklahoma City, 1985, no. 99, illus.).

PROVENANCE: Bought in London, Sotheby's, 11 December 1979, lot 5, illus.

mitrie . p . Odi e . euou . a . Post

partum uirgo inuiolata p

manfisti dei genitrix intercæ

æ pro nobis . p . Diñ cña . euoæ .

V . Sca dei geni
trix uirgo semper
maria . Rf Intercæ
de pnoli ad dñm
deum nrma . Rf .

Dorma

thalamum tuu sy

on et suscipe regem xpi

57 Presentation in the Temple.

Fig. 7. Virgin and Child Adored by a Dominican Monk and Two Nuns, by Jacobellus of Salerno.
Malibu, Calif., J. Paul Getty Museum, MS Ludwig VI. 1, fol. 70.

58 Christ with the Samaritan Woman at the Well
59 Entombment

Two leaves from a Missal with historiated initials F and N. Italy, Perugia, late 13th century. Vellum, 362 x 245 (220 x 63–16–63) mm, 2 columns of 25 lines; both initials are on versos.

P ERUGIAN manuscript illumination of the Gothic era is characterized by delicate ornamentation. In the thirteenth century, the date of these two leaves, this ornamentation consists of bars and foliage that extend from the decorated initials into the margins. The leaves are generally shown with their scalloped edges in profile and highlighted in white. A similar penchant for ornamentation also affects Perugian filigree, which has a tendency to spiral into pinwheel‑like patterns, such as we see on the blue ground of the Entombment. By the fourteenth century, as in the Breslauer Presentation in the Temple (No. 63), Perugian love of fine ornamentation reaches full flower.

The attribution of these two leaves to Perugia is based on the similarity of the secondary decoration, rather than the figural style, to other examples of Perugian illumination of this period. The relative scarcity of studies on Perugian illumination makes an attribution to a specific workshop or hand impossible at this time. The delicate foliage seen in profile and the spiraling filigree can be found in a group of manuscripts attributed to Perugia: Box Hill (Victoria, Australia), St. Paschal's College, Codex S. Paschalis (Margaret M. Manion and Vera F. Vines, *Medieval and Renaissance Illuminated Manuscripts in Australian Collections,* Melbourne, 1984, 28, 37–39, no. 4, pl. 4, figs. 12–23); Gubbio, Archivio di Stato, MS A (*Francesco d'Assisi: documenti e archivi, codici e biblioteche, miniature,* Francesco Porzio, ed., Milan, 1982, 184, no. 4, illus.); London, private collection, historiated initial of Christ and a Kneeling Saint, and four historiated initials in Nuremberg, Germanisches Nationalmuseum, B 32–34 (Filippo Todini, *La Pittura Umbra dal Duecento al primo Cinquecento,* Milan, 1989, I, 116, II, figs. 82, 83); and Paris, Bibliothèque Nationale, MSS lat. 41, 3026, 3990 B, 14278, and 17833 (François Avril and Marie‑Thérèse Gousset, *Manuscrits enluminés d'origine italienne, 2: XIIIe siècle,* Paris, 1984, 119–22, nos. 143–47, pls. I, LXXV–LXXVIII).

Medieval and Renaissance Missals, when illuminated—for they were not always—usually had historiated initials, as we see here, or small miniatures marking the Introit, the opening prayer of the Mass. The subjects of these pictures do not illustrate the Introit, but the Gospel reading for that day. The first Breslauer leaf, illustrating the Gospel for Friday in the third week of Lent (John 4:5–42), shows Christ revealing himself as the Messiah to the Samaritan woman as two disciples arrive, surprised to see their Savior speaking to a woman. The Entombment of the second leaf, illustrating the lengthy reading that recounts Christ's Passion for Tuesday in Holy Week (Mark 14:32–72 and 15:1–46), shows Joseph of Arimathea laying Christ's shroud‑wrapped body in the tomb.

Unlike the Introit initials, the two decorated I's, which mark the beginning of the Epistles, are iconographically related to their texts. In the first leaf (at the lower right) is a bearded Moses supporting a large tome on his shoulders; the Epistle reading, from the Book of Numbers, tells the story of Moses' striking the rock to provide water for the Israelites. In the second leaf, the bearded prophet represents Jeremiah ("Lec[tio] Ieremie p[ro]phe[tae]," Reading of the prophet Jeremiah), from whose Old Testament book the lesson is taken.

The leaf with the picture of the Samaritan woman, while it looks complete, has actually had two of its minor initials cut out, those for the Postcommunion and the Prayer over the People. The initial for the former was replaced by one with a head of a male saint and the latter with a geometric initial. These insertions probably replace less interesting letter forms and were added to make the leaf more attractive.

TEXT: "Fac mecum Domine . . . " (Grant me, O Lord . . .) is the Introit for the Friday ("Feria sexta") of the third week in Lent. "Nos aut[em] gloria[r]i oportet . . . "

(But it behooves us to glory . . .) is the Introit for Tuesday ("F[e]r[ia] t[er]tia," on the recto) in Holy Week.

PROVENANCE: Bought privately in 1975.

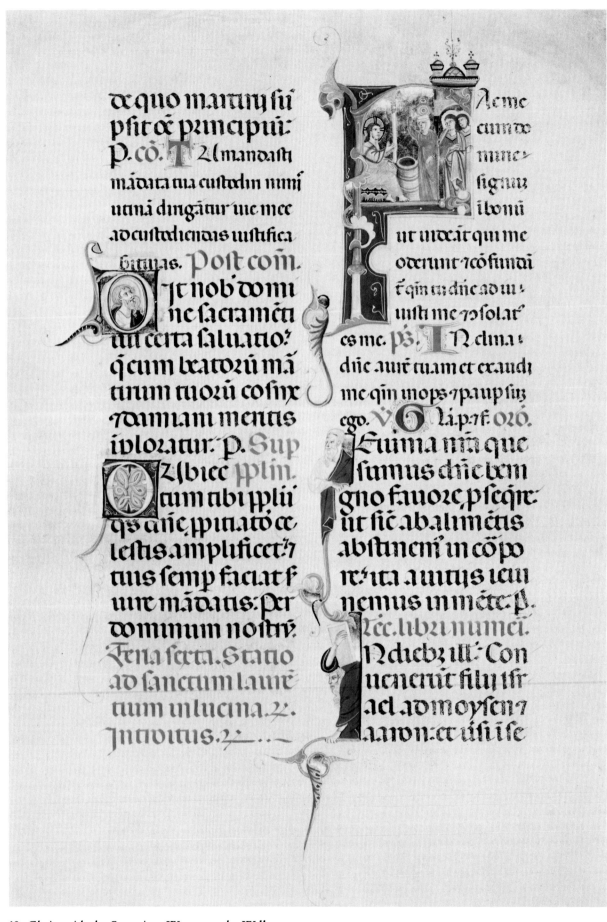

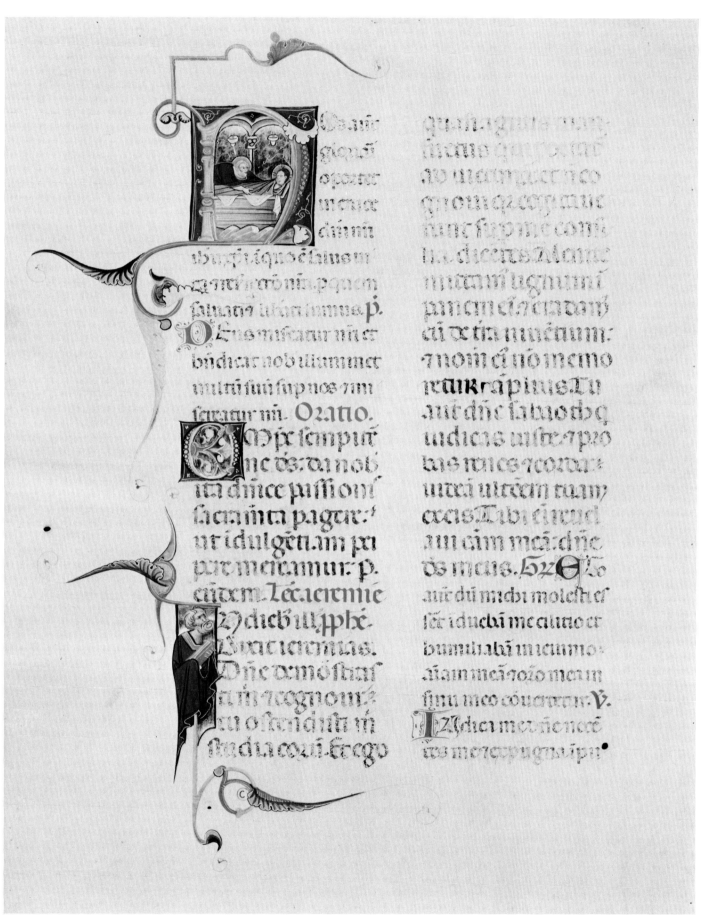

59 Entombment.

60 Ascension

Leaf from a Gradual with a historiated initial V. Italy, Tuscany, ca. 1300. Vellum, 585 x 405 mm, 1 column with 5 staves of 4 red lines; the initial is on a verso.

THIS historiated initial, for the feast of the Ascension, illustrates the Epistle reading for this feast, which is taken from the Acts of the Apostles (1:1–11) and is also excerpted in the Introit. In the biblical passage, Christ is described as being lifted up before the apostles into a cloud, and while they gaze up to heaven, two men robed in white appear among them and ask, "Men of Galilee, why do you stand looking up to heaven?" The Breslauer initial presents at least two variations from the textual source. First, the two men in white are not present and, second, the Virgin has been added to the group of apostles. The inclusion of the Virgin, in the "orans," or praying pose, is an iconographic type found in Early Christian and Byzantine Ascensions, and, in fact, the composition as a whole, with Christ in a mandorla supported by half-length angels and, below, symmetrical groups of apostles, has ancient roots. This type of Ascension can be found, for example, in the sixth-century Rabbula Gospels (Florence, Biblioteca Laurenziana, MS Plut. I. 56) and in the Monza pilgrim flask of the same date (Gertrud Schiller, *Ikonographie der christlichen Kunst,* Gütersloh, 1971, III, 489–90, figs. 459 and 460). That this type of Ascension was popular in Italy in the late thirteenth century is seen not just in the Breslauer initial, but also, among others, in two choir books, both made for the Church of San Francesco in Bologna (Bologna, Museo Civico Medievale, MSS 527 and 530; see Alessandro Conti, *La miniatura bolognese: scuole e botteghe, 1270–1340,* Bologna, 1981, fig. 87; and *Francesco d'Assisi: documenti e archivi, codici e biblioteche, miniature,* Francesco Porzio, ed., Milan, 1982, 357, illus.). Tuscan illuminators and panel painters were reintroducing Byzantine types into Italian painting at this time, and this Ascension can be seen as part of this trend.

The slender figures, with their elegant poses and fine drapery, are reminiscent of the work of Duccio. This similarity has led at least one scholar to attribute this initial to a Duccio follower. The sandals of the apostles, interestingly, are the same as those worn by figures in several panels of the *Maestà,* painted by Duccio between 1308 and 1311. These observations would suggest localizing the Breslauer initial to Siena. However, the border framing the initial, with its alternating gold and blue lozenges on a pomegranate ground, is similar to framing devices found in Florentine illumination. For one of many possible examples, compare the initial with the Virgin from an early-fourteenth-century Gradual made for the Badia di San Salvatore a Settimo near Florence and illuminated by the Master of St. Cecilia (Richard Offner and Miklós Boskovits, *A Critical and Historical Corpus of Florentine Painting: The Fourteenth Century. The Painters of the Miniaturist Tendency,* Florence, 1984, section 3, vol. IX, pl. VIIIa; the Gradual is now in Rome, Santa Croce in Gerusalemme, cor. D [I], fol. 60). The presence of both Sienese and Florentine elements in the Breslauer Ascension makes it impossible to assign it to either center with certainty.

TEXT: "Viri Galilei quid admiramini aspicientes in [celum . . .]" (Men of Galilee, why do you stand looking up to heaven . . .) is the Introit for the feast of the Ascension ("In die asce[n]sio[n]is. ad missam. Int[r]oit[us].").

PROVENANCE: Bought privately in 1979.

anue nic pulſan ti apeꝛie

In vñ. a
ſcenſionꝭ
offin miſ
ſe·7oꝛoꝭ
dñr ꝺ ꝺoꝰ·
pꝛeteríta.

uꝺ alle lu ya

Indie aſcẽ
ſioñſ·aꝺmí
ſam·Intit·

ꝼкi

galile i quiꝺ

uſtatisiſta mũ erimoꝛ

aꝺmira mini aſpicientes in

60 Ascension.

61 Temptation of Christ

Leaf from an Antiphonary with a historiated initial E. Italy, Tuscany, first quarter of the 14th century. Vellum, 510 x 385 mm, 1 column with 6 staves of 4 red lines; the initial is on a verso.

LENT'S forty days of fasting and penance mirror the same number of days Christ spent in the wilderness before he commenced his public ministry. As recounted by Matthew (4:1–11) and Luke (4:1–13), the devil, hoping to catch the Messiah in a moment of weakness, tempted him three times. Hungry, Christ was asked why he did not turn stones into bread, a temptation that elicited the response, "Not by bread alone does man live." Next, the devil took Christ to the pinnacle of the temple and asked why he did not throw himself down and let angels rescue him. Finally, the devil brought Christ to the top of a high mountain and offered him the kingdoms of the world if he would only worship him. Christ's successful resistance to all three temptations is thus the Christian model for the Lenten period of purification. The first Sunday of Lent employs Matthew's version of the Temptation as the Gospel reading for the Mass, and the story is a recurring theme throughout the prayers of the Divine Office for the day (see Abbot Guéranger, *The Liturgical Year. V: Lent,* Westminster, Md., 1949, 121–41). It is thus an appropriate theme for the historiated initial for the first response chanted from the Antiphonary on that day.

The three episodes from the story can be easily recognized in this initial. The devil, as is sometimes the case in depictions of the Temptation, appears not in grotesque form but in the guise of a pilgrim or fellow hermit. Here, bearded and scruffy, he seems quite harmless. One interesting costume detail, however, is worth noting. In both the second and third temptations, the devil wears a brown tunic whose tight sleeves are buttoned along the forearms. The addition of such a detail, nearly invisible to us today, would have been immediately recognizable to the fourteenth-century monks or nuns who sang from this choir book. Buttons, by 1340, made possible the extremely tight clothing that was much condemned throughout the rest of the fourteenth century. In late medieval painting, devils and temptresses were sometimes dressed in contemporaneous clothing, signifying that Satan and the forces of darkness were very much alive and active in the world.

Stylistically this Temptation is related to a single leaf containing a large historiated A with a Last Judgment in the Morgan Library (MS M. 273; reproduced in Roger S. Wieck and Lynn P. Castle, *Paths to Grace: A Selection of Medieval Illuminated Manuscript Leaves and Devotional Objects,* Beaumont, Texas, 1991, no. 1). Both the Breslauer and Morgan initials have the same figural style, light-orange backgrounds, gold stars, and framing devices made of narrow, interlacing strips. In fact, the leaves are so close in style and contain so many of the same stylistic peculiarities—such as the artist's penchant for those forearm buttons mentioned above, and beards that obscure the wearers' mouths—that the same artist must have painted both. Although the dimensions of the Breslauer and Morgan leaves are somewhat different (both have been trimmed), they could be sisters coming from the same Antiphonary.

TEXT: "Ecce nunc tempus acceptabile . . . " (Behold, now is the acceptable time . . .) is the first Matins response for the first Sunday in Lent ("D[omi]nica in xl," on the recto).

SISTER LEAVES: Probably New York, Pierpont Morgan Library, MS M. 273 (Last Judgment).

PROVENANCE: H. P. Kraus, New York; bought in the London trade in 1990.

61 Temptation of Christ.

62 All Saints

Historiated initial G from a Gradual. Italy, Genoa?, second quarter of the 14th century. Vellum, 200 x 125 mm, 1 column with staves of 4 red lines; the initial is on a recto.

THE striking similarity of this initial to one in a choir book (Gradual A, fol. 7) in the Monastery of Santa Maria di Castello makes it clear that they were painted by the same artist (Santa Maria di Castello, *Corali miniati di Santa Maria di Castello*, Genoa, 1976, 73–81, no. 28, pl. V). The initials—both G's of equal widths—are formed by the same type of foliage, have a matching dotted grid background, and are filled with a kindred type of encircled heads. The Genoa initial, which introduces the text for the feast of the third Sunday in Advent, has seven heads, while the Breslauer letter, which originally began the feast of All Saints, has seventeen heads (or parts of heads)—the implication of which is that the number of saints is vast. The manuscript in Genoa is one of two surviving volumes that comprise the Temporale (the major feasts of the year) of what was once a multivolume Gradual. The Breslauer initial, also from a Gradual, probably came from the same set of choir books, but from the Sanctorale (feasts honoring saints). Although these books are housed today in the Monastery of Santa Maria di Castello, liturgical evidence points to the Genoese Monastery of San Domenico (said to have been founded between 1214 and 1220 by St. Dominic himself) as the probable place for and at which they were made. The inclusion of the feast of Corpus Christi, instituted in 1327 in Genoa, and that of the Holy Trinity (included in both Gradual A and its second part, D), instituted in 1334, dates these manuscripts—and thus the Breslauer cutting—to the second quarter of the fourteenth century.

The enigmatic and somewhat old-fashioned style of both the Breslauer and Genoa initials is a combination of Italian and north European elements. The heads, especially, have a linear quality that recalls the graphic style of figures in northern French and Flemish manuscripts of the thirteenth century, and the style points to a scriptorium that must have owned French, Flemish, or English manuscripts. Another choir book, also probably from San Domenico and today in Santa Maria di Castello (Antiphonary E), contains numerous miniatures clearly inspired by Northern, non-Italian models (*Corali miniati,* pls. III and IV, figs. 26–29).

TEXT: G begins the Introit for the feast of All Saints (November 1), "G[audemus omnes in Domino . . .]" (Let us all rejoice in the Lord . . .); on the verso of the initial are fragments of the continuation of the Introit, "gaudent [angeli et c]ollaudant . . . P]s. Exultate . . . . "

PROVENANCE: Carlo Prayer (1826–1900), Milan (his mark appears on the lower right of the recto, Lugt 2044); Maria di Bernasconi, 1971 (signed on the verso); Juan and Felix Bernasconi; bought at their sale in London, Christie's, 24 June 1987, lot 239, illus.

62 All Saints (color plate p. 42).

63　Presentation in the Temple

Historiated initial A, from an Antiphonary, illuminated by the workshop of Marino da Perugia. Italy, Perugia, 1320s. Vellum, 204 x 167 mm, 1 column with staves of 4 red lines.

PERUGIAN illumination from the first quarter of the fourteenth century has a consistent and recognizable style. Three artists, working in similar manners, dominated manuscript production at the time: two anonymous painters nicknamed the "First Perugian Illuminator" and the "Second Perugian Illuminator," and Marino di Elemosina (or, di Oderisio) called Marino da Perugia, who painted panels (a signed one survives) as well as books. These artists preferred large historiated initials whose letter forms often ended in boisterous foliage, deep blue surrounds overlaid with fine white filigree, and decorative patterns applied to areas such as cloth, stone, walls, and backgrounds. As J. J. G. Alexander has related to us and Filippo Todini has published, the Breslauer Presentation can be included among those majestic choir books and single leaves attributed to early-fourteenth-century Perugia. It was a fertile period in which artists began to incorporate into their Gothic illumination Giottesque and other influences from monumental art. Todini, in 1982, noted the closeness of this cutting to the work of Marino da Perugia, and, indeed, the similarity of the form of the initial, the figural style, faces, and drapery to Marino's work make this cutting attributable to his shop. One can compare, for example, the Breslauer initial to one of the same subject that Marino painted in a choir book for San Domenico in Perugia (Perugia, Biblioteca Augusta, MS 2789, fol. 192v; reproduced in both Todini publications cited below: fig. 128 [1989], and illus. p. 233 [1982]). In his corpus on Umbrian painting, Todini further noted the influence of Meo da Siena, a painter from the circle of Duccio active in Perugia from 1319 to 1334, on Perugian illuminators and, in particular, on the painter of the Breslauer Presentation.

An unusual element in this picture, as can be seen by comparing this Presentation to others in the Breslauer Collection (such as No. 57), is the large gold reliquary shrine, with gilt figures, set on a slender column behind the altar. Such shrines were an important art form in the thirteenth and fourteenth centuries. Containing a church's major relics, these chasses were often positioned above the main altar, such as the Shrine of the Three Kings that is still to be seen looming over the high altar of Cologne Cathedral.

TEXT: A begins the first Matins response for the feast of the Purification of the Virgin (February 2), "A[dorna thalamum tuum Syon . . .]" (Sion, adorn your dwelling . . .). The fragment on the back of the initial, "ut. a[ntiphona]. Induere ve- . . . glorie tue cuntas s[an]c[t]i . . . ," has eluded identification.

PROVENANCE: Countess Benckendorff; sold by her in London, Sotheby's, 8 July 1970, lot 25, illus.; bought by Mr. and Mrs. Fielding Lewis Marshall, Chicago (London, Sotheby's, *Exhibition of the Marshall Collection, Which Will Be Sold by Auction by Sotheby & Co. in Several Parts During 1974*

[31 December 1973 to 8 January 1974], London, 78–79, no. 109, illus. [this sale, however, never took place]); bought in London, Bonham's, 28 March 1974, lot 63.

BIBLIOGRAPHY: Filippo Todini, "Gli antifonari di San Domenico e la miniatura a Perugia nel primo Trecento," in *Francesco d'Assisi: documenti e archivi, codici e biblioteche, miniature,* Francesco Porzio, ed., Milan, 1982, 219, illus. p. 222 (as Collezione Marshall), and *La Pittura Umbra dal Duecento al primo Cinquecento,* Milan, 1989, I, 380 (as Chicago, collezione Marshall).

63 Presentation in the Temple (color plate p. 43).

64 Virgin and Child with Saints

Miniature, from a Matricola, illuminated by the Master of the Choir Books of San Lorenzo. Italy, Perugia, 1330s. Vellum, 92 x 138 mm, 1 column; the miniature is on a recto.

MATRICOLE were manuscripts containing a guild's statutes and listing its members. In late medieval Italy these matricole were often illuminated (see, for instance, No. 71 for a Bolognese example painted by the artist Niccolò da Bologna). In Perugia, illuminated matricole, of which nearly two dozen survive, provide an important group of documents for the study of fourteenth-century illumination from this city.

The Breslauer miniature of the Virgin and Child with Saints was painted by the Master of the Choir Books of San Lorenzo, named after the historiated initials he provided for the choir books for the Cathedral of San Lorenzo in Perugia (today in that city's Biblioteca Capitolare, MSS 7, 13, and 14). Active in Perugia in the first half of the fourteenth century, the San Lorenzo Master had a figural style not too dissimilar from that of Marino da Perugia, whose workshop painted the Breslauer Presentation in the Temple (No. 63). The San Lorenzo Master combined a certain elegance from contemporaneous French illumination with an interest, common to Perugian artists at this time, in Giottesque monumental forms.

Although named after his illumination in the San Lorenzo choir books, this master is equally famous for the many matricole he illuminated. These include a matricola for the Dyers' Guild (London, British Library, Add. MS 22497), one for the Shoemakers' Guild, another for the Booksellers' Guild (Perugia, Biblioteca Augusta, MSS 3062 and 3110, respectively), and a single leaf from a matricola for the Notaries' Guild (Venice, Fondazione Giorgio Cini, no shelf number). The Breslauer miniature, from a matricola for the Money Changers' Guild, one of Perugia's more powerful corporations, can now be added to the San Lorenzo Master's oeuvre because of the similarity of its figures and composition to the matricola of the Booksellers' Guild mentioned above (for this illuminator, see Enrica Neri Lusanna, "Le Matricole delle Arti a Perugia," in *Francesco d'Assisi: documenti e archivi, codici e biblioteche, miniature,* Francesco Porzio, ed., Milan, 1982, 260–67, nos. 54–56, illus.; and Filippo Todini, *La Pittura Umbra dal Duecento al primo Cinquecento,* Milan, 1989, I, 120, II, figs. 208–11). Enthroned at the center of the miniature are the Virgin and Child flanked by four male saints. The two mitered saints are probably Herculanus and Constantius—two Early Christian bishops of Perugia and patrons of the city who frequently appear on Perugian matricole. Standing next to the Virgin's throne are Lawrence, patron of Perugia's cathedral (tonsured and dressed in his deacon's dalmatic), and Matthew (barefoot and holding a small chest; before becoming an apostle, Matthew was a tax collector).

Matricola miniatures often included pictures of the guild members, and the Breslauer miniature was undoubtedly the top half of a two-part miniature. The framing bands of color that continue down and the interruption of the text on the back of the leaf indicate that this was the case.

TEXT: On the verso: "Petri & Pauli & gl[or]iosor[um] martiru[m] . . . " (of Peter and Paul and most glorious martyrs . . .) is part of the invocation that headed the list of guild members.

PROVENANCE: Bought in London, Sotheby's, 20 June 1989, lot 16, illus.

64 Virgin and Child with Saints.

65 John the Baptist Preaching to a Crowd

Historiated initial E from an Antiphonary. Italy, Umbria or Tuscany, second quarter of the 14th century. Vellum, 140 x 125 mm, 1 column with staves; the initial is on a verso.

ALTHOUGH it is not the case with the modern liturgy, in the medieval and Renaissance Divine Office the first Matins response for the feast of the Octave of Christmas was "Behold the Lamb of God who takes away the sins of the world. This is he of whom I said, 'After me comes a man who ranks before me, the thong of whose sandal I am not worthy to untie'." It was thus the tradition to illustrate the opening initial E ("Ecce Agnus Dei . . . ") in Antiphonaries with a picture of John the Baptist delivering his words to a crowd and pointing to Christ or, as here, to the Lamb of God. In this initial, the prophet wears, beneath a cloak, his customary rough camel-hair tunic, and has a shaggy beard and unkempt hair. The old man at the front of the crowd raises his hands in a gesture of wonder and surprise.

Localizing this cutting has been problematic, with Siena, Florence, and Pisa all proposed as possible places of execution. Stylistically the initial relates to two large historiated initials, a Christ in Majesty (Cleveland Museum of Art, acc. no. 39.677; Fig. 8, see also Edmund P. Pillsbury, *Florence and the Arts, Five Centuries of Patronage: Florentine Art in Cleveland Collections,* Cleveland, 1971, no. 42, illus.) and a Resurrection with the Three Marys at the Tomb (Yale University Art Gallery, acc. no. 1954.7.1; reproduced in Charles Seymour, *Early Italian Paintings in the Yale University Art Gallery,* New Haven, 1970, 98). Both of these big initials have the same foliage and letter forms set against a gold background. The New Haven leaf has trees like the one in the Breslauer initial, and the Cleveland initial has a number of old men whose beards, wig-like hair, and wrinkled brows are much like those of the man with the upraised hands in the Breslauer picture. But even if one accepts the similarities of the Cleveland and New Haven leaves to the Breslauer cutting and postulates that they may all come from the same Antiphonary, the problem of localization remains. Seymour summarizes the following diverse opinions in the catalogue cited above. Mirella Levi D'Ancona thought the work was Pisan and by an artist close to Francesco Traini. Millard Meiss, however, thought the illumination was by a Sienese working in Umbria rather than its being related to Traini. William Milliken originally published the Cleveland leaf as Florentine (*Pages from Medieval and Renaissance Illuminated Manuscripts from the Xth to the XVIth Centuries,* Berkeley, 1963, 21).

Recently, however, we have been able to determine that two single leaves (Fig. 9 is one) in the Free Library of Philadelphia, each with a large historiated initial, are definitely sisters to the Breslauer cutting. The initials of the Philadelphia leaves contain the same palette, filigree, and figures to be found in the Breslauer example. Interestingly, the two Philadelphia leaves are foliated in the same later hand as the Cleveland leaf. This confirms that it, too, is a sister to those in Philadelphia and, thus, to the Breslauer cutting.

TEXT: E begins the first Matins response, "E[cce Agnus Dei . . .]" (Behold the Lamb of God . . .), from the Octave of Christmas. On the recto of the cutting are fragments from the versicle and response from the same feast, "Ta[m]qu[am] spo[n]sus. Dominus procedens de] thala[mo suo]."

SISTER LEAVES: Cleveland, Museum of Art, acc. no. 39.677 (Christ in Majesty; Fig. 8) and Philadelphia, Free Library, Lewis M74:2 (Christ Appearing to David) and Lewis M74:3 (Christ Appearing to Abraham; Fig. 9).

PROVENANCE: C. H. Hamilton; bought at his sale in London, Sotheby's, 8 December 1975, lot 3.

65 John the Baptist Preaching to a Crowd.

Fig. 8. Christ in Majesty. Cleveland, Cleveland Museum of Art, acc. no. 39.677 (J. H. Wade Fund).

Fig. 9. Christ Appearing to Abraham. Philadelphia, Free Library of Philadelphia, Rare Book Department, Lewis M 74:3 (detail).

66 Pentecost

Leaf from a Laudario with a miniature illuminated by the Master of the Dominican Effigies.
Italy, Florence, ca. 1340. Vellum, 430 x 317 mm; the miniature is on a verso.

THE Master of the Dominican Effigies and the slightly earlier Pacino di Bonaguida were two of the most important and prolific Florentine artists who immediately followed Giotto. Both were panel painters as well as illuminators, and the former, who was influenced by and on occasion collaborated with the latter, was primarily active in the second quarter of the fourteenth century. Richard Offner named the Master of the Dominican Effigies for a panel in Santa Maria Novella that depicts Christ and the Virgin enthroned with seventeen Dominican saints, painted after 1336 (Richard Offner, *Corpus of Florentine Painting: The Fourteenth Century*, New York, 1930, section 3, vol. II, part I, 49, 58, pl. XXV). The artist's earliest dated work is a manuscript of the *Divine Comedy* of 1337 (Milan, Biblioteca Trivulziana, MS 10, 80), and his latest is a polyptych of 1345, now in the Courtauld Institute Galleries in London (*Corpus*, section 3, vol. IX, 55).

Although Offner connected only two other leaves (see Sister Leaves) with the Laudario (a vernacular choir book used by confraternities) from which this leaf comes, Miklós Boskovits has more recently suggested that fourteen others, including one by Pacino di Bonaguida in the Morgan Library (MS M. 742) belonged to the same sumptuous book (*Corpus*, section 3, vol. IX, 52–53). Indeed, if so, the liturgical sequence of the two leaves would be correct, for the Breslauer leaf (fol. 83) depicts Pentecost, while the Morgan leaf (fol. 87) depicts the Trinity, which is celebrated on the first Sunday after Pentecost. The Antwerp leaf (fol. 85), however, should really have followed the Morgan leaf, for it depicts the Last Supper and Celebration of a Mass, which would be appropriate for the feast of Corpus Christi, celebrated on the Thursday after Trinity Sunday. Although the dimensions of the staves of the Breslauer and Morgan leaves agree, the vertical distances between the roundels at the top and bottom of the leaves do not. None of the subjects of the leaves are repeated, and at least two different artists worked on them, which possibly accounts for some differences in layout. A closer physical examination of all the leaves is needed, however, before firm conclusions can be reached. Offner suggested that the Laudario was made for the Company of Santa Maria del Carmine because two Carmelite saints appear on the sister leaf in Washington. Although Ziino pointed out that Santa Maria del Carmine had a special devotion to St. Zenobius (part of his lauda occurs on the Breslauer leaf), he suggested that the Breslauer leaf could also have come from a Laudario commissioned by the Florentine Company of St. Zenobius, known as the Laudesi (*Miscellanea*, 1989, 1471).

The Breslauer leaf depicts the Descent of the Holy Spirit on the Virgin and Apostles (Pentecost), a descent which was promised by Christ, who occupies the roundel at the top of the architectural structure. Although there is no scriptural foundation for the presence of the Virgin, she does occur in the Rabbula Gospels of 586 A.D. (Florence, Biblioteca Laurenziana, MS Plut. I. 56). But her frequent and prominent appearance in later medieval Pentecosts has been connected with, for example, Odilo of Cluny's sermon on the Assumption, where he argued that it would have been impossible to exclude the foremost recipient of the Holy Spirit, linking thereby the earlier descent that brought about the Incarnation (see C. Gardner von Teuffel, "Ikonographie und Archäologie: das Pfingsttriptychon in der Florentiner Akademie an seinem ursprünglichen Aufstellungsort," *Zeitschrift für Kunstgeschichte*, XLI, 1978, 35). The roundels in the borders depict St. Francis and St. Dominic at the top, and a female martyr, male donor, and sainted queen at the bottom.

TEXT: "Spirito santo glorio[so] . . . " (Glorious Holy Spirit . . .) is the beginning of the lauda for Pentecost. On the recto (with folio number LXXXIII) is the end of a lauda for the feast of St. Zenobius (May 25), "a la nostra tenebria e canobio veramente . . . . "

SISTER LEAVES: Antwerp, Museum Mayer van den Bergh, cod. 303 (Last Supper and Celebration of the Mass); Washington, National Gallery of Art, Rosenwald Collection, acc. no. 1959.16.2 (Christ and the Virgin Enthroned with All Saints).

PROVENANCE: New York, H. P. Kraus, Catalogue 95 *(Twenty-Five Manuscripts)*, [1961], 51, no. 14, illus.; H. P. Kraus Catalogue 110 *(Dante and the Renaissance in Florence)*, 1965, 23, no. 9, illus.; H. P. Kraus, private collection, Ridgefield, Conn.; bought from his estate in 1990.

BIBLIOGRAPHY: Wadsworth Atheneum, *An Exhibition of Italian Panels & Manuscripts From the Thirteenth & Fourteenth Centuries in Honor of Richard Offner*, Hartford, 1965, 45, no. 82, illus.; J. De Coo, "L'ancienne Collection Micheli au

66 Pentecost (color plate p. 44).

Musée Mayer van den Bergh," *Gazette des Beaux-Arts,* LXVI, 1965, 370 n. 26; Gary Vikan, ed., *Medieval & Renaissance Miniatures from the National Gallery of Art,* Washington, 1975, 29, fig. 8d; Agostino Ziino, "Laudi e miniature fiorentine del primo Trecento," *Studi musicali,* VII, 1978, 47 and passim, no. 7, fig. 7; Richard Offner and Miklós Boskovits, *A Critical and Historical Corpus of Florentine Painting: The Fourteenth Century. The Painters of the Miniaturist Tendency,* Florence, 1984, section 3, vol. IX, 52 n. 179, 286, pl. CXXb; Agostino Ziino, "La laude musicale del Due-Trecento: nuove fonti scritte e tradizione orale," *Miscellanea di studi in onore di Aurelio Roncaglia a cinquant'anni dalla sua laurea,* Modena, 1989, 1465–1502 passim, fig. 2.

67 Resurrection
68 Man Receiving Communion
69 Beheading of John the Baptist

Historiated initials A, I, and Q, from an Antiphonary, possibly illuminated by Martino di Bartolomeo. Italy, Tuscany, probably Lucca, late 14th century. Vellum, 280 x 212, 260 x 115, and 211 x 180 mm, 1 column with staves of 4 red lines; the first two initials are on rectos, the third undetermined.

LIKE the montage with the miniature of the Birth of John the Baptist (No. 90), these three cuttings are an important testimony to the early appreciation and collecting of single illuminated leaves, as Christopher de Hamel noted in the Sotheby catalogue of the Lord Clark sale. The initials were bought in Lucca in 1838 by the Scottish antiquary James Dennistoun of Dennistoun (1803–55). Dennistoun is best known for his magnum opus, a hefty three-volume study, *Memoirs of the Dukes of Urbino, Illustrating the Arms, Arts and Literature of Italy, from 1440 to 1630,* which appeared in 1851. He went to Italy in 1836 and for twelve years collected material for a projected study on the history of medieval Italian art. Although this study was never completed, Dennistoun passed his material on to his friend Alexander William Crawford Lindsay, earl of Crawford, who incorporated it in his *Sketches of the History of Christian Art,* published in 1847. During these years abroad Dennistoun bought medieval and Renaissance art and returned to his home in Edinburgh with a collection that was admired "especially for the ecclesiastical productions of the 13th to the 16th century" (see G. F. Waagen, *Treasures of Art in Great Britain . . . ,* London, 1854, III, 281).

An early connoisseur of Italian primitives, Dennistoun owned a Crucifixion by Fra Angelico and a Book of Hours with a miniature by Perugino (now in the British Library, Yates Thompson MS 29). He also collected cuttings, assembling 105 of them in an album bound in red morocco (described by A. N. L. Munby, *Connoisseurs and Medieval Miniatures, 1750–1850,* Oxford, 1972, 158). In many cases he recorded when and where he bought them. The first he acquired in Munich in 1836, others from the Duomo in Florence in the next year; he bought more in Siena, Gubbio, and Lucca in 1838, and still others in Padua in 1839. He also bought in Verona, Milan, and Geneva, and received a French miniature as a gift from Luigi Celotti, the abbot turned dealer and early purveyor of illuminations (and the source of Breslauer No. 90). While most of Dennistoun's collection was sold at auction after his death in 1855, the album passed to his granddaughter, Mrs. Henley-Henson, from whom Lord Clark bought it. The cuttings from the album were sold separately or in small groups at the sale of Clark's collections in 1984.

The three Breslauer historiated initials probably all came from the same Antiphonary. The Resurrection and Beheading of John the Baptist are definitely by the same hand—both share figures with large heads and strong features. The Man Receiving Communion, while possibly by a different hand, seems stylistically related. (The cutting contains some fascinating iconographic elements: the words of the consecration in the Missal on the altar, "HOC EST CORPUS MEU[M]," and the beginning of the Hail Mary embossed on the altar cloth, "AVE MARIA GRA[TIA].") All three miniatures have the same early provenance, having been bought the same year in Lucca. Also sharing the Lucca provenance are other cuttings from the Dennistoun album that might have come from the same Antiphonary. These include a Lamb of God, a Levitation of Mary Magdalene, and a Christ Blessing (lots 92, no. 3; 93, no. 3; and 94, no. 1 of the Lord Clark sale). All six of these cuttings, as well as many others in radically different styles, came, according to Dennistoun, from the Charterhouse of Lucca, presumably the Carthusian Abbey of Santo Spirito. This early provenance, too, helps bolster Laurence Kanter's verbal attribution of these cuttings to Lucca and as possibly the work of Martino di Bartolomeo, a Sienese artist active there in the 1390s. The Breslauer initials can be compared with those in a five-volume Gradual painted by Martino for, and still in, Lucca cathedral (Opera del Duomo, MSS 1, 7–10; see Siena, Palazzo Pubblico, *Il gotico a Siena,* Florence, 1982, 308–10, no. 111, illus.; and Clara Baracchini and Antonio Caleca, *Il Duomo di Lucca,* Lucca, 1973, figs. 786–815). The similarity of the initial forms, foliage, and the figural style of the Gradual to those of the Breslauer cuttings makes this attribution tempting, but only a firsthand study of the Gradual can confirm it.

Another possible connection of these initials to Lucca comes from the unfinished coat-of-arms below the

Breslauer Resurrection. This could be a sketch for the arms of Niccolò di Lazzaro Guinigi, archbishop of Lucca from 1394 till his expulsion in 1402 (he was recalled in 1432 and died in 1435). Guinigi's arms, a white cross on a red background, do appear in a miniature that Dennistoun also bought in Lucca as coming from the Abbey of Santo Spirito; it is one of twenty Dennistoun miniatures by Niccolò da Bologna that Lord Clark sold in 1962 (see New York, H. P. Kraus, Catalogue 172 [Illuminations . . .], 1985, 18–23, no. 3, illus.). Did Guinigi's expulsion from Lucca in 1402 interrupt work on the Antiphonary from which these three initials come—an Antiphonary, perhaps, that was commissioned by him? It is a tempting theory, but, with the arms below the Resurrection unfinished, it must remain a postulation.

TEXT: Resurrection: "An[ge]lu[s] [Do]m[ini descendit de celo . . .]" (An angel of the Lord descended from heaven . . .) is the first Matins response for Easter; the response continues on the verso, "[la]pide[m] et sup[er eum s]edit et dixit [mulie]ribus noli[te tim]ere scio e[nim . . . .]" Communion: I begins the first Matins response for the feast of Corpus Christi, "I[mmolabit haedum multitudo filiorum Israel . . .]" (With the whole assembly of Israel present . . .); the response continues on the verso, "[pane]s. v. [Pascha nost]ru[m immolatus est] xpistus . . . . " John the Baptist: undetermined.

PROVENANCE: Bought by James Dennistoun (1803–55), Edinburgh, in Lucca in 1838 (his nos. 67, 82, and 75); Mrs. Hensley-Henson, Dennistoun's granddaughter and wife of the Bishop of Durham, Auckland Castle; bought from her by Kenneth Clark in 1930; bought at his sale in London, Sotheby's, 3 July 1984, lot 92, illus.

BIBLIOGRAPHY: A. N. L. Munby, Connoisseurs and Medieval Miniatures, 1750–1850, Oxford, 1972, 158 (mentions Dennistoun's album of miniatures); John Pope-Hennessy, Learning to Look, New York, 1991, 29 (as Uncle Denny's scraps).

67 Resurrection (color plate p. 45).

68 Man Receiving Communion.

69 Beheading of John the Baptist.

70 Three Marys at the Tomb

Leaf from an Antiphonary with a historiated initial A illuminated by Niccolò da Bologna. Italy, Bologna, ca. 1365. Vellum, 740 x 525 mm, 1 column with 5 staves of 4 red lines; the initial is on a recto.

NICCOLÒ di Giacomo di Nascimbene, called Niccolò da Bologna, was Bologna's leading illuminator during the second half of the fourteenth century. Active from about 1330 to 1403, he directed a workshop that produced a large body of work, both religious and secular. (See Patrick M. De Winter, "Bolognese Miniatures at the Cleveland Museum," *Bulletin of the Cleveland Museum of Art,* LXX, 1983, 332–38, for the latest discussion, with bibliography.) Evidence of Niccolò's financial success are two houses he owned in Bologna and nine pieces of land. He had a penchant—rare in the fourteenth century—for signing his creations. Such is the case, for example, with two of his manuscripts in the Morgan Library, an Ordinal (MS M. 800) whose large Crucifixion is signed and a leaf from a register of creditors of a Bolognese lending society (MS M. 1056). Signed also was the Antiphonary from which the Breslauer leaf came—the sister leaf with the Ascension (Los Angeles County Museum of Art) bears the inscription, "EGO NICHOLAU[S] D[A] BOLONIA FECIT" (I, Niccolò of Bologna, made this).

Niccolò's earthy painting style is easily distinguished. His figures, while stocky, have great energy and his large broad faces, much force and emotion. Thick, heavy drapery gives the figures volume and weight. Later in his career, for example in the St. Dominic (No. 71), the second work by this artist in the Breslauer Collection, his figures become a little more rigid.

As is revealed by two other Antiphonary leaves for Easter (Nos. 46 and 84), the theme of the three Marys at the tomb was a popular and appropriate subject for decorating the large A that began the Matins response for that important feast. The theme is a direct illustration of events that took place early on Easter morning, events described in the text of the response itself: "An angel of the Lord descended from heaven, and came and rolled back the stone and sat upon it. And he said to the women, 'Do not be afraid, for I know that you seek the Crucified. He has already risen. Come, see the place where He lay, alleluia'." At the bottom of the tomb Niccolò has added the soldiers who slept through Christ's resurrection. The angel has been provided with a glowing red face, a reference to the biblical description that "his countenance was as lightning." The half-length portrait of St. Dominic that Niccolò painted in the foliage of the bottom border indicates that the Antiphonary from which this leaf came was probably made for a Dominican monastery.

This was the first leaf Bernard Breslauer bought for himself, and is the cornerstone of his collection.

TEXT: "Angelus Domini descendit de celo . . . " (An angel of the Lord descended from heaven . . .) is the first Matins response for Easter.

SISTER LEAVES: London, Sotheby's, 11 July 1966, lot 190, illus. (David Leading a Group in Prayer; ex-Lansburgh); Los Angeles County Museum of Art, acc. no. M.75.3 (Ascension; ex-Lansburgh).

PROVENANCE: Leo S. Olschki, Florence, 1912; Léonce Rosenberg, Paris, 1913; Mark Lansburgh, Colorado Springs; sold by him in London, Sotheby's, 11 July 1966, lot 191.

BIBLIOGRAPHY: Paolo D'Ancona, "Di alcune opere inedite di Nicolò di Giacomo da Bologna," *La Bibliofilia,* XIV, 1912, 281–84, fig. 3; Seymour de Ricci, *Catalogue d'une collection de miniatures gothiques et persanes appartenant à Léonce Rosenberg,* Paris, 1913, 21, no. 52, pl. VIII.

70 Three Marys at the Tomb (color plate p. 46).

71 St. Dominic

Leaf, from a register of the Shoemakers' Guild, illuminated by Niccolò da Bologna. Italy, Bologna, ca. 1386. Vellum, 350 x 245 (258 x 154) mm, 1 column of 33 lines; the decoration is on a recto.

LIKE the preceding leaf, this illumination was painted by Niccolò da Bologna, who was appointed that city's official illuminator by the late 1380s. In this capacity he illuminated a large number of matricole (statutes with registers) of the city's various guilds, in addition to many liturgical and legal texts. The registers included those of the guilds of haberdashers, goldsmiths, blacksmiths, apothecaries, and money lenders. The present leaf and its sister were originally part of a register of the Shoemakers' Guild; both leaves have shields displaying a leather cutter's knife, a shoe, and a sandal. This leaf lists the guild members for the quarter of San Procolo, including the parishes of Sts. Proculus, Dominic, and Catherine. Differences in handwriting indicate those men who were guild members at the time the register was commissioned and those who joined later. Additions, to one side of the name, of a small cross or the word *mor* (short for *mortem*) indicate the death of a member, who was then remembered in the guild's prayers.

This leaf shows a standing St. Dominic dressed in a black cloak and hood over a white robe, the habit of the Dominican order. He holds a red-covered book and a stem of lilies, one of his attributes. Although neither this leaf nor its sister is signed by Niccolò, the style of the large figures and their strong features indicate his authorship. Indeed, similar figures of both Dominic and Francis appear on a creditors' register signed by Niccolò, in the Morgan Library (MS M. 1056), as well as on the register of the Lending Society dated 1394 (Bologna, Archivio di Stato, MS 3, fol. 1). The style of the figures and foliate borders of these last two registers is somewhat broader than the Breslauer leaf; this helps confirm the slightly earlier date (as Patrick De Winter has indicated) for the St. Dominic. The frontal, somewhat rigid figures of the Breslauer leaf and its sister, however, are characteristic of the painter's later years.

TEXT: The leaf contains the guild members' names from Bologna's quarter of San Procolo ("De q[ua]rterio p[ro] S[an]c[t]i P[ro]culi"), including the parishes of Sts. Proculus and, on the back, Dominic and Catherine.

SISTER LEAVES: London, Sotheby's, 19 June 1990 (Korner collection), lot 17, illus.

PROVENANCE: Bought from Heinrich Eisemann by Eric Korner, London (his no. 21); bought at his sale in London, Sotheby's, 19 June 1990, lot 16, illus.

BIBLIOGRAPHY: Patrick M. De Winter, "Bolognese Miniatures at the Cleveland Museum," *Bulletin of the Cleveland Museum of Art,* LXX, 1983, 350 n. 29 (as London, private coll.).

De qrteno. p. fci. pculi.

De cap. fci Proculi.

D Andreas proculi.
D Jacobs proculi.
D Gloias Jacobi bodi.
D Petrus fil dni albti.
D Paulus dnti.
D Matte miegoli.
D franeischus albti petriani.
D Petrus guidonis.
D Guido petri guidonis.
D Jacobs fili fil odifiti mani
D Paulus. fris Jacobi de bopoll.
D Unichus Jacobi proculi.
D. matteus albti petriani
D Guasparinus mater alberti petriani
D Simon francisci Gregorii
D Unichus petri Proluii
D. Johanes odam Blaxy dugolly de latuke
D. Btholomeus johanis olim Blaxy delatuiez

D. Peregrinus Jachobi olim Blaxy delatuiez
D. Franeischus y ambo fratres z fily simonis odam Franeisa
D. Johanes olim gregory:
D. Lucas petri olim lupi de chalanchis.
D. Petrus nanie olim rogi
D. Johanes filius luce olim petri olim lupi de calanchis

71 St. Dominic (color plate p. 46).

72 Adoration of the Magi

Leaf from a Gradual with a historiated initial E illuminated by Don Simone Camaldolese and his workshop. Italy, Florence, late 1380s. Vellum, 592 x 415 mm, 1 column with 5 (normally 6) staves of 4 red lines; the initial is on a verso.

DON Simone Camaldolese, Don Silvestro dei Gherarducci, and Lorenzo Monaco were all somehow associated with Santa Maria degli Angeli, the most important monastic center of manuscript and panel painters in Florence from 1375 to 1425. Although the monastery dates only from about 1300, the Camaldolese order itself was founded, according to tradition, by St. Romuald in the eleventh century. Santa Maria degli Angeli first rose to artistic prominence about 1370 under Don Silvestro. Don Simone, who was of Sienese origin, was not documented in Florence until 1380, when he received payment for a miniature executed for the church of San Pancrazio. From the surviving documents, it seems that Simone worked mostly on commissions for other institutions, for between 1386 and 1389 he decorated a Missal and several Antiphonaries for San Miniato al Monte and in 1388 and 1389 worked on several choir books for Santa Maria del Carmine (see Mirella Levi D'Ancona, *Miniatura e miniatori a Firenze dal XIV al XVI secolo: documenti per la storia della miniatura,* Florence, 1962, 239–41). The most recent list of works attributed to Simone can be found in Miklós Boskovits, *Pittura fiorentina alla vigilia del Rinascimento, 1370–1400,* Florence, 1975, 426–30.

According to Mirella D'Ancona this Adoration probably belongs to the group of manuscripts that Simone illuminated for San Miniato al Monte (letter of 3 January 1991). She is currently identifying other members of the same group. The leaf would have been folio 41 of a Gradual, since it bears that number on its verso. A slightly more elaborate layout, also with prophets holding scrolls, can be found in a Nativity of about 1390–95 in Santa Croce sull'Arno (Collegiata di San Lorenzo, cor. I, fol. 7v), for which see Boskovits ("Su Don Silvestro, Don Simone e la 'Scuola degli Angeli'," *Paragone,* XXIII, no. 265, 1972, fig. 26). The style of the figures in the Breslauer leaf, however, appears quite different from the signed and dated Simone that was more recently acquired (No. 73); a possible explanation is that Simone designed the leaf with the Adoration and an assistant painted it.

In the Breslauer Adoration, the Virgin sits on an inlaid throne, and the eldest Magus extends his hand to the blessing Christ Child. The two other Magi calmly and reverentially await their turns. The gold haloes, as in contemporary panel painting, are tooled. In the background a servant whips an unruly camel, an iconographic tradition that may refer to the belief that the Magi were previously bitter enemies (see Charles Sterling, "Fighting Animals in the Adoration of the Magi," *Bulletin of the Cleveland Museum of Art,* LXI, 1974, 357). The lay confraternity known as the Compagnia de' Magi, established in Florence by 1390, staged elaborate festivities on the feast of Epiphany (January 6), which included elaborate costumes, stage sets, and processions (see Rab Hatfield, "The Compagnia de' Magi," *Journal of the Warburg and Courtauld Institutes,* XXXIII, 1970, 107–61).

TEXT: "Ecce a[d]venit dominator Dominus . . . " (Behold the Lord the ruler is come . . .) is the Introit for the feast of Epiphany ("In die epyphanie. Introitus."). The recto contains part of the text for the feast of the Circumcision.

PROVENANCE: Bought in Olten, Switzerland, from Museion, in 1984.

72 Adoration of the Magi (color plate p. 47).

73 Resurrection and Three Marys at the Tomb

Historiated initial R, from a Gradual, illuminated by Don Simone Camaldolese. Italy, Florence, dated 1388. Vellum, 280 x 240 mm, 1 column; the initial is on a verso, the recto blank.

THIS leaf, one of the last added to the collection, complements in a remarkable way the previous entry, for it is both signed and dated on the lower border of the initial: "HOC OPVS FECIT D[ON] S[IMONE] O[RDINIS] K[AMALDULENSIS] ANNO D[OMINI] MCCCLXXXVIII" (This work was made by Don Simone of the Camaldolese Order in the year of Our Lord 1388). In his earliest and only other signed and dated (1381) work, an Antiphonary Don Simone made for San Pancrazio (Florence, Biblioteca Laurenziana, cor. 39), he still referred to his Sienese origin ("Simon de Senis monachus ordinis camaldulensis"; for the complete citation see Paolo D'Ancona, *La miniatura fiorentina (secoli XI–XVI), II, Catalogo descrittivo*, Florence, 1914, 59). The upper and side borders of the Breslauer leaf are virtually identical to those of his opening initial A (of "Aspiciens") of an Antiphonary in the church of Santa Croce in Florence (cod. A, fol. 4v), which Boskovits dates about 1385 to 1390 (p. 427 in the work cited below; reproduced in D'Ancona, pl. XX and Bolaffi, fig. 429). A similar border was also used for his initial A (of "Aspiciens") in the aforementioned San Pancrazio Antiphonary, but the figural style is less developed and the foliage making up the letter is less vigorous and elaborate (reproduced by Mario Salmi, *La miniatura fiorentina gotica*, Rome, 1954, pl. XL). This more elaborate style is also found in Simone's last signed work, a historiated initial H with a Nativity in another Antiphonary in Santa Croce (cod. B, fol. 5v). The inscription reads "OP[US].FEC[IT].DON.SIMO[NE].ORDI[NI]S.CAMALD[ULE]N[SIS]," and Boskovits dates this Nativity from about 1405 to 1410 (p. 427; reproduced in Salmi, pl. XLI). The present leaf, which has unfortunately been damaged and somewhat repainted (especially the face of the angel), comes from the middle period of his documented activity.

The compositional formula used in the Breslauer initial, with the two parts of the letter devoted to two separate scenes, the Resurrection and the Three Marys at the Tomb, was popular in both northern and southern Europe: see, for example, the late-thirteenth-century initial from Regensburg in the Breslauer Collection (No. 35) and an R similar to the Breslauer initial by the Master of the Dominican Effigies reproduced in Richard Offner (*Corpus of Florentine Painting: The Fourteenth Century*, New York, 1957, section 3, vol. VII, pl. XXb). The Marys at the Tomb illustrates the Gospel reading for Easter (Mark 16:1–7): "Mary Magdalene, and Mary the Mother of James and Salome . . . came to the sepulcher. They saw a young man sitting on the right side, clothed with a white robe."

TEXT: R begins the Introit for the feast of Easter, "R[esurrexi et adhuc tecum sum . . .]" (I arose and am still with you . . .). Since the recto is blank, the leaf probably was the first folio in the Gradual, a fact that might also account for its somewhat damaged condition.

PROVENANCE: Bought in 1992.

BIBLIOGRAPHY: Kunsthistorisches Museum, *Europäische Kunst um 1400*, Vienna, 1962, 198, no. 167 (and in the French edition, *L'art européen vers 1400*, 178, no. 167); Bernhard Degenhart and Annegrit Schmitt, *Corpus der italienischen Zeichnungen, 1300–1450: Teil I, Süd- und Mittelitalien, Band I*, Berlin, 1968, 263, fig. 373; Miklós Boskovits, *Pittura fiorentina alla vigilia del Rinascimento, 1370–1400*, Florence, 1975, 430, fig. 379; Giulio Bolaffi, ed., *Dizionario enciclopedico Bolaffi dei pittori e degli incisori italiani*, Turin, 1975, X, 315; Domenico Gus Firmani, "Don Simone Camaldolese and Manuscript Production in Late Trecento Florence: A Codicological Examination," Ph.D. diss., University of Maryland, College Park, 1984, 22, 172, fig. 157.

73 Resurrection and Three Marys at the Tomb.

74 Ascension

Historiated initial V, from a Gradual, designed by Lorenzo Monaco but completed by Bartolomeo di Fruosino and, possibly, Fra Angelico. Italy, Florence, ca. 1423–24. Vellum, 402 x 324 mm, 1 column; the initial is glued to wood.

LORENZO MONACO (Piero di Giovanni) was not only the most important painter and illuminator associated with the Camaldolese monastery of Santa Maria degli Angeli in Florence, he was also the most important Florentine artist of the first quarter of the fifteenth century. Entering the monastery late in 1390, he assumed the name Lorenzo and took simple vows. He entered minor orders on 10 December 1391, and was ordained sub-deacon in September 1392 and deacon in 1396. Soon thereafter Lorenzo took up residence outside the monastery and set up a large workshop. Although there are some documents recording payments for panels and miniatures (Eisenberg, 209–16), only one work is signed, the *Coronation of the Virgin* executed in 1414 for the high altar of Santa Maria degli Angeli now in the Uffizi. He may have died about 1423 or 1424, because his last documented payment, for an altarpiece at Sant'Egidio, was in August 1422.

Lorenzo's earliest illuminations are found in an Antiphonary dated 1394 made for Santa Maria degli Angeli (Florence, Biblioteca Laurenziana, cor. 5). This Ascension comes from a Gradual that was made for the same monastery (Laurenziana, cor. 3) and was apparently begun by Lorenzo in 1409, the year when the writing of the text was completed, but the illustration was never finished. According to Mirella Levi D'Ancona, the Gradual's missing folio 59 would have contained a miniature of the Ascension within an initial V ("I Corali di S. Maria degli Angeli, ora nella Biblioteca Laurenziana, e le miniature da essi asportate," *Miscellanea di studi in memoria di Anna Saitta Revignas,* Florence, 1978, 226). Eisenberg has proposed that the miniature is, indeed, the present Ascension, "designed by Bartolomeo di Fruosino under the supervision of Lorenzo Monaco, and painted in the milieu of Fra Angelico, whereas the figures in the leafy swirls of the initial and in the surrounding frame were designed and painted by Bartolomeo." Boskovits (in the Christie's sale catalogue) thinks that the main figural group was painted by Zanobi Strozzi on Don Lorenzo's design, but agrees with Eisenberg that the border was painted by Fruosino. A comparison with the drapery found in Lorenzo's signed *Coronation of the Virgin* of 1414, however, leaves little doubt that he designed the Ascension. Laurence Kanter has recently suggested that the main figural group may have been painted by the young Fra Angelico, who he believes studied with Lorenzo (note especially the head of the angel who faces the viewer within the initial). Another leaf, originally folio 31 from the same manuscript, depicting the Procession of the Holy Innocents, has also been attributed to Fra Angelico (reproduced in Metropolitan Museum of Art, *Woodner Collection: Master Drawings,* New York, 1990, no. 3).

TEXT: V begins the Introit for the feast of the Ascension, "V[iri Galilaei . . .]" (Men of Galilee . . .).

PARENT MANUSCRIPT: Florence, Biblioteca Laurenziana, cor. 3.

SISTER LEAVES: Washington, National Gallery of Art, Woodner Collection on deposit (Procession of the Holy Innocents).

PROVENANCE: London, Sotheby's, 18 December 1945, lot 638; bought by Scharf for Baron Paul Bernard Hatvany (1899–1977), London; bought at his sale in London, Christie's, 24 June 1980, lot 2, illus.

BIBLIOGRAPHY: Noël Annesley, "Baron Hatvany," *Christie's Review of the Season, 1980,* John Herbert, ed., New York, 1981, 103, color illus.; Marvin Eisenberg, *Lorenzo Monaco,* Princeton, 1989, 110–11.

74 Ascension (color plate p. 48).

75 Annunciation and Brigittine Nuns at Choir

Leaf from a Gradual, illuminated by Bicci di Lorenzo for Il Paradiso, the Brigittine convent in Florence. Italy, Florence, ca. 1435. Vellum, 555 x 370 mm, 1 column with 1 stave of 4 black lines; the miniature is on a verso.

ALTHOUGH Bicci di Lorenzo (ca. 1368–1452) was a pupil of his father, Lorenzo di Bicci, he was also influenced by the leading artists of his time, Lorenzo Monaco, Gentile da Fabriano, and Fra Angelico. His son, Neri di Bicci, was also a painter. One of the most prolific artists of his time, Bicci painted many panels and altarpieces and over a dozen frescoes (see Bernard Berenson, *Italian Pictures of the Renaissance: A List of the Principal Artists and Their Works with an Index of Places. Florentine School,* London, 1963, I, 27–32). Most of Bicci's documented works, including a piece of sculpture, fall between 1420 and 1446 (see Raimond van Marle, *The Development of the Italian Schools of Painting,* The Hague, 1927, IX, 1–37, figs. 1–19). Now, however, thanks to Laurence Kanter's recent attribution, this leaf becomes the first manuscript illumination to be added to his oeuvre. The Annunciation shares a number of specific details with a fresco of the same subject at the Church of San Marco in Florence that has been attributed to Bicci's father, Lorenzo: the two-storied architecture, God the Father surrounded by cherubim, and the golden rays emitted from the dove as well as the hand of God the Father (reproduced in the periodical *Les Arts,* II, no. 14, 1903, 33, and further discussed in no. 16, v). The San Marco Annunciation, in turn, was partly influenced by the miraculous Annunciation in the Church of the Annunziata in Florence (for which see Eugenio Casalini et al., *Tesori d'arte dell'Annunziata di Firenze,* Florence, 1987, 78–81, 96, fig. 1).

The Annunciation is compositionally connected with the scene below. St. Bridget, holding a red pilgrim's Jerusalem cross and a scroll, and nine Brigittine nuns occupy the outer space, while the niche with the altar and cross form a separate architectural unit, as does the cubicle containing the Virgin. The cubicle, as the *thalamus virginis,* or bridal chamber of the Virgin, undoubtably reminded the nuns of their own vows as brides of Christ. Bridget (1302–73), whose rule was confirmed by Pope Urban V in 1370, was herself never a nun. The mother of eight children, one of whom was St. Catherine of Sweden, she is shown wearing a widow's wimple. The crown beneath her feet reflects the Italian belief that she was a Swedish princess. The nuns are all wearing the habit of the Order of the Holy Savior, as it was known, including the headdress with five red dots symbolizing the five wounds of Christ. They are singing from a choir book, and one of them is about to turn the page, which is otherwise held down by a weighted cord.

According to Julia Bolton Holloway (in a letter of 10 March 1991), the choir book was probably commissioned for Il Paradiso, the Brigittine convent in Florence founded by the Alberti family in 1394, three years after St. Bridget was canonized by Boniface IX. The convent was built on the land of the Alberti Palace, where some of the greatest Florentine minds participated in Neoplatonic gatherings. In her research at the State Archives in Florence, Professor Holloway found that it was not unusual for nuns to come from the most important Florentine families, such as the Alberti, Macchiavelli, Frescobaldi, and Ghiberti; in one case even an illegitimate Alberti daughter (Camilla) was accepted. About the time this leaf was made, the convent witnessed renewed activity under the patronage of the city of Florence, especially in the construction of a dependent house, S. Maria del Popolo. The Gradual for Il Paradiso was probably commissioned by either Margherita di Domenico di Agnolo da Montevarchi, elected as the third abbess in 1421, or Tommasa di Filippo da Diacceto, elected in 1430 (see Domenico Maria Manni, *Osservazioni istoriche sopra i sigilli antichi de' secoli bassi,* Florence, 1742, X, 70).

TEXT: The words on the recto, "in eternum." (in eternity), are a later addition.

PARENT MANUSCRIPT: We are grateful to Christopher de Hamel for informing us that the leaf was once the frontis-piece of a Brigittine Gradual sold in London, Sotheby's, 24 June 1986, lot 121, and which was previously sold in London, Christie's, 17 July 1985, lot 302, illus.

PROVENANCE: Il Paradiso, Florence; bought in London, Christie's, 17 July 1985, lot 294, illus.

75 Annunciation and Brigittine Nuns at Choir (color plate p. 49).

76 Saint Praying

Historiated initial I, from a choir book, illuminated by Cristoforo Cortese. Italy, Venice, 1430s. Vellum, 163 x 88 mm, 1 column with staves of four red lines.

THE Venetian artist Cristoforo Cortese, active from the late 1390s to the mid-1440s, ranks among Italy's most important illuminators from the first half of the fifteenth century. The first major artist in Venice to paint in the late Gothic style, Cortese was an extremely prolific artist who steered the course of Venetian illumination during his lifetime (see Palazzo Reale, *Arte in Lombardia tra Gotico e Rinascimento,* Milan, 1988, 230–39). Cortese produced over fifty manuscripts, designed woodcuts, and was probably a panel painter. Ironically, only one illumination signed by him has been identified, a historiated initial A with the Death of St. Francis (Paris, Musée Marmottan). The inscription reads: "XFORV. CŌTEXE. VENETVS. F." (Cristoforo Cortese of Venice made this). His style, however, is easily recognizable, and the large body of work now given to him has a consistent high quality that makes the attributions convincing.

Cortese painted in two manners. The first, his early so-called fine manner, which can be found, for example, in a Morgan Library manuscript of Petrarch's *Libro degli huomini famosi* (MS G. 36), of about 1405, consists of small, very delicately drawn figures. The Breslauer cutting exemplifies Cortese's second manner, the so-called bold style he practiced late in his career, in which larger figures, often half-length, are painted with a bolder brush in brighter colors (see Simona Cohen, "Cristoforo Cortese Reconsidered," *Arte Veneta,* XXXIX, 1985, 22–31). The careful attention to facial features seen in the Breslauer figure, especially in the eyes and hair, and the fine web of thin white lines overlaid on the foliage, are typical of Cortese's style throughout his career. Similar powerful figures, also half-length, occur in a Gradual in Milan (Biblioteca Nazionale Braidense, MS AB XVII, 28) and in a cutting in Venice (Fondazione Giorgio Cini, MS 2171; both works are reproduced in the Palazzo Reale catalogue cited above). The Breslauer cutting, like the Milan Gradual and the Cini initial, sets the figure and foliate initial against a decorative background that is then given a wide framing band of color. The orange frame of the Breslauer initial is further decorated with pseudo-Kufic writing that simulates Arabic calligraphy. Cortese's use of big figures set within large foliate initials is thought to derive from similarly constructed initials painted by the late-fourteenth-century Florentine illuminator Silvestro dei Gherarducci in choir books made for the Camaldolese monasteries of San Michele and San Mattia in Murano, near Venice. (Giordana Mariani Canova, in her article, "Miniatura e pittura in età tardogotica (1400–1440)," in *La pittura nel Veneto: Il Quattrocento,* Mauro Lucco, ed., Milan, 1989, I, 193–222, discusses Cortese and the influence of Gherarducci on his work.) The Morgan Library has a large collection of grand historiated initials by Gherarducci of this type (see, for example, M. 478.16 and .17, reproduced by Roger S. Wieck and Lynn P. Castle, *Paths to Grace: A Selection of Medieval Illuminated Manuscript Leaves and Devotional Objects,* Beaumont, Texas, 1991, nos. 5 and 6).

TEXT: The fragment on the back of the cutting, "n[?]ichil / . . . r[?]it in," has eluded identification.

PROVENANCE: Bought privately in the mid-1980s.

76 Saint Praying.

77 Circumcision

Historiated initial I, probably from an Antiphonary, illuminated by the Master of the *Vitae Imperatorum*. Italy, Milan, 1430s. Vellum, 122 x 75 mm, 1 column with staves of 4 lines (1 red); the initial is on a verso.

THE Master of the *Vitae Imperatorum* was one of the most important illuminators active in Milan during the second quarter of the fifteenth century. He is named after his earliest dated work, an Italian translation of Suetonius's *Lives of the Emperors* illuminated in 1431 for Filippo Maria Visconti, duke of Milan (Paris, Bibliothèque Nationale, MS ital. 131). His artistic personality was first established by Pietro Toesca (*La Pittura e la miniatura nella Lombardia dai più antichi monumenti alla metà del Quattrocento,* Milan, 1912), and most recently discussed by Anna Melograni ("Appunti di miniatura lombarda: Ricerche sul 'Maestro delle *Vitae Imperatorum*'," *Storia dell'arte,* no. 70, 1990, 273–314). The Master of the *Vitae Imperatorum*, along with his contemporary Belbello da Pavia, executed numerous manuscripts for Filippo Maria Visconti and his circle. Belbello finished the magnificent Visconti Hours (Florence, Biblioteca Nazionale, MSS Banco Rari 397 and Landau Finlay 22), begun by Giovannino dei Grassi for Filippo Maria's father, Giangaleazzo Visconti. Indeed, the styles of both Belbello and the Master of the *Vitae Imperatorum* derive from and continue the international Gothic art practiced in Lombardy by such illuminators as dei Grassi and Michelino da Besozzo. The style of the *Vitae* Master, however, is somewhat harder and more linear, and should be distinguished from the more painterly Olivetan Master whose works have sometimes been attributed to him (see Alison Stones, "An Italian Miniature in the Gambier-Parry Collection," *Burlington Magazine,* CXI, 1969, 7–12, and Ilaria Toesca, "In margine al 'Maestro delle Vitae Imperatorum'," *Paragone,* XX, no. 237, 1969, 73–77).

The feast of the Circumcision of Christ is celebrated on January 1, for, according to the Old Testament law, every Jewish male child was to be circumcised on his eighth day (Leviticus 12:3). It was also the custom to name the child on the same day. This miniature is particularly unusual because Christ places his hand on the circumciser's hand, perhaps indicating he was a willing participant. According to the popular thirteenth-century *Golden Legend* of Jacobus de Voragine—which Emile Mâle regarded as one of the fundamental books for understanding medieval culture—the circumcision represented the first shedding of Christ's blood for mankind and the beginning of redemption. Further, Christ allowed himself to be circumcised to show that he had really assumed human form, and it was said that an angel carried the sacred flesh to Charlemagne, who enshrined it at Aix-la-Chapelle.

TEXT: The I probably begins the first Matins response for the feast of the Circumcision, "I[n principio . . .]" (In the beginning . . .). Since the back of the cutting bears a folio number (possibly LX), the initial is on the verso of the leaf.

SISTER LEAVES: Germany, private collection (two initials, the Virgin in Glory and Martyrdom of St. Hippolitus, probably come from the same manuscript; both also have staves with 1 red line).

PROVENANCE: Bought privately about 1980.

77 Circumcision (color plate p. 50).

78 Ducal Privilege

Taxation exemption granted by Duke Francesco Sforza of Milan to Facino de Tanciis and Gaspare da Vimercate, illuminated by the Hippolyta Master. Italy, Milan, dated 29 September 1462. Vellum, 295 (350 with bottom flap unfolded) x 440 mm.

THIS and another illuminated document (No. 87) are examples of the deluxe charters, diplomas, and other archival documents issued by the chancery serving, successively, the Visconti and Sforza dukes of Milan. These documents were elaborately decorated with foliate borders, coats-of-arms, family emblems, mottoes, and, sometimes, portraits of the dukes themselves. Sixteen such illuminated documents are listed by Elisabeth Pellégrin in her study of the Visconti-Sforza library (*La bibliothèque des Visconti et des Sforza, ducs de Milan, au XVe siècle,* Paris, 1955, 410–12). The Gaspare da Vimercate mentioned in this document, a count and governor of Genoa, was commander of the Sforza troops. He donated the land upon which the Dominican church of Santa Maria delle Grazie in Milan was built, and where he was buried in 1467.

When Francesco Sforza (1401–66) wed Bianca Maria Visconti in 1441, one of Italy's most powerful *condottieri* married into the family that had ruled Milan since the thirteenth century. When Bianca's father, Filippo Maria Visconti, died in 1447 without a male heir, Francesco Sforza (whose surname, assumed by his father, means "the forcer") usurped the dukedom. As an outward sign of legitimacy, and to lend a sense of continuity to Milan's Visconti past, Francesco adopted many of the heraldic devices of his wife's family. One such example on this document is the red (flayed?) baby swallowed by the large viper, here given feet to form the initial F of the opening word, "Franciscus." Various devices employed by Francesco decorate the top of the document: a golden quince, a brush with the motto "Merito et Tempore" (Merit and Time), a greyhound tied to a pine tree accompanied by Francesco's initials, the Sforza arms (including, again, the hungry Visconti viper), the greyhound repeated in mirror image, a horse's bit, a lone pine tree gripped by a hand, and three intertwined diamond rings. At the bottom is a medallion with a portrait of the duke encircled by the inscription, "Franciscus Sfortia Dux Mediolani Quartus" (Francesco Sforza, fourth duke of Milan). Flanking the medallion, but nearly hidden among the foliage, is another Sforza emblem, waves with palm branches.

As Albinia de la Mare has observed, the decoration of this document can be attributed to the Hippolyta Master. The anonymous artist receives his name from a copy of Domenico Cavalca's *Vite di Santi Padri* that Francesco and Bianca presented to their daughter Hippolyta at her marriage in 1465 to Alfonso of Calabria, the Aragonese heir to the throne of Naples (Paris, Bibliothèque Nationale, MS ital. 1712; see Bibliothèque Nationale, *Dix siècles d'enluminure italienne (VIe-XVIe siècles)*, Paris, 1984, no. 136). This artist worked for Francesco in the last years of the duke's life, and then did even more work for his son Galeazzo Maria Sforza (1444–76). The Hippolyta Master, for example, painted the historiated initials, foliate borders, and many heraldic devices in a Book of Hours for Galeazzo that was recently auctioned in London (Sotheby's, 21 June 1988, lot 58, illus.). He also illuminated a manuscript on Roman history written by Galeazzo's fifteen-year-old brother, Ludovico, in 1467 (Turin, Biblioteca Reale, MS 75; see Francesco Malaguzzi Valeri, *La corte di Lodovico il Moro,* Milan, 1913–19, I, illus. p. 24, and III, figs. 128–30). The style of the portraits in that manuscript is close to that of the portrait of Francesco in the Breslauer document. As François Avril has noted (in the 1984 Bibliothèque Nationale catalogue cited above), the Hippolyta Master's style—seen here at its best in the fine greyhounds, trees, and foliate border—continues trends established by the north Italian illuminator known as the Master of the *Vitae Imperatorum,* whose work is also represented in the Breslauer Collection (No. 77).

PROVENANCE: Bought privately about 1980.

78 Ducal Privilege (color plate p. 50).

79 Adoration of the Magi

Historiated initial E, possibly from a Gradual, illuminated by Franco dei Russi. Italy, Veneto, 1470s. Vellum, 150 x 157 mm, 1 column with staves of 4 red lines; the initial is probably on a verso.

THIS Adoration, which was first attributed to Franco dei Russi by J. J. G. Alexander, closely resembles, in style, a signed cutout historiated initial B with a Virgin and Child that was recently purchased by the Victoria and Albert Museum (E. 1275–1991, bought at Sotheby's, London, 29 November 1990, lot 22, illus.). Although Franco's contributions to the great Bible of Borso d'Este (Modena, Biblioteca Estense, MS lat. 422–23, V. G. 12)—regarded as one of the most magnificent monuments of Italian art—are not signed, his participation is documented. The Bible, carried out with Taddeo Crivelli and at least two others, was begun in 1455; although completed in 1461, Franco did not receive the last payment for his work until 1465 (the documentation is given in the complete facsimile by Giovanni Treccani and Adolfo Venturi, *La Bibbia di Borso D'Este,* Milan, 1937, I, 41–58). His hand can be seen in the illustrations for Leviticus and Matthew. Two other signed works are known, a cutting showing an author or scholar in a chariot pulled by owls, from an album of miniatures mostly taken from Venetian dogal documents (London, British Library, Add. MS 20916, fol. l), and the frontispiece to a Bible printed in Venice in 1471 by Vindelinus de Spira (Wolfenbüttel, Herzog August Bibliothek, Slg. 2°). Both are discussed by J. J. G. Alexander, "A Manuscript of Petrarch's Rime and Trionfi," *Victoria and Albert Museum Yearbook,* II, 1970, 27–40. Although Franco was born in Mantua, where he may have been influenced by Belbello da Pavia (see Mirella Levi D'Ancona, "Contributi al problema di Franco dei Russi," *Commentari,* XI, 1960, 34), his activity is first documented in Ferrara. Thereafter he appears to have worked both in Urbino, for Federico da Montefeltro (where he was referred to as "maestro Franco de Ferrara"), and in Venice. According to Lilian Armstrong, Franco was one of the illuminators who played a role in the formation of the new style of decorating books with illusionistic letters and frontispieces incorporating classical decorative motifs and architectural forms (*Renaissance Miniature Painters and Classical Imagery: The Master of the Putti and His Venetian Workshop,* London, 1981, 8).

In this Adoration of the Magi, probably an early work of Franco, the eldest Magus is about to kiss the foot of the infant Jesus, a motif derived from the late-thirteenth-century *Meditations on the Life of Christ:* "Each one offered Him gifts . . . and with reverence and devotion they kissed His feet. Perhaps at this the judicious Child . . . blessed them. They bowed and joyously took leave." (Isa Ragusa and Rosalie B. Green, eds., *Meditations on the Life of Christ: An Illustrated Manuscript of the Fourteenth Century, Paris, Bibliothèque Nationale, MS. Ital. 115,* Princeton, 1961, 51.) The calm of the Magi is contrasted with the rather mean-looking horses; one has a piercing glance, the other shows his teeth—perhaps reflecting the rare theme from a mystery play that the Magi were mortal enemies before the star brought them together (Charles Sterling, "Fighting Animals in the Adoration of the Magi," *Bulletin of the Cleveland Museum of Art,* LXI, 1974, 357). The meaning of the inscription "DOM" on the stocking of the youngest magus has not been determined.

As Christopher de Hamel has pointed out, the remaining text and music around the initial was painted out in black, as with some cuttings in the Wallace Collection in London, a common early-nineteenth-century practice disguising the painting's original function as part of a manuscript.

TEXT: The E possibly begins the Introit for the feast of Epiphany, "E[cce advenit dominator Dominus . . .]" (Behold the Lord the ruler is come . . .).

PROVENANCE: Bought in New York, Sotheby's, 14 December 1983, lot 89, illus.

79 Adoration of the Magi (color plate p. 51).

80 Sacrifice of Isaac
81 God the Father Blessing
82 Two Male Saints

> Four leaves (God the Father Blessing is part of a bifolio) from an Antiphonary with historiated initials L, I, and A, the first two illuminated by Francesco d'Antonio del Chierico and the third by Ricciardo di Nanni. Italy, Florence, early 1460s. Vellum, 577 x 400, 575 x 385, and 570 x 403 mm, 1 column with 5 staves of 4 red lines; the first initial is on a recto, the second and third on versos.

THESE four leaves come from a set of choir books consisting of eleven Antiphonaries, five Graduals, and a Kyriale. Today these volumes are in the archives of the Church of San Lorenzo in Florence, but they were originally made for the Augustinian abbey at Fiesole, under Cosimo de' Medici's patronage, which began in the 1440s with the rebuilding of the church. Cosimo's campaign included the commissioning of a new set of choir books, for which payment documents dating from 1459 to 1467 survive. (See Elisabetta Landi, "I corali medicei della Badia Fiesolana. I: I documenti; II: Le miniature di Francesco d'Antonio e di Ricciardo Nanni," *Prospettiva*, VIII and X, both 1977, 7–17; 31–39; and Annarosa Garzelli, "Note su artisti.")

The first two initials, the Sacrifice of Isaac and God the Father Blessing, were painted by Francesco d'Antonio del Chierico, active from the late 1450s until his death in 1484. He is documented as working on the choir books for the Badia Fiesolana from 11 January 1461 to 27 April 1465, for which he received a substantial sum. Francesco was one of Florence's leading illuminators in the second half of the fifteenth century, and the handsome payment he received for his work on the Badia Fiesolana choir books is a reflection of the esteem in which he was held, even at this early date in his career. The choir books are among Francesco's major illuminations; other important works by him include a Bible for Federigo da Montefeltro (Vatican City, Biblioteca Apostolica Vaticana, MS Urb. lat. 1, 2), the Breviary of Lorenzo the Magnificent (Florence, Biblioteca Laurenziana, MS Plut. XVII. 28), and numerous Petrarchs, including one for the same Lorenzo (Paris, Bibliothèque Nationale, MS ital. 548). Much of Francesco's fame comes from the large number of humanistic texts—Petrarch, Plutarch, Virgil, among others—that he illustrated for his eminent patrons. Favored by the Medici, he soon became Florence's most sought-after illuminator.

The initial of the Two Male Saints is the work, as Garzelli has observed, of Ricciardo di Nanni da Castelfiorentino, active from the 1450s to 1480. Payment records indicate that Ricciardo and two assistants were active from 23 February 1461 to 14 April 1462 on some Antiphonaries, a Psalter, and another book for the abbey in Fiesole. Ricciardo's style, although similar to Francesco's, is somewhat harder and more schematized. Ricciardo also worked for the Medici—Cosimo's sons Piero and Giovanni—and his major works include illustrated manuscripts of classical and patristic texts (Plautus, Pliny, Seneca, Petrarch, etc.), a Gospel Lectionary of 1468 for Santa Maria del Fiore (Florence, Biblioteca Laurenziana, MS Edili 115), and a miniature of the Corpus Domini in Gradual D for the Church of the Santissima Annunziata, for which he was paid in 1473 and which is still in the church library.

Two of the initials, the Sacrifice of Isaac and the Two Male Saints, were identified by Garzelli in 1985 as belonging to the Badia Fiesolana Antiphonaries, which had been described by Paolo D'Ancona early in this century (*La miniatura fiorentina, secoli XI–XVI,* Florence, 1914, II, 545, 552, nos. 1078 and 1086). His description also mentions an initial of a "male saint, merely sketched in" within an initial I (p. 547, no. 1080). We have been able to identify this initial with the Breslauer God the Father Blessing on the basis of its liturgical position in the choir book. The sketchy character noticed by D'Ancona refers to the very light treatment of the head, beard, and hands of God the Father, which he seems to have perceived as unfinished.

The somewhat unusual subjects of the three Breslauer initials can be best understood by examining their broader liturgical contexts. The first two lessons and responses for Quinquagesima (the Sunday before Ash Wednesday) tell the story of God's covenant with Abraham, thus making the Sacrifice of Isaac an appropriate theme for its major decorated initial. The office for the Monday after Pentecost makes frequent mention of God the Father, probably providing the inspiration for the God the Father Blessing in the initial. The third initial presents something of a puzzle. It contains two crowned male saints in pseudo-antique armor, one of whom holds palm branches of

mus ei .℣. Nan te.

Dantis ℟.

est dominus

ɩo abraam diccns egit

dcit dc tẽrɩa tua ɩd cognati

80 Sacrifice of Isaac.

81 God the Father Blessing (color plate p. 52).

82 Two Male Saints (color plate p. 53).

martyrdom. As the illustration for the Common of Several Martyrs, this depiction of two martyr saints is generically appropriate. An initial with Two Virgin Saints (on fol. 109; see Landi, "I corali medicei," I, fig. 10) for the Common of Virgins from the parent manuscript employs a similar composition with two half-length female saints and a half-length God the Father supported by cherubs. While the Breslauer male saints are not given any particular attributes, they could have called to the fifteenth-century mind any number of Early Christian martyrs, some of whom were particularly significant to Tuscany, such as Sts. Pergentinus and Laurentianus whose cult was in nearby Arezzo. Particularly popular in Florence were Sts. Cosmas and Damian, and their presence in this Antiphonary could reflect specifically Medicean iconography, but these doctor saints were traditionally represented wearing long robes and holding medicine jars and pincers.

TEXT: Sacrifice of Isaac: "Locutus est Dominus ad Abraam . . . " (The Lord spoke to Abraham . . .) is the first Matins response for Quinquagesima (the Sunday before Ash Wednesday). God the Father: "Iam non dicam vos servos . . . " (No longer do I call you servants . . .) is the first Matins response for the Monday ("feria s[e]c[un]da") after Pentecost; the bifolio leaf attached to this sheet contains the end of the texts for the feast of Pentecost. Two Male Saints: "Absterget Deus omnem lacrimam . . . " (God will wipe away every tear . . .) is the first Matins response for the Common of Several Martyrs.

PARENT MANUSCRIPT: Choir books from the Badia Fiesolana now in Florence, Archivio della Basilica di San Lorenzo. The Sacrifice of Isaac was originally fol. 119 (so foliated) from cor. C 202; the leaves with God the Father were originally fols. 125–126v (so foliated) from cor. E 204; and the Two Male Saints was originally fol. 42v from cor. L 210.

PROVENANCE: God the Father and Sacrifice of Isaac: London, Sotheby's, 11 December 1968, lots 175 and 176, respectively; both lots possibly bought in; bought privately in November 1973. Two Male Saints: London, Sotheby's, 18 June 1962, lot 107, pl. 5; Maggs, London; Mark Lansburgh ("Lansburgh '63" inscribed on the lower right edge of verso); Blumka Gallery, New York; bought in 1979.

BIBLIOGRAPHY: Mark Lansburgh, "Medieval and Renaissance Manuscripts and Graphic Arts at the Colorado College," *Colorado College Magazine,* II, Summer 1967, n.p., illus., and "The Illuminated Manuscript Collection at Colorado College," *Art Journal,* XXVIII, 1968, 66, fig. 9; Annarosa Garzelli, *Miniatura fiorentina del Rinascimento, 1440–1525: un primo censimento,* Florence, 1985, I, 60, II, figs. 168, 223, and "Note su artisti nell'orbita dei primi Medici: individuazioni e congetture dai libri di pagamento della Badia fiesolana (1440–1485)," *Studi Medievali,* XXVI, 1985, 440, 441.

83 Christ Calling St. Peter
84 Three Marys at the Tomb

Two leaves from an Antiphonary with historiated initials S and A illuminated by
Pellegrino di Mariano. Italy, Siena, dated 1471. Vellum, 530 x 380 and 577 x 394 mm,
1 column with 5 staves of 5 red lines; both initials are on rectos.

THESE two leaves came from a set of choir books commissioned for Siena's Spedale di Santa Maria della Scala by Niccolò Ricoveri, the hospital's rector between 1456 and 1476/77. At the bottom of each leaf is a coat-of-arms (later repainted) that originally contained, in the left half, the hospital's emblematic ladder against a black field and, in the right half, Ricoveri's rampant griffin on a gold field.

These leaves are the work of Pellegrino di Mariano Rossini, who was active in Siena by 1449 and died in 1492. Pellegrino, as Carl Strehlke in *Painting in Renaissance Siena* informs us, was both an illuminator and a panel painter. His only signed and dated panel is the *Madonna with Sts. John the Baptist and Bernardino* of 1450 in Memphis (Brooks Memorial Art Gallery). Slightly earlier is his illumination in a Gradual (Siena, Biblioteca Comunale, cod. H.I.2) to which Giovanni di Paolo, probably Pellegrino's teacher, also contributed three miniatures. Between 1444 and 1450 Pellegrino was decorating a chapel at the Spedale di Santa Maria della Scala under the rector Urbano di Pietro del Bello. In the early 1460s, he, Sano di Pietro, and a third artist illuminated choir books for Pope Pius II's cathedral in Pienza. And from 1465 to 1481, Pellegrino, along with Sano di Pietro, Liberale da Verona, Girolamo da Cremona, and Francesco Rosselli, was painting choir books both for Siena's cathedral and the Spedale. The Breslauer leaves come from this last period of activity, for inside the wreath surrounding the coat-of-arms on the leaf with Christ Calling St. Peter is the date 1471.

Both of the compositions on the Breslauer leaves were repeated by Pellegrino, with some variations, in other works he illuminated. The artist added Andrew to the boat and transformed his Christ Calling St. Peter into a Christ Calling Andrew and Peter (for the feast of St. Andrew on November 30) in an Antiphonary now in the Museo dell'Opera del Duomo (cod. 11. M, fol. 4; reproduced in M. G. Ciardi Dupré, *I Corali del Duomo di Siena*, Siena, 1972, pl. 73). Pellegrino's three Marys make a second appearance for Easter in another Antiphonary in the Museo dell'Opera del Duomo (cod. 9. I, fol. 3; reproduced by Ciardi Dupré, pl. 63).

TEXT: "Symon Petre antequa[m] de navi vocarem te . . . " (Simon Peter, before I called you from the ship . . .) is the first Matins response for the feast of Sts. Peter and Paul (June 29) (not, as in *Painting in Renaissance Siena*, for the feast of the Chair of St. Peter). "Angelus Domini descen[dit de celo . . .]" (An angel of the Lord descended from heaven . . .) is the first Matins response (not, as in *Painting in Renaissance Siena*, an antiphon) for Easter.

PARENT MANUSCRIPT: The choir books (Antiphonaries and Graduals) commissioned for the Spedale di Santa Maria della Scala by Niccolò Ricoveri are much mutilated, and many leaves with historiated initials are missing. The remaining volumes are in Siena's Museo dell'Opera del Duomo. Christ Calling St. Peter may come from cod. 90. L

and the Three Marys from cod. 86. F (see Daniela Gallavotti Cavallero, *Lo Spedale di Santa Maria della Scala in Siena: vicenda di una committenza artistica*, Pisa, 1985, 231).

SISTER LEAVES: Cambridge, Fitzwilliam Museum, MS 197 (Creation of Heaven and Earth), and, as pointed out to us by Christopher de Hamel, possibly Cleveland, Museum of Art, acc. no. 52.282 (Nativity, by the workshop of Benvenuto di Giovanni).

PROVENANCE: Christ Calling St. Peter: bought in Italy in the 1970s. Three Marys: bought by T. Rogers in London, Sotheby's, 9 December 1974, lot 22, illus.; bought in London, Sotheby's, 26 November 1985, lot 15, illus.

BIBLIOGRAPHY: Keith Christiansen et al., *Painting in Renaissance Siena, 1420–1500*, New York, 1988, 243–46, nos. 39a and 39b, illus.

S mon

pe

tre antequá de na

ui voca rem te

no ni

83 Christ Calling St. Peter (color plate p. 54).

ce sepulchro alla. Qi p nob pependit

iligno

alla.

Nge

lus

comi in descen

84 Three Marys at the Tomb (color plate p. 55).

85 Pentecost

Historiated initial D, from an Antiphonary, illuminated by Girolamo Dai Libri. Italy, Verona, late 1480s. Vellum, 163 x 176 mm, 1 column with staves of 4 red lines; the initial is on a recto.

WHILE the connection of Girolamo Dai Libri to the large body of illumination that has recently grown up around his name is somewhat circumstantial, the evidence pieced together by Gino Castiglioni and Hans-Joachim Eberhardt (in the 1986 publication cited below) is convincing. From Vasari we learn that Francesco Dai Libri, a skilled illuminator, was the father of Girolamo (1474–1556), who at an early age excelled his father. Already at sixteen Girolamo painted an altarpiece for the Lischi Chapel of Santa Maria in Organo in Verona that brought him great fame. In addition to numerous panels, Vasari continues, Girolamo was also known for the many choir books he illuminated. In spite of this telling biography, there exist no signed or securely documented miniatures by either Francesco or Girolamo with the exception of a miniature that has been associated with the father. The miniature occurs in a dated manuscript of 1503 in Padua (Biblioteca del Seminario, MS 432, fol. 112v) whose colophon states, "Et magister Franciscus miniator de sancto paulo Veronae miniavit" (And Master Francesco, illuminator of St. Paul's of Verona, illuminated this). All attributions to the father and son are based on this manuscript. There exist two different, but obviously stylistically related, bodies of work that have been grouped, one around the father and the other around Girolamo. The attribution of the body of work to Girolamo is buttressed by Castiglioni's identification of five of the seven choir books specifically mentioned by Vasari with existing manuscripts (or fragments). Furthermore, a group of six books, either dated or securely datable from 1492 to 1502, forms a chronological anchor around which other manuscripts can be grouped and this in turn has helped establish a picture of Girolamo's stylistic development.

The Breslauer Pentecost is considered among the earliest illuminations by Girolamo and is given to the late 1480s when the artist was but a teenager. The composition is stable, the figures quiet, and the initial forms relatively simple—three things that Girolamo will change. In the course of his career his compositions became progressively more complex, his figures more mobile, and the initial forms increasingly complicated. The style and initial forms of this Pentecost are similar, although markedly simpler, to those in another early work of Girolamo's, the historiated initials he painted for an Antiphonary today in London (Victoria and Albert Museum, MS A.M. 4929–1866; reproduced in Castiglioni and Marinelli, figs. IV. 20–22 and illus. p. 239). The Antiphonary made for the Monastery of Sts. Nazarius and Celsus and dated 1492 is, according to Castiglioni, one of Girolamo's commissions mentioned by Vasari.

TEXT: D begins the first Matins response for Pentecost, "D[um complerentur dies Pentecostes . . .]" (When the day of Pentecost had come . . .); on the verso of the cutting is a fragment from the second Lauds antiphon for Pentecost, "[Spi]ritus Domini [replevit o]rbem terraru[m]."

SISTER LEAVES: possibly ex-Kann collection, nos. 80 (Nativity) and 82 (Annunciation).

PROVENANCE: Rodolphe Kann, Paris (his sale, 1907); Duveen Brothers; Mrs. Collis P. Huntington, San Marino, Calif.; Norton Simon Foundation (their no. 30431); sold by them in London, Sotheby's, 8 July 1974, lot 18, and bought by Breslauer.

BIBLIOGRAPHY: Jules Mannheim and Edouard Rahir, *Catalogue of the Rodolphe Kann Collection: Objets d'Art*, Paris, 1907, I, 64, no. 81; William Suida, "Italian Miniature Paintings from the Rodolphe Kann Collection," *Art in America*, XXXV, 1947, 21–22, fig. 2; Los Angeles County Museum, *Mediaeval and Renaissance Illuminated Manuscripts*, Los Angeles, 1953, 35, no. 127; Gino Castiglioni and Sergio Marinelli, *Miniatura veronese del Rinascimento*, Verona, 1986, 120, fig. IV.24 (as ubicazione ignota).

85 Pentecost.

86 Hawking

Miniature, from the Hours of Bona Sforza, illuminated by Giovanni Pietro Birago for Bona Sforza. Italy, Milan, ca. 1490. Vellum, 115 x 85 mm; the miniature is on a verso.

THE parent manuscript for this leaf is the Book of Hours commissioned from the artist Giovanni Pietro Birago, active first in Brescia and then mainly in Milan in the last third of the fifteenth century, by Bona of Savoy (1449–1503), widow of Galeazzo Maria Sforza, duke of Milan. This Book of Hours, now in the British Library, has been identified with one ordered by Bona and mentioned in a letter by Birago. The manuscript has a fascinating history. After part of the Hours had been completed by the artist and delivered to his patron, a major part of the rest was stolen from Birago by a certain Fra Gian Jacopo. As Mark Evans informs us (in the monograph on the Sforza Hours cited below), the stolen portion was valued by the artist at the enormous sum of over 500 ducats, a figure that can be compared to Leonardo da Vinci's 100-ducat valuation of his London *Virgin of the Rocks*. Although Birago sought compensation and the thief Jacopo was imprisoned, the stolen folios were apparently never returned. They soon came into the possession of Giovanni Maria Sforzino, bastard half-brother of Galeazzo Sforza. Bona's unfinished Book of Hours passed, upon her death in 1503, to her nephew, Duke Phillibert II of Savoy, and, upon his death the following year, to his widow, Margaret of Austria, regent of the Netherlands. When Margaret moved to the Netherlands she commissioned the scribe Etienne de Lale to finish writing the manuscript and the artist Gerard Horenbout to furnish sixteen miniatures. The manuscript may then have been presented by Margaret to her nephew, Emperor Charles V, a gift that would account for its removal to Spain.

To date, three leaves from the stolen portion of Bona's Hours have come to light: an Adoration of the Magi, the calendar miniature for May (both now in the British Library), and the present leaf. The Breslauer miniature shows a handsome couple on horseback. Assisted by two youths and a pair of growling dogs, they are hawking. In the background men carry baskets of grapes to a wine press. The text on the back of the miniature, the feasts for the last third of September, indicates that this scene was the calendar illustration for the month of October and originally preceded the text for that month. The painting is remarkable for many reasons. One, pointed out by Mark Evans in the *British Library Journal* (cited below), is the fact that it is full-page. Such large calendar miniatures were actually rare in Books of Hours before the early sixteenth century and then appear mainly in Flanders. Evans postulates that the large calendar miniatures in Jean de Berry's *Très Riches Heures* might have led Bona to seek the same in her Hours. Unusual, too, is the aristocratic theme of the hunt for this fall month; the background subject, the vintage, is the usual labor for October. Bona's entire cycle may have had this aristocratic emphasis, for the London May miniature also places the traditional peasant labor, mowing, in the background while showing, in the foreground, an aristocratic picnic.

Like the British Library's May, the Breslauer October miniature is sandwiched between glass, the top layer of which has unfortunately (also like the London miniature) cracked; water damage has caused some smudging.

TEXT: The recto of the leaf has the last third of the month of September, beginning with the 20th, the Vigil of the feast of St. Matthew.

PARENT MANUSCRIPT: London, British Library, Add. MS 34294.

SISTER LEAVES: London, British Library, Add. MS 45722 (Adoration of the Magi) and Add. MS 62997 (May).

PROVENANCE: Commissioned by Bona Sforza; stolen, with other leaves, from Birago by Fra Gian Jacopo; Giovanni Maria Sforzino, bastard half-brother of Galeazzo Sforza; probably Charles Fairfax Murray, London; probably Tammaro de Marinis; bought in Switzerland in 1984.

BIBLIOGRAPHY: Mark Evans, *The Sforza Hours,* New York, 1992, 11–12, 29, fig. 2. The following citations all refer to two calendar miniatures, of which the Breslauer leaf may be one, once in the de Marinis collection: Paul Wescher, "Francesco Binasco, Miniaturmaler der Sforza," *Jahrbuch der Berliner Museen,* II, 1960, 80, and "Birago, Giovanni Pietro," *Dizionario biografico degli italiani,* 1968, X, 592; Mark L. Evans, "A Newly Discovered Leaf of 'The Sforza Hours'," *British Library Journal,* XII, 1986, 23.

86 Hawking (color plate p. 56).

87 Ducal Privilege

Senatorial appointment by Duke Lodovico Maria Sforza of Milan to Ugo Cavazzi della Somaglia. Italy, Milan, dated 21 July 1495. Vellum, 362 (452 with bottom flap unfolded) x 600 mm.

LIKE Breslauer No. 78, this illuminated document is an example of the deluxe charters, diplomas, and other archival documents issued by the ducal chancery of the Sforza of Milan. This one was issued by Lodovico Maria Sforza, called Il Moro (1451–1508), second son of Francesco, who became duke of Milan when Sforza's grandson Giangaleazzo died in 1494. The document has some of the devices and arms seen in the earlier example. At the left the Visconti viper swallowing the red baby forms the initial L of the opening "Ludovicus." The Sforza arms at the top center are surmounted by the Visconti ducal crown intersected by laurel and palm fronds; the arms are flanked by flaming branches from which hang buckets of tar. At the bottom a mermaid holds the Sforza brush and a merman displays a horse's bit; they originally flanked a wax seal that is now lost.

On the lower right of the document is the inscription, "B. Chalcus," the signature of Bartolomeo Calco. Calco was ducal secretary under Giangaleazzo, who granted him the title of *cavaliere* in 1489 on the occasion of the ceremonial entry of the duke and his wife, Isabella of Aragon, into Milan (Francesco Malaguzzi Valeri, *La corte di Lodovico il Moro,* Milan, 1913, I, 343, 458). Under Lodovico, who also held him in high esteem, Calco became head of the ducal chancery, with the title of *primo segretario ducale.* As a central figure in the administration of the court, Calco was responsible for overseeing business transactions with merchants, tailors, goldsmiths, embroiderers, shoemakers, as well as granting to scholars, *litterati,* and bibliophiles, the privilege of borrowing books, drawings, and maps from the ducal library.

Although we do not know who illuminated this leaf, Giordana Mariani Canova has compared its style, in conversation with us, to that of the Second Master of the Canzoniere Grifo, a painter active in Milan in the 1490s. No matter who the artist, it is instructive to compare this document with the Sforza one painted over thirty years earlier (No. 78). The illuminator of 1495, in keeping with artistic developments of the late fifteenth century, has painted his foliage, pearls, and viper with a trompe⁄l'oeil three⁄dimensionality that visually lifts them from the vellum surface.

PROVENANCE: Acquired privately about 1979.

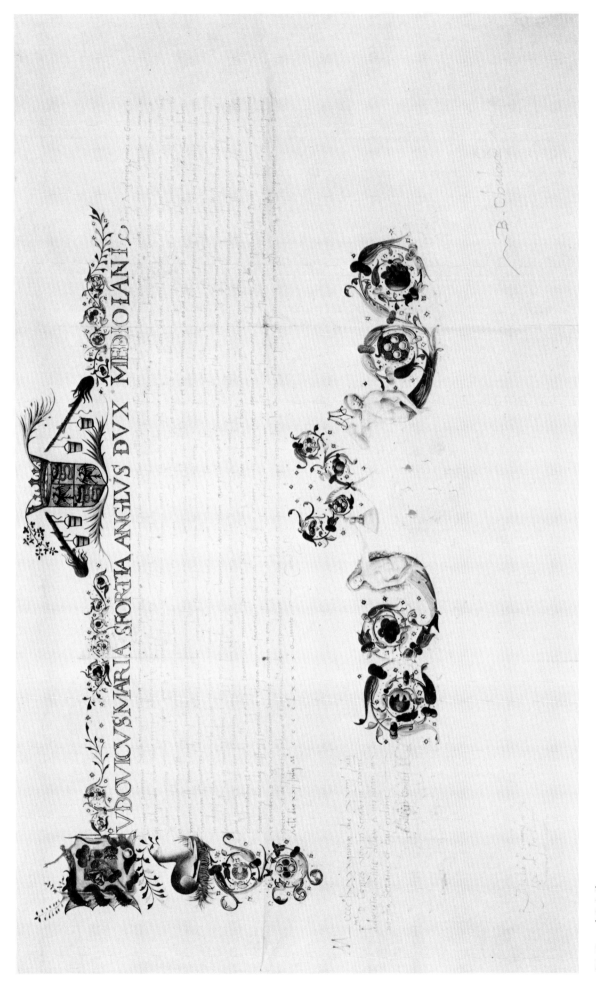

87 Ducal Privilege.

219

88 Crucifixion

Miniature probably from a Book of Hours. Italy, possibly Lombardy or Naples, late 15th century. Vellum, 185 x 141 mm; the miniature is glued to paperboard.

THIS miniature presents something of an art-historical puzzle. The statuesque figures, heavy drapery, and arid foreground landscape are Italianate. On the other hand, there is also something very Northern about the style of the miniature, and the gold cityscape and half-length angels look very much like those to be found in French illumination of the 1480s, such as in the work of Jean Colombe. Also unusual is the Virgin's white robe, which may suggest the leaf was part of a book made for Carthusians, whose habit was white.

But even if one accepts an attribution of this miniature to Italy, confusion continues to reign. A localization to north Italy is suggested by Laurence Kanter and Pia Palladino who have compared (in conversation with us) this Crucifixion to the work of Jacopino de Mottis, a painter active in the last quarter of the fifteenth century who did work for the Certosa in Pavia. While this Crucifixion bears some resemblance to de Mottis's work, it is actually closer to a panel of the Entombment that is only tentatively attributed to him (see Mina Gregori, *Pittura a Pavia dal Romanico al Settecento*, Milan, 1988, 228–29, pls. 81–88). The figures in the Entombment, like those in the Crucifixion, have a habit of holding their mouths open. On the other end of the spectrum, an attribution to the south Italian city of Naples is suggested by the similarity of this Crucifixion to a Deposition in a private German collection (see Joachim M. Plotzek, *Andachtsbücher des Mittelalters aus Privatbesitz*, Cologne, 1987, 233–34, no. 78, illus.). While the landscapes are very different, the figures, their faces and drapery, and their sense of quiet dignity are similar in both the Crucifixion and Deposition. Otto Pächt, in the Sotheby sale catalogue (13 July 1977, lot 17) for the Deposition, compared the style to Neapolitan Hispano-Flemish painting from the end of the fifteenth century. To Pächt's comparisons we might add the panels in Naples with scenes from the legend of St. Vincent Ferrer whose figures and faces resemble those in the Breslauer miniature (see Raimond Van Marle, *The Development of the Italian Schools of Painting*, The Hague, 1934, XV, figs. 218–21). Furthermore, John Plummer pointed out some similarity of the Crucifixion to miniatures in a Book of Hours painted in Naples around 1497 (L. M. J. Delaissé et al., *The James A. De Rothschild Collection at Waddesdon Manor: Illuminated Manuscripts*, Fribourg, 1977, 374–94, no. 18, figs. 22–26). The Waddesdon Manor Hours, although clearly by a different hand and of inferior quality, does contain a Crucifixion whose Christ bears an uncanny resemblance to that in the Breslauer miniature. There is something, too, of the style of the French artist Jean Bourdichon in both the Crucifixion and the Deposition and, indeed, Bourdichon's art exerted an influence on Neapolitan painting at this time. But the connection between the Crucifixion and the Deposition remains conjectural, and they could prove to be by two different hands.

There is one area of confusion concerning this leaf that can be clarified. Plotzek, in the catalogue cited above, mistakenly relates the Deposition to a group of eleven leaves that share a common provenance—they were all once owned by the Marquess of Londonderry. These eleven miniatures, by Simon Bening and his shop, apparently all come from the Hours of Albrecht of Brandenburg. Sandra Hindman will demonstrate in her forthcoming catalogue of the Northern miniatures of the Robert Lehman Collection that they have nothing to do with either the Deposition or the Breslauer Crucifixion.

PROVENANCE: Bought in the London book trade in 1992.

88 Crucifixion (color plate p. 57).

89 Penitent David

Leaf from a Psalter, with a historiated initial B. Italy, Florence, ca. 1500. Vellum, 620 x 450 (412 x 258) mm, 1 column of 13 lines; the initial is on a recto.

THIS imposing historiated initial, one of the largest of the Renaissance, can be directly connected with the famous Penitent David painted by Monte di Giovanni del Fora for King Matthias Corvinus of Hungary. One of Monte's chief works, it served as the frontispiece for the last of a three-volume Bible that began with the book of Psalms (Florence, Biblioteca Laurenziana, MS Plut. XV. 17, fol. 2v). Because of Corvinus's death in 1490, however, the Bible was never finished, and it remained in Florence, perhaps even in Monte's studio (he died in 1529). Monte's David influenced the as yet unidentified artist of the present leaf, the illuminator Giovanni di Giuliano Boccardi (Boccardino Vecchio, 1460–1529), and others. For the related miniatures see Annarosa Garzelli, *Miniatura fiorentina del Rinascimento 1440–1525: un primo censimento,* Florence, 1985, pl. XVI, figs. 903–14 (for Monte), 1071–72 (for Boccardi), and 1077; and J. J. G. Alexander, "Constraints on Pictorial Invention in Renaissance Illumination: The Role of Copying North and South of the Alps in the Fifteenth and Early Sixteenth Centuries," *Miniatura,* I, 1988, figs. 8–9). Indeed, Monte's brother Gherardo and Boccardi knew each other, for they collaborated on at least one commission (see Mirella Levi D'Ancona, *Miniatura e miniatori a Firenze dal XIV al XVI secolo,* Florence, 1962, 149–54), and it is likely that the artist responsible for the Breslauer leaf may have been associated with them as well.

Within the initial B, David kneels and raises his hands in prayer to God the Father, who is surrounded by blue cherubim and from whom golden rays descend on David. His scepter, psaltery, and crown lie on the ground. Through the cave-like formation on the left, the youthful David can be seen picking up rocks for his sling, and in the right background, before the city of Jerusalem, he is about to sever the head of the fallen Goliath.

The figures in the roundels surrounding the initial are either Benedictines, authors, or sources of inspiration named in the titles of the Psalms themselves. David, of course, was regarded as the chief author and editor of the Psalms. The ten figures in the borders of the page opposite the David in the Corvinus Bible, which have heretofore not been recognized as authors or sources of inspiration for the Psalms, are all identified by inscriptions, and are the bases for our identifications here.

At the top is Pope Gregory the Great, a Benedictine, who can be identified by his attribute, the small dove by his ear. According to the *Golden Legend* of Jacobus de Voragine, the Holy Ghost, in the form of a dove, had often descended on Gregory's head, presumably inspiring his writings. Gregory contributed much to the form of the liturgy and its music. The two figures flanking Gregory, and the pair flanking the letters, "eatus vir," are Moses, Solomon, Jeduthun (Ethan), and Asaph, all mentioned in the *tituli* of the Psalms as authors or models of Psalms. The pair flanking the middle of the letter are St. Justina of Padua, who was venerated by the Benedictine order (her attribute is the knife in her chest), and St. Scholastica, the sister of St. Benedict. At the bottom, shown against a continuous colonnaded wall, are St. Benedict (in the middle, holding his discipline) and Sts. Placidus and Maurus, his early missionaries (these three identifications are based on inscriptions in a grouping by Boccardi, see Garzelli, fig. 1074). Boccardi executed commissions for several Benedictine houses, including St. Peter's in Perugia and Monte Cassino, and there is no question that the present leaf was commissioned for a Benedictine establishment as well.

TEXT: "Beatus vir . . . " (Happy is the man. . .) is the opening of Psalm I, which continues on the verso (marked as folio 1).

PROVENANCE: Bought in London, Christie's, 22 June 1988, lot 216, illus.

89 Penitent David (color plate p. 58).

90 Birth of John the Baptist

Composite leaf with a miniature by Vincent Raymond. Italy, Rome, ca. 1523. Vellum,
320 x 250 mm; the montage is pasted on card.

THIS leaf has a fascinating history, one that tells us a great deal about sixteenth-century patronage, eighteenth-century looting, and nineteenth-century collecting. Like its sister leaves, this leaf is actually a montage, a cleverly arranged composite of separate fragments carefully cut, juxtaposed, and pasted together to look like an integral creation. The fragments originally came from a service book, probably a one- or multivolume Missal commissioned by Pope Clement VII (reigned 1523–34) or his cousin Pope Leo X (1513–21) for use in the Sistine Chapel. This and the sister miniatures frequently contain the arms, name, and date of election of Clement; but the appearance of Leo's name on at least one leaf indicates that the book could have been commissioned by him but completed for Clement. The manuscript remained in the Sistine until Napoleon's troops looted the chapel in 1798. The parent manuscript, or fragments from it, were collected by Luigi Celotti, an abbot turned art dealer who enriched himself by marketing books, manuscripts, miniatures, and fragments in the early nineteenth century. In 1825, for example, Celotti sold, in three Sotheby sales in London, some four thousand lots of manuscripts and books. In the same year, at Christie's (then better known for selling pictures), he sold 97 lots of fragments from Sistine Chapel manuscripts, including the Breslauer miniature. It was probably Celotti who arranged the fragments in their present form, presenting the illumination like an easel picture, and without its "distracting" text. (Importing fragments evidently also allowed Celotti to avoid the import taxes on bound books and manuscripts imposed in England at that time.) Celotti's sale in 1825, which was extremely successful, marks the real beginning of the collecting of individual medieval and Renaissance miniatures. (Sandra Hindman and Michael Heinlen, "A Connoisseur's Montage: The *Four Evangelists* Attributed to Giulio Clovio," *Art Institute of Chicago Museum Studies,* XVII, 1991, 155–78, discuss, with citations to earlier literature, Celotti's important sale.)

The Breslauer leaf, like its sisters, is made up of five separate panels. (The two examples from the Victoria and Albert Museum, Figs. 10 and 11, have extra strips inset into their "original" frames.) The two vertical side panels include, among classical decoration, medallions with figures of evangelists, a pope and a bishop, and the emblem of Clement VII. This *impresa* consists of a glass sphere through which two rays of sun pass, the first setting a tree on fire, the second falling on a white banner with no ill effect. On the banner is written Clement's motto, "Candor ilesus," which means "whiteness undamaged" or "innocence unharmed." The device, invented by the pope's treasurer, Domenico Buoninsegni, is based on his observation that sunlight, intensified when passing through crystal, will burn all objects except the whitest. Clement used the emblem to demonstrate that the innocence of his soul was not offended by his enemies. (See Marilyn Perry, "'Candor Illaesvs': The 'Impresa' of Clement VII and Other Medici Devices in the Vatican Stanze," *Burlington Magazine,* CXIX, 1977, 676–86.) The top horizontal border fragment contains another Medici device, used by both Leo X and Clement VII, a diamond ring accompanied by three colored feathers and a scroll inscribed "Semper" (Always). At the bottom are the Medici papal arms. The miniature of the Birth of John the Baptist at the center shows Elizabeth handing her swaddled newborn to a woman, while Zachariah writes the name of his son on a scroll. Below the miniature is written a sentence from the Gospel of John (1:6): "Fuit homo missus a Deo cui nomen erat Iohannes" (There was a man sent from God, whose name was John).

The miniatures on this and the sister leaves have traditionally been attributed to Vincent Raymond (Vincent de Lodève or Vincenzo Raimondi), a French illuminator whose long career spanned the courts of Leo X to Paul IV (1555–59). Paul III (1534–49) appointed him papal miniaturist in 1549 with a life tenure, a position he held until his death in 1557. For him, Raymond painted a luxurious Psalter (Paris, Bibliothèque Nationale, MS lat. 8880) and a Constitutions of the Sistine Chapel (Vatican City, Biblioteca Apostolica Vaticana, MS Cappella Sistina 611). Stylistic features of the Breslauer miniature—especially the crisp drapery and the somewhat pinched facial features—are generally comparable to elements in the somewhat later Constitutions (see Roger S. Wieck and Eric M. Zafran, *Splendor of the Popes: Treasures from the Sistine Chapel and the Vatican Museums and Library . . . ,* Baltimore, 1989, 22, no. 7, illus. and frontispiece). Stylistic, as well as iconographic, similarities of the miniature to another work by Raymond can also be cited; a historiated initial, also containing the Birth of John the Baptist, in an Antiphonary for the Sistine Chapel (Vatican City, Biblioteca Apostolica Vaticana, MS Cappella Sistina 11, fol.

90 Birth of John the Baptist (color plate p. 59).

34) is quite similar and helps confirm the attribution to Raymond. (The historiated initial is reproduced by Léon Dorez, *Psautier de Paul III,* Paris, 1909, pl. XXIII; see also José María Llorens Cisteró, "Miniaturas de Vincent Raymond en los manuscritos musicales de la Capilla Sixtina," *Miscelánea en homenaje a Monseñor Higinio Anglés,* Barcelona, 1958–61, I, 485.) The quality of the miniatures from one sister leaf to another varies, however, and there is clearly the assistance of shop hands in the medallion figures. Carl Nordenfalk argues that the Florentine miniaturist Blasius, mentioned in payment documents from 1523 to 1525, is the artist of these leaves ("Tre nyförvärvade bokmålningar," *Stockholm Nationalmuseum Bulletin,* XV, 1991, 74–81). Mirella Levi D'Ancona (in her article cited below) attributes the sister leaf with the Last Judgment to another Florentine, Jacopo del Giallo. But, since Blasius, to whom no other illuminations at present are attributed, and Jacopo del Giallo are something of art-historical ghosts, and the Last Judgment is stylistically different from all the other leaves of this group, it seems prudent, especially in light of the comparisons offered here, to retain the attribution to Raymond.

TEXT: "Fuit homo missus a Deo cui nomen erat Iohannes" (There was a man sent from God, whose name was John) is the beginning of the Gradual prayer from the Mass of the Vigil of the Nativity of John the Baptist. The inscription, however, could be nineteenth-century.

PARENT MANUSCRIPT: Two Missals (MS A.I.9 and A.I.14) of Pope Clement VII, described in an early-eighteenth-century inventory of the Sistine Chapel sacristy manuscripts, contain numerous Masses that could have been illustrated by this group of leaves and are thus candidates for having been parent manuscripts.

SISTER LEAVES: The Celotti sale in London, Christie's, 26 May 1825, contained, from the parent manuscript(s), the following 19 lots (for which locations are provided when known): lot 57 (8 border fragments); 58 (border fragments); 59 (8 border fragments); 60 (8 border fragments); 61 (Martyrdom of St. Catherine; Stockholm, Nationalmuseum, NMB. 2339); 62 (Martyrdom of Pope Clement I; London, private collection [ex-Sotheby's, 16–17 November 1925, lot 115, illus.]); 63 (Vision of Pope Leo I; Cambridge, Fitzwilliam Museum, Marlay Cutting It. 35); 64 (Stigmatization of Francis); 65 (Martyrdom of Sebastian); 66 (Decapitation of Two Saints); 67 (Martyrdom of Lawrence; London, Sotheby's, 11 April 1961, lot 117); 68 (Cosmas and Damian; London, Victoria and Albert Museum, E.4577–1910, Fig. 10); 69 (Assumption of the Virgin; London, British Library, Add. MS 35254 L); 70 (the Breslauer leaf); 71 (Decollation of Paul; Lon-

don, Victoria and Albert Museum, E.4578–1910, Fig. 11); 72 (Sts. Paul, Stephen, Lawrence, Sebastian, and other Martyrs); 73 (Clement VII in Procession); 74 (Deposition; Cambridge, Fitzwilliam Museum, Marlay Cutting It. 34); 75 (Last Judgment; Cambridge, Mass., Harvard University, Houghton Library, Hofer bequest, MS Typ 734). Also from the parent manuscript(s), but not identifiable in the Celotti sale, are a Martyrdom of St. Blaise (London, British Library, Add. MS 35254 M) and additional borders (Berlin, Staatliche Museen Preussischer Kulturbesitz, Kunstbibliothek, 4013 aus D 130; Cambridge, Fitzwilliam Museum, Marlay Cutting It. 33; London, British Library, Add. MS 21412, fol. 29, and Add. MS 35254 I; and London, Sotheby's, 16–17 November 1925, lot 117; and 25 April 1983, lot 213).

PROVENANCE: Parent manuscript made for Pope Clement VII (reigned 1523–34) or possibly originally commissioned by Pope Leo X (1513–21); looted by the French army, probably in February 1798; acquired (as a whole or in fragments) by Abbot Luigi Celotti (ca. 1768–ca. 1846); his sale, London, Christie's, 26 May 1825, lots 57–75. This fragment: Celotti lot 70; bought by Neville for £ 8/5; William Horatio Crawford of Lakelands; his sale, London, Sotheby's, 11 April 1961, lot 118, illus.; bought by Martin Breslauer, London, Catalogue 101, no. 26, illus.; acquired from the firm after 1970.

BIBLIOGRAPHY: Mirella Levi D'Ancona, "Jacopo del Giallo e alcune miniature del Correr," *Bollettino dei Musei Civici Veneziani,* VII, no. 2, 1962, 21 n. 12.

Fig. 11. Decollation of Paul, by Vincent Raymond.
London, Victoria and Albert Museum, E.4578–1910. Courtesy of the
Board of Trustees of the Victoria and Albert Museum.

Fig. 10. Cosmas and Damian, by Vincent Raymond.
London, Victoria and Albert Museum, E.4577–1910. Courtesy of the
Board of Trustees of the Victoria and Albert Museum.

227

91 Crucifixion

Leaf from a Missal with a miniature by Vincent Raymond. Italy, Rome, ca. 1545.
Vellum, 372 x 260 (268 x 178) mm, 1 column of 29 lines; the miniature is on a verso.

LIKE the French Crucifixion (No. 4), this miniature of the crucified Savior is taken from a Missal. It became the practice early on in Missals to mark the beginning of the Canon of the Mass (the text starting with the words "Te igitur") with a full-page picture of the Crucifixion. This miniature is particularly big, and it most likely came from a Missal made for a pope, probably Paul III, who reigned from 1534 to 1549. An eighteenth-century inventory of the manuscripts in the Sistine Chapel sacristy, which was looted by Napoleon's troops in 1798, lists two Missals (MSS A.II.14 and B.I.6) owned by Paul III and makes mention of their Crucifixions; one of these could have been the Missal from which this leaf came.

This Crucifixion can be attributed to Vincent Raymond, the artist to whom we also attribute the Birth of John the Baptist in the Breslauer montage (No. 90). Raymond, as we discussed earlier, was a French illuminator whose long career spanned the papacies of Leo X (1513–21) to Paul IV (1555–59). Paul III appointed him papal miniaturist in 1549 with life tenure, a position Raymond held until his death in 1557. Paul III was Raymond's major patron, and the artist painted for him a luxurious Psalter (Paris, Bibliothèque Nationale, MS lat. 8880) and a Constitutions of the Sistine Chapel (Vatican City, Biblioteca Apostolica Vaticana, MS Cappella Sistina 611). The Crucifixion in the Constitutions (reproduced in Roger S. Wieck and Eric M. Zafran, *Splendor of the Popes: Treasures from the Sistine Chapel and the Vatican Museums and Library . . . ,* Baltimore, 1989, 23) is similar to the Breslauer depiction, including a comparable landscape and distant city, and both scenes exhibit the pinched facial features characteristic of the artist. In addition, the Vatican and Breslauer miniatures have similar framing devices composed of gold architectural elements inset with black panels incorporating the same textual fragment taken from the Office of the Exaltation of the Holy Cross, "Qui passus es pro nobis IHV XPE miserere n[obis]" (You who suffered for us, O Jesus Christ, have pity on us). The Breslauer miniature was probably painted about 1545, the date of the Constitutions, and therefore was probably made for Paul III.

TEXT: On the recto is the end of the Preface and the entire Sanctus, "[con]fessione dicentes. Sanctus, sanctus, sanctus . . . " (while we say with lowly praise: Holy, holy, holy . . .). The frame of the miniature is inscribed, "Qui passus es pro nobis IHV XPE miserere n[obis]" (You who suffered for us, O Jesus Christ, have pity on us), part of a response taken from the feast of the Exaltation of the Holy Cross, and, at the bottom, "Adoram[us] te Christe et benedicimus tibi quia [per crucem tuam redemisti mun-dum]" (We adore you, Christ, and we bless you, because [by your holy cross you have redeemed the world]), an antiphon from the same feast.

PROVENANCE: Sir Thomas Phillipps, Middle Hill; bought by H. P. Kraus at his sale, London, Sotheby's, 28 November 1973, lot 614, pl. 33; H. P. Kraus private collection, Ridgefield, Conn.; bought from his estate in 1990.

BIBLIOGRAPHY: London, Sotheby's, 30 November 1976, lot 893, where the Breslauer leaf, referred to as Bibliotheca Phillippica, N. S. Medieval VIII, 614, is mistakenly thought to have come from the same Missal as a Pietà by the artist Apollonio dei Bonfratelli.

91 Crucifixion (color plate p. 60).

92   Adoration of the Shepherds

Historiated initial P, probably from a Gradual. Italy, Rome, mid-16th century. Vellum, 260 mm in diameter; the initial is pasted on card and glued to wood.

ALREADY in the fifteenth century, and even more so in the sixteenth and seventeenth centuries, prints were widely used as sources, not only by illuminators, but also by painters and other designers, including majolica decorators. In Rome, moreover, an engraving business was established by Marcantonio Raimondi (ca. 1480–ca. 1534) and continued by his assistants and immediate followers, such as Agostino Veneziano (ca. 1490–1540). These engravers were especially known for the numerous prints they made after famous paintings by Raphael, Giulio Romano, Michelangelo, and others; they also copied prints by Northern artists such as Dürer and Lucas van Leyden. Motifs taken from these prints could both honor the original artist and compliment those who recognized their sources.

Sometimes sources from several prints were used, and in this Adoration of the Shepherds, no less than three—based on works by Giulio Romano, Titian, and Dürer—have been identified. The main composition derives from an Adoration by Giulio Romano engraved by Agostino Veneziano in 1531 (Fig. 12; see *The Illustrated Bartsch*, XXVI, 28, no. 17); in the Romano, however, the brilliant light emanating from the body of Christ, described in the Revelations of St. Bridget of Sweden, is more dramatic, causing distorted shadows on the walls and in the foreground. According to Bridget, the Virgin also showed the shepherds the nature and male sex of the child, for they wished to know whether the newborn child was a savior or a savioress.

The shed, including the two birds and the tree on the right, are derived, as Peter Dreyer kindly pointed out, from Giovanni Britto's woodcut after Titian's *Adoration of the Shepherds* (Fig. 13). The reverse print has been dated to the late 1530s (see David Rosand and Michelangelo Muraro, *Titian and the Venetian Woodcut*, Washington, 1976, 196–97).

To judge by the frequent copies of Dürer's engraved *Madonna and Child with the Monkey* (ca. 1498), both in Germany and Italy, it must have been one of his most popular prints. But it was the German cottage in the background that seems to have fascinated Italian artists because it not only occurs in this Adoration but also in at least two other Italian prints: Giulio Campagnola's *Zeus and Ganymede,* and Cristofano Robetta's *Adam and Eve with Infants Cain and Abel.* The building was taken from a copy in reverse, perhaps one by Giovanni Antonio da Brescia (Fig. 14), who signed (Z A) at least five such copies and dated one of them 1503. (For the identification of Z A with Giovanni Antonio rather than Zoan Andrea see Suzanne Boorsch, "Mantegna and his Printmakers," in *Andrea Mantegna,* Jane Martineau, ed., London, 1992, 56–66.) The buildings on the hill in the background are probably also based on a print.

The small papal arms (Medici, but all six balls are red whereas one is supposed to contain the fleur-de-lis) at the top of the letter and the initials (R S) and date (1516) at the bottom appear to be spurious. Our Adoration, because of the Titian source, could not have been painted before the late 1530s.

TEXT: Although the historiated initial is so closely trimmed that it resembles an O, it is probably the top of a P, the letter beginning the Introit for the third (main) Christmas Mass, "P[uer natus est . . .]" (A Child is born . . .).

PROVENANCE: Bought privately in 1979.

92 Adoration of the Shepherds (color plate p. 61).

Fig. 12. Adoration of the Shepherds, engraving by Agostino Veneziano after
Giulio Romano. London, British Museum.

Fig. 13. Adoration of the Shepherds, chiaroscuro woodcut by
Giovanni Britto after Titian. New York, The Metropolitan
Museum of Art, 22.73.3–162 (Rogers Fund, 1922).

Fig. 14. Virgin and Child with Monkey,
engraving by Giovanni Antonio after Dürer.
Vienna, Graphische Sammlung Albertina.

93 Presentation in the Temple

Miniature. Italy, probably Rome, last quarter of the 16th century. Vellum, 267 x 205 mm; the back is blank.

THE commerce in prints that had been inaugurated by Marcantonio Raimondi in Rome was continued in the third quarter of the sixteenth century by Cornelis Cort (1533–78), among others. Cort, a Dutchman, took up residence in Rome in 1566, where he established an art academy; Agostino Carracci was one of his notable students. Leading artists, among them Federico Zuccaro and Giulio Clovio, commissioned Cort to make prints of their works. Both Zuccaro and Clovio, incidentally, used print sources in their own works. Zuccaro's drawing of the Holy Trinity and Four Angels of about 1563 is based on Dürer's 1511 woodcut of that subject (see E. James Mundy, *Renaissance into Baroque: Italian Master Drawings by the Zuccari, 1550–1600*, Milwaukee, 1989, no. 55). Clovio's Adam and Eve in the Farnese Hours (Morgan Library, MS M. 69, fol. 27) borrows details from Dürer's 1504 engraving of the Fall of Man.

The Presentation, except for the Holy Family group, is based on Cort's print after the *Presentation of the Virgin in the Temple* by Federico Zuccaro's brother, Taddeo, who died in 1566 (Fig. 15; see *The Illustrated Bartsch,* LII, 29, no. 21). Since the print, which is nearly identical in size to the miniature, is dated 1570, it provides a terminus post quem for the miniature. For other copies of the print, which was reissued into the seventeenth century, see J. C. J. Bierens de Haan, *L'oeuvre gravé de Cornelis Cort, graveur hollandais, 1533–1578,* The Hague, 1948, 46, no. 21. Camillo Procaccini (ca. 1555–1629), a successful north Italian painter, used the same composition for his *Presentation of the Virgin in the Temple* of about 1616 (see Nancy Ward Neilson, *Camillo Procaccini: Paintings and Drawings,* New York, 1979, fig. 239). In the Breslauer leaf, the transformation from the Presentation of the Virgin to that of Christ was accomplished by the substitution of the Holy Family for the Virgin and St. Anne and the addition of three doves. Two are placed in the foreground (they are usually carried as a required sacrificial offering), and the other (here a symbol of the Holy Spirit) is above Simeon, who came by the Spirit into the temple so that he might see Christ before his own death (Luke 2:26–27).

Whether this leaf was created as an independent picture or belonged to a series on the life of Christ, as did the Cort print, has not been established, for no other related leaves have been identified.

PROVENANCE: Estelle Doheny (1875–1958), Camarillo, Calif.; Edward Laurence Doheny Memorial Library, St. John's Seminary, Camarillo; bought at the Doheny sale in London, Christie's, 2 December 1987, lot 178, illus.

93 Presentation in the Temple (color plate p. 62).

Fig. 15. Presentation of the Virgin in the Temple, engraving by Cornelis Cort after Taddeo Zuccaro. New York, New York Public Library (Astor, Lenox and Tilden Foundations).

Ten leaves with twenty miniatures from a prayer book. Italy, probably Rome, late 16th century. Vellum, 78 x 52 mm (average).

ALTHOUGH these leaves are presently framed, they had previously been set into vellum leaves and bound in full red morocco gilt, for they are so described when they were in the collection of Adolph Lewisohn (died 1938), the only other known owner. The leaves were in the sequence given above, beginning with the Annunciation, continuing with the Passion of Christ, and ending with a selection of saints. But the cycle of pictures may have been fuller, perhaps similar to Dürer's *Small Passion* of 1511, upon which some of the miniatures are based. The Dürer cycle of thirty-seven engravings also included the Entombment, Resurrection, and Ascension, which are surprisingly lacking in the Breslauer cycle.

Dürer's *Small Passion,* of course, was an immediate success in both Germany and Italy. According to Vasari, Marcantonio Raimondi made such deceptive copies of it (including the initials A. D.) that Dürer complained before the Signoria in Venice. The only satisfaction he received, however, was that Marcantonio could no longer use Dürer's initials on the prints (see Jan Bialostocki, *Dürer and His Critics, 1500–1971: Chapters in the History of Ideas Including a Collection of Texts,* Baden-Baden, 1986, 45). The Breslauer Betrayal, Agony in the Garden, Christ Crowned with Thorns (the kneeling figure sticking out his tongue), Ecce Homo, and the Descent from the Cross are all based on the *Small Passion* (Figs. 17, 19, and 20).

Most of the other miniatures are probably also based on prints, some of which are Italian in origin. The Flagellation, for example, is based on two prints by Adamo Ghisi (ca. 1530–74); one, after an anonymous painter, for the composition and flagellators (Fig. 18), and the other, based on Michelangelo, for the figure of Christ (*The Illustrated Bartsch,* XXXI, 153–54, nos. 1–2). St. Martha, on the other hand, is virtually a copy, and nearly the same size as the Martha in Marcantonio's series of saints (*The Illustrated Bartsch,* XXVI, 178, no. 182). More interesting is the source for St. Barbara, which is based on Marcantonio's print after Raphael's *Peace* (Fig. 21); the print was described by Vasari as Love offering an olive branch to Peace (*The Illustrated Bartsch,* XXVII, 85, no. 393). The source for the Presentation, however, is the most important, for the date of the print, 1568, provides a terminus post quem for the cycle of miniatures. The engraving (Fig. 16) was made by Cornelis Cort after a painting by Federico Zuccaro (*The Illustrated Bartsch,* LII, 62, no. 51).

Since the mannerist style and the prints under discussion remained popular into the seventeenth century and no documented works by the same illuminator have been identified, it is difficult to date these miniatures precisely.

PROVENANCE: Adolph Lewisohn (his bookplate), New York; Esther Rosenbaum, Chicago and New York; her sale, London, Sotheby's, 25 April 1983, lot 218, illus.; Arturo Pregliasco, *Miniatura Gotico-Rinascimentale,* Turin, 1984, no. 32, illus.; bought in 1984.

94 Annunciation.

94 (verso) Adoration of the Shepherds.

Fig. 16. Presentation in the Temple, engraving by Cornelis Cort after Federico Zuccaro. Dresden, Staatliche Kunstsammlungen Dresden.

Fig. 17. Betrayal, engraving from Dürer's *Passio Christi*. New York, The Pierpont Morgan Library, PML 4084.

95 Adoration of the Magi (color plate p. 63).

95 (verso) Presentation in the Temple (color plate p. 63).

Fig. 16

96 Agony in the Garden.

96 (verso) Betrayal (color plate p. 63).

Fig. 17.

97 Christ Crowned with Thorns
(color plate p. 63).

97 (verso) Flagellation
(color plate p. 63).

Fig. 18.

98 Ecce Homo
(color plate p. 63).

98 (verso) Way of the Cross
(color plate p. 63).

Fig. 19.

99 Crucifixion.

99 (verso) Deposition
(color plate p. 63).

Fig. 20.

Fig. 18. Flagellation, engraving by Adamo Ghisi after an anonymous painting. Vienna, Graphische Sammlung Albertina.

Fig. 19. Ecce Homo, engraving from Dürer's *Passio Christi*. New York, The Pierpont Morgan Library, PML 4084.

Fig. 20. Descent from the Cross, engraving from Dürer's *Passio Christi*. New York, The Pierpont Morgan Library, PML 4084.

Fig. 21. Peace or the Reconciliation of Minerva and Cupid, engraving by Marcantonio Raimondi after Raphael. Boston, Museum of Fine Arts.

100 Virgin Mary?

100 (verso) Mary Magdalene.

101 St. Catherine
(color plate p. 63).

101 (verso) St. Martha.

Fig. 21.

102 St. Barbara.

102 (verso) St. Dominic.

103 St. Jerome.   103 (verso) St. John the Baptist.

104 Lamentation

Miniature illuminated by Francesco Grigiotti. Italy, Rome, first third of the 17th century. Vellum, 472 x 340 mm; the back is blank.

VERY little is known about Francesco Grigiotti, and this miniature signed "D. Franciscus de Grigiottis F[ecit]" may be his only surviving work. He was born in Cortona, but was active in Rome from 1604 to 1635, where he illuminated Urban VIII's copy of a Missal that had been printed by Plantin in 1620 (Ulrich Thieme and Felix Becker, *Allgemeines Lexikon der bildenden Künstler . . .*, Leipzig, 1922, XV, 32). According to Sisto Ramón Parro (*Toledo en la mano,* Toledo, 1857, I, 686), there were Pontificals and Missals illuminated by him and Antonio Maria Antonozzi in Toledo Cathedral, but these, except for the present single leaf, were not mentioned in Bordona's survey of the illuminated manuscripts in Spain. Lastly, in an inventory of 1623, among items willed by Archbishop Maffeo Barberini (later Urban VIII) to his brother Don Carlo Barberini, was a Flight into Egypt on vellum by Grigiotti (Marilyn Aronberg Lavin, *Seventeenth-Century Barberini Documents and Inventories of Art,* New York, 1975, 317, no. 520).

Antonozzi, Grigiotti's collaborator, is only slightly better documented. Four large leaves by him from a volume made for Urban VIII were described in the Celotti sale catalogue (London, Christie's, 26 May 1825, lots 91–94). These include a Crucifixion signed A. M. Ant. (lot 93) with exactly the same dimensions as this Lamentation, suggesting that it might have come from the same or another volume made for Urban VIII. The papal court, it seems, was one of the last patrons of manuscript illumination. Although the Breslauer leaf has no papal arms, the border contains four bees (part of the Barberini arms) and laurel leaves (as do lots 91 and 94 in the Celotti sale). Barberini, however, also had laurel leaves surrounding his arms while he was still cardinal (*The Illustrated Bartsch,* XL, 84, no. 86). The Celoti leaves have not been traced, so the styles of the two artists cannot be compared.

Grigiotti, at least in this Lamentation, was greatly influenced by prints, and at least four different sources can be identified. The sensuously displayed body of Christ is derived from Annibale Carracci's celebrated *Pietà* in Naples (Fig. 22, Museo di Capodimonte), which is itself partly inspired by that of Michelangelo. Painted about 1599–1600 for Cardinal Odoardo Farnese, Carracci's *Pietà* was widely known, copied, and engraved (see Donald Posner, *Annibale Carracci: A Study in the Reform of Italian Painting around 1590,* London, 1971, 52, no. 119, fig. 119a). The postures and gestures of the Virgin and John are derived from Cornelis Cort's engraving after Taddeo Zuccaro's *Lamentation,* while the standing figures of Joseph of Arimathea and the centurion, the cross, ladder, and sky are based on Cort's engraving (Fig. 23) after Girolamo Muziano's *Lamentation* (*The Illustrated Bartsch,* LII, 107, no. 89, 105, no. 87).

The two grisaille vignettes in the border, which oddly enough resemble prints, depict events before and after the Lamentation. At the top, in the foreground, the two thieves await crucifixion while a hole is dug to receive one of their crosses. In the background Christ's cross is raised and the Virgin is comforted by John and one of the holy women. At the bottom is the Entombment, which is rendered with hatching; it is based on one of the small scenes (Fig. 24) surrounding an engraving of the Virgin of Sorrows by Giorgio Ghisi (*The Illustrated Bartsch,* XXXI, 51, no. 16; see also Suzanne Boorsch et al., *The Engravings of Giorgio Ghisi,* New York, 1985, no. 54).

PROVENANCE: Toledo Cathedral; Dr. Guy Fink Errera, Brussels; bought in London, Sotheby's, 29 November 1990, lot 25, illus.

BIBLIOGRAPHY: Jesús Domínguez Bordona, *Manuscritos con pinturas,* Madrid, 1933, II, 201, no. 1836, fig. 593.

104 Lamentation (color plate p. 64).

Fig. 22. Pietà, painting by Annibale Carracci.
Naples, Museo di Capodimonte.

Fig. 23. Lamentation, engraving by Cornelis Cort
after Girolamo Muziano. Amsterdam, Rijksmuseum,
Rijksprentenkabinet.

Fig. 24. Entombment, detail from an engraving of the
Virgin of Sorrows by Giorgio Ghisi.
Philadelphia Museum of Art.

INDICES

ARTISTS AND SCRIBES

ICONOGRAPHY

Old Testament

New Testament

Secular scenes

Butchering hog: 34
Capricorn: 34
Crippled archer: 31

Hawking: 86
Man clubbing dog: 51
Mermaids: 87
Wine making and tasting: 14, 86
Shoes: 71

TYPES OF MANUSCRIPTS

Acuña, Don Luis d', Treaty of Utrecht: 13
Antiphonary: 14–15, 30, 37, 38, 39, 45–46, 49, 57,
    61, 63, 65, 67–69, 70, 77, 80–82, 83–84, 85
Beatus of Liébana, *Commentarius in Apocalypsim*: 29
Bible: 56
Boccaccio, Giovanni, *Des cas des nobles hommes et femmes*:
    5–7
Book of Hours: 8–11, 17, 18, 21, 22, 23–26, 86, 88
Choir Book: 76
Documents: 78, 87
Gradual: 12, 35–36, 43, 47, 50–54, 60, 62, 72, 73, 74,
    75, 79, 92

Gratian, *Decretum Gratiani*: 16
Laudario: 66
Lectionary: 1, 40
Matricola: 64, 71
Missal: 3, 4, 44, 48, 55, 58–59, 90, 91
Peter Lombard, *Liber Sententiarum*: 2
Prayer Book: 22, 94–103
Psalter: 18, 19–20, 32, 33, 34, 89
Psalter-Hours: 31
Register: 71
Spiegel menschlicher Behältnis: 41–42
Undetermined: 27, 93, 104

PROVENANCE

Arenberg, Dukes of: 34
Arroyo, San Andrés de, Cistercian Convent: 29
Augsburg, Monastery of Sts. Ulrich and Afra: 44
Aycelin, Gilles, Narbonne: 4
Benckendorff, Countess: 63
Bernasconi, Felix, Juan, and Maria di: 62
Blumka Gallery, New York: 82
Bodmer, Martin and Alice, Geneva-Cologny: 28
Bologna, San Guglielmo, Dominican Convent: 57
Bologna, Shoemakers' Guild: 71
Bonham's, London, 28 March 1974, lot 63: 63
Boycott, Thomas: 17
Brandt, Mortimer, New York: 33
Breslauer, Martin, London: 3, 22, 28, 90
Brummer, Ernest: 34
Brunschwig, Dr. Silvain S.: 38
Camarillo, Calif., St. John's Seminary, Edward
    Laurence Doheny Memorial Library: 93
Cavazzi della Somaglia, Ugo, Milan: 87
Celotti, Abbot Luigi: 90
Christie's, London
  26 May 1825, lot 70: 90
  11 July 1974, lot 1: 40
  11 July 1974, lot 6: 8

  11 July 1974, lot 7: 11
  24 June 1980, lot 2: 74
  17 July 1985, lot 294: 75
  24 June 1987, lot 239: 62
  2 December 1987, lot 178: 93
  22 June 1988, lot 216: 89
Clark, Lord Kenneth: 67–69
Clement VII, Pope: 90
Crawford, William Horatio, of Lakelands: 90
Dennistoun, James, Edinburgh: 67–69
Diacceto, Tommasa di Filippo da: 75
Doheny, Estelle, Camarillo, Calif.: 93
Duveen Brothers: 85
Eisemann, Heinrich: 71
Errera, Dr. Guy Fink, Brussels: 104
Ferrini, Bruce, Akron, Ohio: 33
Fiesole, Badia, Augustinian Abbey: 80–82
Fleming, John, New York: 32, 37
Florence
  Il Paradiso, Brigittine Convent: 75
  San Miniato al Monte: 72
  San Zenobio, Company of (Laudesi): 66
  Santa Maria degli Angeli: 74
  Santa Maria del Carmine, Company of: 66

3 July 1984, lot 92: 67–69
26 November 1985, lot 15: 84
24 June 1986, lot 8: 35–36
21 June 1988, lot 22: 46
6 December 1988, lot 17: 30
20 June 1989, lot 16: 64
5 December 1989, lot 15: 2
19 June 1990 (Korner collection), lot 16: 71
19 June 1990 (Korner collection), lot 32: 17
19 June 1990 (Korner collection), lot 38: 49
19 June 1990, lot 53: 18
29 November 1990, lot 6: 34
29 November 1990, lot 25: 104

Sotheby's, Monte Carlo, 13 June 1982, lot 126: 13
Sotheby's, New York, 14 December 1983, lot 89: 79
Spitz, Joel, Glencoe, Ill.: 34
St. Katharinenthal, Dominican Convent: 37
Tanciis, Facino de: 78
Toledo, Cathedral: 104
Urban VIII, Pope: 104
Vatican City, Sistine Chapel: 90
Vilain, Jean-François, New York: 14–15
Vimercate, Gaspare de: 78
Wien, Rudolf: 17
Witten, Laurence: 56

MANUSCRIPTS CITED

Akron, Ohio, Bruce P. Ferrini: 12, 37
Amiens, Bibliothèque Municipale, MS 19: 3
Antwerp, Museum Mayer van den Bergh, cod. 303: 66
Augsburg, Diözesanmuseum, Inv.-Nr. DMI 11: 44
Augsburg, Maximilianmuseum: 44
Baltimore, Walters Art Gallery
    MS W. 33: 35–36
    MS W. 460: 12
Berlin, Antiquariat Tiedemann: 37
Berlin, Staatliche Museen Preussischer Kulturbesitz,
    Kunstbibliothek
    4000–99,332: 34
    4013 aus D 130: 90
Berlin, Staatliche Museen Preussischer Kulturbesitz,
    Kupferstichkabinett, cod. 78 A 7: 34
Berlin, Staatsbibliothek Preussischer Kulturbesitz,
    MS lat. fol. 830: 12
Bern, Dr. Ernst and Sonya Böhlen: 47
Bologna, Archivio di Stato, MS 3: 71
Bologna, Museo Civico Medievale
    MS 518: 56
    MS 527: 60
    MS 530: 60
Bonn, Universitätsbibliothek, MS 384: 39
Box Hill, Victoria, Australia, St. Paschal's College,
    Codex S. Paschalis: 58–59
Bruges, Groot Seminarie, MS 55/171: 19–20
Burgos, Biblioteca Provincial: 29
Cambridge, Fitzwilliam Museum
    MS 197: 83–84
    Marlay Cuttings It. 33–35: 90
Cambridge, Magdalene College, Pepys' Calligraphical
    Coll., I: 8–11
Cambridge, Trinity College MS B. 11. 7: 18

Cambridge, Mass., Harvard University,
    Houghton Library
    pfMS Lat 186: 12
    MS Typ 270: 41–42
    MS Typ 701: 55
    MS Typ 734: 90
Chantilly, Musée Condé
    MS 65 (Très Riches Heures): 86
    MS 1695: 31
Chicago, Art Institute
    acc. no. 11.142.B: 57
    acc. no. 24.671: 34
Claremont, Calif., Scripps College, Denison Library,
    MS Perkins 4: 12
Cleveland, Cleveland Museum of Art
    acc. no. 39.677: 65
    acc. no. 52.282: 83–84
    acc. no. 63.256: 21
    Otto F. Ege deposit, TR 12828/15: 38
Cologne, Erzbischöfliche Diözesanbibliothek, MS 1 B:
    39
Copenhagen, Royal Library, Ny kgl. Saml. 168, quarto:
    19–20
Donaueschingen, Fürstlich Fürstenbergische
    Hofbibliothek, cod. 309: 34
Dublin, Chester Beatty Library, MS W. 99: 22
Edinburgh, National Library of Scotland, MS 8999:
    8–11
Esztergom, Főszékesegyházi Könyvtár, MS I. 3: 47
Evreux, Bibliothèque Municipale, MS 78: 32
Florence, Archivio della Basilica di San Lorenzo
    cor. C 202: 80–82
    cor. E 204: 80–82
    cor. L 210: 80–82

Private collections
    Belgium: 21
    Germany: 37, 38, 44, 47, 57, 77, 88
    London: 58–59, 90
    New York: 17, 47
    Paris: 5–7
    Switzerland: 37

Whereabouts unknown: 8–11, 37